PUBLICATIONS ON THE NEAR EAST

PUBLICATIONS ON THE NEAR EAST

Poetry's Voice, Society's Song: Ottoman Lyric Poetry
Walter G. Andrews

The Remaking of Istanbul: Portrait of an Ottoman City in the Nineteenth Century, Zeynep Çelik

The Tragedy of Sohráb and Rostám from the Persian National Epic, the Shahname of Abol-Qasem Ferdowsi
Translated by Jerome W. Clinton

The Jews in Modern Egypt, 1914–1952
Gudrun Krämer

Izmir and the Levantine World, 1550–1650
Daniel Goffman

Medieval Agriculture and Islamic Science: The Almanac of a Yemeni Sultan, Daniel Martin Varisco

Rethinking Modernity and National Identity in Turkey
Edited by Sibel Bozdoğan and Reşat Kasaba

Slavery and Abolition in the Ottoman Middle East
Ehud R. Toledano

Britons in the Ottoman Empire, 1642–1660
Daniel Goffman

Popular Preaching and Religious Authority in the Medieval Islamic Near East, Jonathan P. Berkey

The Transformation of Islamic Art during the Sunni Revival, Yasser Tabbaa

Shiraz in the Age of Hafez: The Glory of a Medieval Persian City, John Limbert

The Martyrs of Karbala: Shi'i Symbols and Rituals in Modern Iran, Kamran Scot Aghaie

Ottoman Lyric Poetry: An Anthology, Expanded Edition,
Edited and translated by Walter G. Andrews, Najaat Black, and Mehmet Kalpaklič

Party Building in the Modern Middle East
Michele Penner Angrist

Party Building in the Modern Middle East

MICHELE PENNER ANGRIST

UNIVERSITY OF WASHINGTON PRESS
Seattle and London

For Ezra

PUBLICATION OF THIS BOOK IS SUPPORTED BY A GRANT FROM THE INSTITUTE OF TURKISH STUDIES, WASHINGTON, D.C.

Printed in the United States of America
Designed by Pamela Canell
12 11 10 09 08 07 06 5 4 3 2 1

University of Washington Press
P.O. Box 50096, Seattle, WA 98145
www.washington.edu/uwpress

Library of Congress Cataloging-in-Publication Data
Angrist, Michele Penner, 1970–
Party building in the modern Middle East /
Michele Penner Angrist.
p. cm.— (Publications on the Near East)
Includes bibliographical references and index.
ISBN 0-295-98646-8 (hardback : alk.paper)
ISBN 13:978-0-295-98646-3
1. Political parties—Middle East.
2. Middle East—Politics and government—1979–
3. Authoritarianism—Middle East.
I. Title. II. Series: Publications on the Near East, University of Washington.
JQ1758.A979A64 2006 324.20956—dc22 2006016244

The paper used in this publication is acid-free and 90 percent recycled from at least 50 percent post-consumer waste. It meets the minimum requirements of American National Standard for Information Sciences—Permanence of Paper for Printed Library Materials, ANSI Z39.48-1984. ♾♻

CONTENTS

ACKNOWLEDGMENTS vii

INTRODUCTION: Party Systems and Regime Formation in the Middle East 3

Part I *Explaining Party System Characteristics*

1 The Emergence of the Preponderant Single-Party Systems 31

2 The Emergence of the Multiparty Systems 54

3 The Emergence of Bipartism in Turkey 73

Part II *The Impact of Party Systems on Regime Formation*

4 Preponderant Single Parties and Immediate Authoritarian Rule 103

5 Polarization, Mobilizational Asymmetry, and Delayed Authoritarian Rule 123

6 Depolarization, Increased Mobilizational Symmetry, and the Consolidation of Competitive Politics in Turkey 158

CONCLUSION: The Arguments in Middle East and Comparative Perspective 188

NOTES 205

BIBLIOGRAPHY 219

INDEX 237

ACKNOWLEDGMENTS

In these few pages I want to thank the people and the institutions that supplied the professional and personal support without which this book could not have been written.

I was fortunate to receive financial support for the research and writing of the original manuscript on which the book is based from a number of sources, including a National Science Foundation Graduate Research Fellowship and fieldwork funding from the American Research Institute in Turkey, the Institute for Turkish Studies, and Princeton University's Center for International Studies and Council on Regional Studies. A fellowship from the Society of Fellows of the Woodrow Wilson Foundation and two Princeton University summer stipends supported the writing process. During one of those summers, the participants in a fabulous SSRC writing workshop, ably led by Joel Migdal and Steven Heydemann, provided timely and critical input as I was developing my arguments.

I must also thank the many who made my fieldwork year a productive one. First and foremost I wish to acknowledge the librarians, archive staffs, scholars, and politicians in Turkey and Tunisia who gave me their time and attention. In Turkey the staffs of the American Research Institutes in Ankara and İstanbul ably provided research support as well as homes away from home. In Tunis, Jeanne Mrad of the Centre d'Etudes Maghrebines à Tunis supported me both professionally and personally in important ways. To her I will always be grateful.

Throughout the project I benefited immensely from truly fine advising.

John Waterbury provided timely, careful, invaluable input on the comparative and Middle East dimensions of the study. When new professional challenges called him away from Princeton, neither the promptness nor the quality of his attention flagged, for which I am grateful. Atul Kohli's intellect and curiosity helped hook me on comparative politics, and his personal support subsequently helped keep me in the field. His ability to go right to the heart of the analytic issues that often swirled around unformed in early chapter drafts was tremendously helpful to me as I developed my arguments. Nancy Bermeo, too, has shaped this work in important ways. As a scholar, teacher, colleague, mother, and mentor, she has been for me a wise and treasured role model.

Beyond Princeton, of course, there are myriad individuals and institutions to which I must also give my heartfelt thanks for supporting me as I crafted the final book manuscript. I received valuable feedback as to the strengths and weaknesses of the manuscript from Sheri Berman, participants in a series of workshops titled "Bringing the Middle East Back In . . . to the Study of Political and Economic Reform," and several anonymous reviewers who commented diligently and intelligently on the work.

Most recently, my professional home has been the Department of Political Science at Union College in Schenectady, New York. A friendly home it has been, with colleagues who are as personally likeable as they are incredibly talented teachers and researchers. There I owe Carol Cichy a debt of thanks for her assistance in preparing the final manuscript.

For their interest in and support of the book project, I wish to express my gratitude to Michael Duckworth and his colleagues at the University of Washington Press. The same is due to Charlotte Borst, Dean of Arts and Sciences at Union College, and the Institute of Turkish Studies; both provided generous subvention funds to facilitate the book's publication.

Finally, thanks go to my mother, in whose bloodlines my intellectual instincts undoubtedly find their origins, and to my dad, who has all along been my most zealous cheerleader. My son, Jordan, with his zest for living and especially for the playground, forced me to retain some semblance of balance in my life as the book took final form. To my husband, Ezra, I cannot sufficiently express my gratitude. Our relationship closely spans the years spent working on the original manuscript and subsequent book. It has sustained me through rocky patches and has always been a source of joy. It is to him that I dedicate the book.

Party Building in the Modern Middle East

INTRODUCTION

Party Systems and Regime Formation in the Middle East

In 1950, Mustafa Kemal Atatürk's ruling Republican People's Party allowed free and fair elections to go forward in Turkey. To the surprise of many in the party, the opposition Democrat Party won a large parliamentary majority in those elections. Faced with defeat at the ballot box, the Republican People's Party assumed the role of loyal opposition while its rival took control of the Turkish ship of state. This peaceful transfer of power—a rare phenomenon in the Middle East—ushered in a new, pluralistic era in Turkish political history. Since 1950, except for very brief intervals of military rule, competitive party politics and free and fair elections have determined who governs Turkey. Yet of all the modern states to emerge this century from the ruins of the Ottoman Empire, Turkey alone evolved competitive political institutions that persisted into the contemporary era. Centered on an inflexible parliamentary quota system, a competitive regime functioned in Lebanon for nearly thirty years but then gave way to civil war. Everywhere else in the Muslim Middle East, armies, families, hegemonic single parties, or monarchs came to dictate the rules and parameters of politics.

The Question Posed

Competitive political norms in Turkey have traveled a bumpy road. The military has intervened in civilian affairs on at least three occasions since 1950.[1] After 1961, the military acquired the constitutional right to constrain civilian decision-making processes through the institution of the National

Security Council, a body of military and civilian leaders possessing what amounted to veto power over cabinet initiatives. Yet while post-1950 Turkish politics has not been "democratic,"[2] the norm that competitive procedures should determine who holds power has remained an entrenched one in the Turkish political community. After all three coups, military leaders returned power to civilian politicians in short order (after between one and three years). Despite repeated military interventions, for the half century following 1950, Turkey's party system manifested significant continuity in the organization and leadership of the main center-left and center-right parties. In the first elections following the 1980 coup, victory went to the party most independent of the military. Competitive elections and parliamentary processes thus have been understood by a majority of Turks to be the legitimate mechanisms that govern cabinet formation and political representation. In this respect, Turkish politics has been, by orders of magnitude, more competitive than that of any other Muslim state in the region.

With the exception of Lebanon, the remaining Muslim Middle East states settled into various forms of authoritarian rule in the postcolonial era, and authoritarianism has proven to be tremendously resilient in the region. No Middle East state made a transition to democracy between 1974 and 1990, for instance. During these years, dubbed by Huntington (1991) as the "Third Wave," a significant democratizing trend touched southern Europe, Latin America, eastern Europe, the former Soviet Union, and parts of Asia and sub-Saharan Africa. Yet the Middle East remained seemingly immune to such developments. Some political liberalization—and even some democratizing reforms—were instituted in the region during the Third Wave,[3] but in no country did a democratic experiment with free and fair elections occur that contained the possibility of real change in the locus of political power. Instead, authoritarian rule continued to be *the* rule in the region through the end of the millennium. While several liberalizing and/or democratizing developments have transpired recently in the wake of two dramatic "shocks" to the region (the U.S. military intervention in Iraq and the death of Yasser Arafat),[4] numerous serious obstacles remain in the way of substantial regionwide democratization.[5]

Why, in a region so homogeneously authoritarian, was Turkey able to evolve competitive political institutions? How did patterns of political development there contrast with those of the rest of the postcolonial, Muslim Middle East to yield Turkey's exceptional regime outcome? These are the questions this book sets out to answer. Understanding the macrohistorical dynamics underlying regime formation and regime type has long been a central research concern in comparative politics. On intellectual grounds, then, the puzzle of Turkish exceptionalism calls out for investigation. More important perhaps, in an era when U.S. foreign policy toward the Middle East now explicitly aims at democratizing that region, comparative scholarly work offering insights into the ingredients that were necessary to achieve plural politics in the region's one success story in this regard is of practical, policy-informing value as well.

Contending Theories of Middle East Authoritarianism

What explains the emergence of competitive electoral politics in Turkey and authoritarian regimes nearly everywhere else in the post-Ottoman, Muslim Middle East? The argument presented here locates the origins of regional regime configurations in the relationships that held among political parties when countries in the region first gained independence in the early to mid-twentieth century. Several characteristics of the nascent party systems that were in existence at the crucial independence juncture significantly affected the shape of the political regimes that would emerge in the region. With its focus on party system characteristics as pivotal explanatory variables, this study takes a different theoretical approach from the extant literature on regime type in the Middle East, which tends to attribute outcomes to local political cultures, levels of socioeconomic development, or class structures.

POLITICAL CULTURE

One school of thought on the emergence of authoritarian rule in the Middle East assigns predominant causal weight to culture. "Political culture" can refer to the beliefs, attitudes, and feelings held by individuals concerning the proper organization of their political community (Almond and Verba 1963; Inglehart 1988 and 1997), patterns of political behavior (Waterbury 1970), and/or practices of "meaning making" among political actors (Wedeen 2002). However culture is operationalized as an independent variable, resulting hypotheses tend to share a common intuition: culturally patterned beliefs and behaviors have an important, tangible impact on the stuff and functioning of political regimes. A given political culture either is or is not propitious for the founding and/or consolidation of a given kind of regime. More specifically, democracy's development, solidification, and stability will require a certain set of supportive cultural underpinnings. According to this perspective, authoritarian regimes in the Middle East find their anchor in the attitudes, orientations, and behaviors of their citizens.[6]

Perhaps the most prominent cultural take on regional authoritarianism casts Islam as the culprit. Many argue that the emergence of democracy in the Middle East was (and is) unlikely because democratic ideals and institutions find little to no echo in Islamic sacred texts or political theory.[7] Others, however, have identified nonreligious elements of Middle Eastern cultures as obstacles to the emergence of democracy. Sharabi asserts that a constellation of values, attitudes, and authority relations featuring repressive paternal roles and emphasizing individuals' subordination to personalized rather than legal-rational authority is responsible for thwarting democratic development in the Arab world (1988). Hammoudi suggests that a widely held "master-disciple" norm governs individuals' behavior in the region. Here, authoritarianism is buttressed by a social pyramid of men who show obedient, submissive behavior to those above them in the hierarchy while simultaneously showing authoritarian, domineering behavior toward those below them (1997).

While such arguments may seem reasonable and intuitive, three important liabilities mean that political culture is not an ideal theoretical starting-point for answering the comparative regime-formation question posed in this study. First, the argument alleging Islam's authoritarian affinity is overly simplistic, reductionist, and untenable, as any religion will generate a range of competing interpretations and derivative societal prescriptions. For example, while some Islamic jurists commanded believers to obey their temporal authorities come what may, over the centuries other important strains of Islamic political philosophy disapproved of arbitrary leaders, conceived of rule as being necessarily contractual and consensual, and commanded disobedience of bad rulers (Lewis 1996, 55). Second, cultural accounts of regime type encounter the "chicken-and-egg" problem that it is difficult to determine whether culture molds structures (e.g., regime type), whether structures mold culture, or whether and how reciprocal causation occurs. Both Sharabi and Hammoudi, for instance, discuss specific socioeconomic and political structures that might well account for the cultural-behavioral patterns they identify as facilitating authoritarian rule; the reader is thus left unconvinced as to culture's role.

Third, cultural accounts of regime formation have difficulty when they acknowledge and encounter subnational cultural pluralism. Often they are unable to explain or predict which or whose culture(s) will matter for regime outcomes. For example, Entelis (1989) identifies Islam, Arabism, and Moroccanism as elements of a common Moroccan cultural "core" but disaggregates the political arena into four subcultures: monarchism, modernism, militarism, and messianism. However, once he does so, he must outline five possible regime trajectories that the Moroccan monarchy might take, for he cannot predict which subculture will triumph.

The larger analytical problem is that cultural approaches tend to present correlations between cultural traits and political outcomes without addressing issues of agency. Inglehart (1997), for example, argues that economic development facilitates democratic development and consolidation not only through its impact on social structures but also through its impact on cultural norms and values. Postmaterialist values emphasizing individual freedom, self-expression, and participation spread among populations, which then demand and defend democratic institutions. At the level at which Inglehart is theorizing, however, little can be said about who will go about constructing democracy, how, and under what conditions. This study views regime type as the product of struggles among concrete, purposive political actors over what the "rules of the game" will be. Linking cultural attributes to regime outcomes without specifying the relevant actors and arenas of struggle is ultimately unsatisfactory. Therefore, while it assuredly must matter in that it will partially inform key agents' preferences, norms, and worldviews, political culture is not the most useful analytical point of departure for this investigation into regime formation dynamics.

LEVELS OF SOCIOECONOMIC DEVELOPMENT: MODERNIZATION THEORY

A second important macrohistorical tradition in the study of regime formation and regime type is the modernization paradigm. Modernization theory concerned itself with the processes and implications of industrialization and economic growth in the non-Western world, both for individuals[8] and for polities. In terms of the latter, work in this tradition conceives of democratizing political change as arising from industrialization and economic growth and the various societal changes that these effected. Lipset asserted that urbanization and rising wealth and education levels, as well as decreasing income gaps across social classes, created populations that were oriented to moderate parties, a requisite for making democracy work (1959). Others hypothesized along more functionalist lines. Lerner conceived of democracy as "an institutional outgrowth of needs internal to an increasingly participant society" (1958, 68). Similarly, Huntington argued that political systems would become more sophisticated, secular, rational, and democratic to successfully manage societies that were increasingly complex and variegated (in terms of class structure, culture, and so on) (1991, 65).

Some have argued that modernization theory explains the prevalence of authoritarian rule in the Middle East. Issawi concluded that the region lacked the economic and social foundations necessary for democracy to "strike root and flourish," including communications infrastructures, higher levels of more equitably distributed income, larger middle classes, industrial and commercial growth, urbanization, improved educational attainment, and growth in the number of cooperative associations (1956). Lerner asserted that much of the Middle East lacked the levels of urbanization, literacy, and mass media communications that would produce well-informed, participatory citizenries and thus democratic governance; by contrast, Turkey was the Middle East's "most impressive example of modernization" (1958, 105).

Yet the empirical record raises questions about the utility of modernization theory for investigating the type of comparative regime-formation question that is posed here. Democratic development in the United States preceded industrialization, for instance. Argentina and Brazil saw economic growth go hand in hand with the breakdown of democracy (O'Donnell 1973). Post-1989 sub-Saharan Africa witnessed a number of democratic experiments in the absence of substantial industrialization, urbanization, or mass literacy. If most of the Middle East was insufficiently modern for democracy in the 1950s, in 1991 Huntington wrote that "Middle Eastern economies and societies were approaching the point where they would be too wealthy and too complex for their various . . . systems of authoritarian rule" (315). Yet, more than a decade later, authoritarian rulers still hang on to power across the region. Economic development thus seems to be neither a necessary nor a sufficient condition for political pluralization. In Przeworski and Limongi's words, "democracy is or is not established by political actors pursuing their goals, and it can be initiated at any level of development" (1997, 177).

As the preceding quote suggests, the main theoretical drawback to modernization theory for the purposes of this study is that, like political culture arguments, it analyzes observed correlations (economic growth and democracy) without addressing either the struggles through which specific regime configurations emerge or the agents who are party to such struggles. Lipset assumes democratic rules and then theorizes about modernization's production of citizens who act in ways that do not threaten such rules. But he cannot tell us how democratic institutions get built in the first place. Similarly, while Lerner analyzes in great depth the human agents of *modernization*—the "Transitionals" in a given society—he is silent about agency where the construction of *democracy* is concerned. Modernization theory's inability to specify when and under what conditions actors are likely (or unlikely) to put democratic institutions into place suggests that it is not the most useful approach for the research question at hand.

There remains much to be said for the insights that derive from modernization theory. Global economic development, communications improvements, and scientific and technological progress struck at centralized state power and undermined authoritarian regimes, helping to drive the Third Wave of democratic transitions (Pye 1990). An impressive number of quantitative analyses probing Lipset's "optimistic equation" between economic development and democracy have confirmed the correlation and demonstrated that the former appears to be causal of the latter.[9] And while Przeworski and Limongi question that claim, they affirm that, once established, democracy is stabilized and sustained by economic development (1997). Indeed, countries' levels of development will always be relevant to understanding the types of regime they harbor, because while

> history is not moved by some hidden economic hand, but by people and the variety of interests, values, and unique historical factors that motivate them . . . changing social and economic conditions—including economic development and its consequences—powerfully frame those interests and values and conjunctures. (Diamond 1992, 116)

Still, to explore in an intellectually satisfying way the origins of modern Middle East regime types, this study places a primary focus on the "interests, values, and unique historical factors that motivate[d]" the concrete actors whose choices shaped political institutions.

CLASS

Like modernization theory, class approaches to regime formation see the development of the capitalist mode of production as the most important causal factor driving changes in political institutions. Unlike modernization theorists, however, analysts in this tradition *do* specify who the relevant agents are in regime-building processes. A main claim is that capitalist middle classes are the standard-bearers in struggles for democracy because representative institutions provide them with the public goods they require if they are to flourish (Moore 1966, Hobsbawm 1968). Following a similar logic, the literature assumes that where a labor-repressive, large-landholding aristocracy is the dominant social class, the emergence of democracy is unlikely (Moore 1966; Rueschemeyer, Stephens, and Stephens 1992).

Those who use class to account for regime type in the Middle East argue that states in the region evolved authoritarian rather than democratic systems in the postcolonial period because they lacked sufficiently large and autonomous middle classes (Bellin 2000) and because they instead tended to possess significant, large landlord classes (Gerber 1987). At the same time, a prominent argument about the emergence of competitive party politics in Turkey attributes this outcome to the preferences and activism of the Turkish middle class. It posits that by 1946, the commercial and industrial middle class was unhappy with the Republican People's Party regime's economic policies and arbitrary tendencies. This middle class is argued to have reacted by forming the opposition Democrat Party and driving a democratizing transition to secure its interests (Keyder 1987; Ahmad 1993).[10]

As intuitively plausible as the arguments appear, class analysis is handicapped as a general, solo approach to regime formation and regime type by a number of shortcomings. First, the notion of one or another class in society acting in concert for a given political objective is problematic because, empirically, classes often are divided (Bellin 2000; Przeworski and Sprague 1986; Vitalis 1995). Second, a broad consensus exists that class interests cannot be deduced from objective relationships to modes of production; instead, interests are contingent (Bellin 2002; Kohli and Shue 1994; Przeworski and Limongi 1993). Third, class analysis tends to be too quick to assume collective action when it is actually the case that members of a given class *may or may not* act collectively in pursuit of commonly held goals (Katznelson 1986). Finally, a society's division along class lines does not inevitably mean that politics will be organized in terms of class; other types of identity—including religion, race, ethnicity, language, and region—may motivate individuals in the political sphere (Przeworski and Sprague 1986).

If classes often are divided, if their interests are contingent, if their ability to act collectively is determined by other variables, and if politics is not necessarily dominated by class concerns, then taking a strictly class approach to the research question posed here is not advisable. Such an approach offers little hope of generating predictions or general statements about the conditions under which, and as a result of whose agency, democratic institutions will emerge. That said, class considerations often matter greatly to political outcomes. Indeed, this study will show that actors' class positions and material interests were very relevant to Middle Eastern regime outcomes. However, complementing class considerations with an analytical focus on parties is crucial for generating systematic accounts of regime type in the region.

The Analytical Approach of the Book: Why Parties?

This study proceeds on the premise that the contours of political regimes are drawn during struggles for power among purposeful agents—and that political parties are agents that deserve our analytical attention.[11] Interestingly, scholars working in the class tradition often end up writing extensively about parties. In a seminal work, Luebbert (1991) argues that class characteristics and patterns of class alliances determined regime outcomes in interwar western Europe. His work is widely characterized as class analysis (Thelen 1998, 5; Ertman 1998, 494)[12] but revolves around parties and party behavior because parties are, in his words, the "representatives" of social classes. Rueschemeyer, Stephens, and Stephens also pay significant attention to parties because they "emerged in a crucial role as mediators" between class interests and political outcomes (1992, 9). Though their dependent variable is not regime type, Przeworski and Sprague argue about party rather than class attributes because they find that parties' strategies affect the salience of class for political outcomes (1986, 9).

More generally, the fact that political parties are collective actors gives us sound theoretical reason to expect them to play important roles in regime formation processes. Parties can link together large numbers of individuals and, as a result, can affect political outcomes in significant ways. In his classic work on political parties, Michels stressed that, "be the claims economic or be they political, organization appears the only means for the creation of a collective will. Organization . . . is the weapon of the weak in their struggle against the strong" (1962, 61–62). The ability to mobilize and command the loyalty of large constituencies gives party leaders more potential political influence than that wielded either by individual actors or by smaller, clique-like groups. When the dependent variable to be explained is a macro-level phenomenon such as regime type, parties therefore are likely to be pivotal actors.

The nature of the goals toward which party leaders direct their regime-shaping influence is, of course, an open question. Twentieth-century history furnishes a number of examples wherein political leaders used powerful parties to build authoritarian regimes: Mao Tse-Tung and the Communist party in China and Adolf Hitler and the Nazi party in Germany are but two examples. Political parties have proved to be effective instruments for the creation and maintenance of authoritarian regimes, both in the Middle East and around the globe.

At the same time, party-centered competition and opposition can play key roles in moving a polity toward democracy. For instance, the establishment of authoritarian rule can be thwarted—or at least made more difficult—when at least two groups possessing approximate parity in organization and resources confront one another and contend for power. In such a situation, competitive institutions may emerge as a second-best solution that all parties agree to because none is strong enough to impose its own top preferences on the political arena (Rustow 1970; O'Donnell and Schmitter 1986). Where an authoritarian regime already exists, the existence of a party-based opposition can trigger democratizing regime change. Due to their collective character, the emergence of party-based opposition can be a threatening development to authoritarian rulers. If opposition parties grow too large and institutionalized to buy off and too extensive to repress without the incursion of intolerable political costs, they can put pressure on those in power to accommodate them by pluralizing the rules of the game.

Not only can parties bring substantial pressure to bear on authoritarian regimes; they may also be a boon to the success of pacted democratizing transitions. Pact participants will be more likely to sign on if they are confident that their partners will deliver on promises made—for example, not to push beyond agreed-upon policy agendas, not to mobilize too widely, not to prosecute leaders accused of human rights violations, and so on. Cohesive, disciplined parties that are able to keep members and constituents in compliance with pact principles and the evolving rules of a new political game can help supply this confidence (O'Donnell and Schmitter 1986, 40–41, 47; Bruhn 1997, 9).

The historical record also shows that, in many places, competition between two or more political parties has served as an engine of democratic deepening over the long term. This has tended to take the form of suffrage extension and mobilization, processes pushed as competing parties sought to further broaden the bases of their support. Competition between the Liberal and Conservative parties in nineteenth-century England, for example, led to a series of suffrage rights extensions (Sartori 1976, 21). Similarly, Aldrich argues that "the mass party was created for, and was critical to, the extension of democratic practices in nineteenth-century America" (1995, 295–96).

Finally, the democratization and parties literatures contain consistent assumptions about the importance of political parties to the healthy functioning of democracies. To quote Schattschneider, "modern democracy is unthinkable save in terms of parties" (1942, 1). Indeed, parties play several crucial political functions in democratic systems. They are intermediate institutions connecting citizens to the government. They order the political game by aggregating and articulating citizens' preferences, by reducing information costs and facilitating voter participation at elections, and so on (Mainwaring and Scully 1995, 2–3). They recruit citizens into public office and shape public policy (Mair 1990, 1), and they serve to hold elected officials collectively responsible for policy action (Aldrich 1995, 3).

The Argument (I): How Party Systems Shaped Regimes in the Modern Middle East

As the states of the Middle East broke free from the yoke of the Western imperial powers (France and Britain) in the mid-twentieth century, political parties played important roles in shaping the founding regimes that would emerge in ten countries: Tunisia, South Yemen, Algeria, Morocco, Iran, Iraq, Jordan, Syria, Egypt, and Turkey.[13] Following Collier and Collier, this study defines "regime" as the "structure of state and governmental roles and processes," including "the method of selection of the government and of representative assemblies (election, coup, decision within the military, etc.), formal and informal mechanisms of representation, and patterns of repression" (1991, 789). By "founding regimes" the study refers to the first set of stable rules governing cabinet formation, representation, and repression that emerged in the states of the region after the departure of the imperial powers. The characteristics and behavior of the political parties that were in existence at this historic juncture had an important impact on the types of founding regimes that would be established.

The cases subdivide into three categories (see table 1). In three cases—

TABLE 1. Number of Parties and Regime Outcomes

Country	*Independence*	*Parties after Independence*	*Founding Regime*	*Type*
TUNISIA	1956	Neo-Destour	1956–present	(immediate) authoritarian
SOUTH YEMEN	1967	National Liberation Front	1967–1990	(immediate) authoritarian
ALGERIA	1962	Front de Libération National	1962–present	(immediate) authoritarian
IRAN	(1941)	Tudeh/Communists Iran Liberals Democrats Patriots National Union	1953–1979	(delayed) authoritarian
IRAQ	1932	Istiqlal National Democrats Communists Ba'th Constitutional Union Socialist Nation	1968–2003	(delayed) authoritarian
JORDAN	1946	Communists Ba'th National Socialists Muslim Brotherhood Liberation Community Arab Constitutionalists	1957–present	(delayed) authoritarian
SYRIA	1946	Communists Arab Socialists Ba'th People's National	1963–present	(delayed) authoritarian

Country	Independence	Parties after Independence	Founding Regime	Type
EGYPT	1936	Muslim Brotherhood Young Egypt Communists Wafd Liberal Constitutionalists Sa'dists Independent Wafdist Bloc Watani Ittihad Sha'b	1952–present	(delayed) authoritarian
TURKEY	1923	Republican People's Party PRP>FRP>DP	1950–present	(delayed) competitive

Tunisia, South Yemen, and Algeria—an authoritarian founding regime was established immediately at independence. In six cases, founding regimes were established only after significant transitional periods had unfolded. During these periods, the rules governing cabinet composition, representation, and repression were in flux as political parties and other actors jockeyed for position. Transitional periods were characterized by inconsistent methods of forming governments and managing representation—methods that were associated with different levels of repression. Transitional periods ended and founding regimes began in these countries when a consistent, replicated rule governing cabinet formation, representation, and repression emerged for the first time after independence. In Iran, Iraq, Jordan, Syria, and Egypt, founding regimes were authoritarian. In Turkey, however, a competitive regime was constructed.[14]

Three party system characteristic variables help explain this variation in founding regime outcomes. The first is the number of parties. In Tunisia, South Yemen, and Algeria, a single preponderant party monopolized the domestic political stage at independence (see table 1). These parties were "preponderant" in that they were mass parties organized and exerting social control in all (or nearly all) rural and urban areas. The term "social control" refers to the fact that these parties commanded the loyalty of the majority of nonelite actors in these areas. In all three cases, the existence of single, preponderant, mass-mobilizing parties facilitated the immediate establishment of one-party authoritarian regimes at independence. When the imperial powers departed, these parties faced no significant challengers for power. What's more, they constituted extremely effective tools with which elites could construct authoritarian rule. In Tunisia, South Yemen, and Algeria, party leaders used them to suppress their would-be rivals, to take over the state, and to craft the new political rules of the game in their favor.

The remaining countries under consideration here—Iran, Iraq, Jordan, Syria, Egypt, and Turkey—saw multiple parties contending with one another for power at independence. No single actor could impose its will and craft the rules of a stable founding regime right away as had been the case in Tunisia, South Yemen, and Algeria. Instead, in all six cases an interim transitional period of political contestation unfolded between independence and the time when founding regimes put down roots.[15] During these transitional periods, the rules of the game were fluid, contested, and unstable. Importantly, multiple parties competed with one another for influence in political arenas in which, at the outset, competitive elections and parliaments to a significant extent determined representation and cabinet formation. For this reason, all six states had an opportunity to evolve competitive institutions. Of the six, however, only Turkey did so. In the remaining five cases, nascent competitive politics gradually gave way to authoritarian rule over the course of transitional periods.

Why did the norm of electoral competition flourish only in Turkey? Two additional variables sort the multiparty cases in a manner that helps to answer this question: the presence or absence of polarization, and the presence or absence of "mobilizational asymmetry" in party systems. The theoretical context from which these variables derive is what Waterbury dubbed the "contingency school in explaining the initiation and institutionalization of democracy" (1997). Put forth by Rustow (1970) and formalized by Przeworski (1988, 1991), this perspective pays primary attention to relationships among agents during periods of regime flux. It conceives of democracy as occurring when "bargained equilibria lead to the establishment of institutional arrangements from which no significant actors have any incentive to defect" (Waterbury 1997, 387).

The fundamental insight here is that democratic regimes are special sets of rules put into place by concrete historical actors. They are "special" because, by specifying that elections and parliamentary politics will determine the content of governmental policy, they introduce levels of uncertainty into the political process that are unmatched in authoritarian contexts (Przeworski 1986). At the end of the day, in a polity governed by democratic rules, no actor can be sure that its rivals will not come to power.

Democratic institutions, therefore, cannot survive unless all key actors are prepared to live with the fact that no guarantees exist as to the identity of those who will wield policymaking power. Democracy is viable only if all actors make the calculation that they can accept open-ended governance outcomes.

In democracies, elections are the route to power, and parties are the vehicles used by elites to gain the votes they need to defend their interests in parliament. As parties are pivotal to the processes that determine who will wield policymaking power, party-system characteristics will influence elites' calculations about their ability to defend their interests in a democratic context. If viable democracy is a bargain struck by elite actors—a bargain that no actor wishes to terminate—then party-system characteristics should bear greatly on actors' decisions as to whether or not they can tolerate democracy.

For any given party elite, this calculation entails two considerations. The first is an assessment of what rival parties bring to the competitive electoral table, platform-wise. If an opposing party were to win power, what kind of policies would it be likely to implement? How threatening would those be to one's interests? If the answers to these questions suggest that a given party elite's interests would come under substantial threat, those actors will be less likely to remain allegiant to democratic institutions.[16] For this reason, high levels of polarization in party systems lower the probability that democratic rules will survive. Taking its cues from Waldner (1999), this study defines "polarized" party systems as those in which one or more parties advocate policies that threaten one or more segments of the political elite's ability to reproduce their elite status over the long term.

The second consideration is an assessment of what rival parties bring to the competitive electoral table mobilizationally relative to one's own party. How well equipped to capture votes are one's opponents, as compared with one's own party's ability to get the vote out? Can one's own party muster sufficient votes to defend one's interests democratically? These questions are important because they bear on the probability that one's opponents will have the opportunity to carry out alternative policy agendas. If the answers to these questions suggest that one's own party is significantly handicapped in the vote-getting arena relative to its opponents, one will be less likely to remain faithful to democratic rules—especially if polarization exists. In party systems characterized by "mobilizational asymmetry"—that is, the existence of significant gaps in contending parties' respective abilities to get out the vote—the probability that democratic rules will survive is low.[17]

Polarization and mobilizational asymmetry characterized nascent party systems in newly independent Iran, Iraq, Jordan, Syria, and Egypt. In the elections and parliaments that functioned during transitional periods, conservative forces committed to maintaining the political-economic status quo confronted challenger forces intent on significantly altering that status quo through land reforms and nationalization of industry. Depending on the case, conservatives and challengers fought over three additional polarizing issues: borders, foreign allegiances, and regime type. Conservative forces failed to build parties at all or formed nonideological parties whose political support rested on a limited base of patron-client ties. Challenger forces, meanwhile, were building modern and encompassing party structures with articulate, strident ideological platforms. In doing so, the latter were laying the building blocks for a capacity in the long term to substantially outpoll conservatives. Threatened by this development, conservatives defected from nascent democratic rules by rigging elections, suppressing challenger parties, and supporting monarchs and foreign powers in antidemocratic actions. Faced with such defections, challenger parties also defected from democratic rules, turning to alternative arenas such as the streets and the army in the pursuit of power. These dynamics hollowed out and ultimately destroyed democratic arenas, paving the way for the establishment of authoritarian regimes.

Turkey began its postindependence transitional period with a party system that closely resembled those of the breakdown cases. At the beginning of the period, two parties squared off in the political arena. The challenger party's policy agenda threatened the status-quo party's leaders' ability to sustain their elite status and looked to be mobilizationally superior to the status-quo party. Sensing its inability to defend its interests in a competitive context, the status-quo party defected from nascent democratic norms and suppressed the opposition. Unlike in the breakdown cases, at this point the opposition did *not* defect from democratic norms and seek out alternative arenas through which to pursue power. Instead, it lay low, buying Turkey important time during which nascent democratic institutions had the potential to be salvaged. Over time, challenger parties deradicalized while the status-quo party dramatically grew its grassroots apparatus. Depolarization and increased mobilizational symmetry facilitated Turkey's turn to a largely stable competitive regime in 1950 when the status-quo party, feeling confident of its ability to defend its interests democratically, agreed to compete with its opponent in free and fair elections.

The Argument (II): The Factors That Shaped Party System Characteristics

If variation in party system characteristics was so pivotal for founding regime outcomes, what explains that variation? Why did these countries arrive at the independence juncture with such divergent nascent party systems? These questions bring into focus a second analytical dimension of this study, which treats party system characteristics as dependent variables.

Single, preponderant, mass-mobilizing parties in Tunisia, South Yemen, and Algeria were the product of the impact of imperial powers' policies on the sociopolitical standing of traditional elites in those societies. In these three cases, imperialists' modes of occupation significantly disrupted traditional elites' patron-client relationships. In addition, the imperial powers were intransigent in the face of traditional elites' demands for independence. They did not establish parliamentary bodies in which indigenous elites could wield some measure of influence, and they made few if any concessions to early nationalist demands. Both dynamics critically weakened traditional elites' power in society. As a result, control over nationalist movements eventually passed into the hands of "second-generation" elites. These were men of comparatively humble, rural social origins who were willing, able, and motivated to mobilize on a mass basis (whereas traditional elites were not). Second-generation elites were the motor force behind the construction of single, preponderant, mass-mobilizing parties.

Multiparty postindependence political arenas emerged in countries whose traditional elites were *not* weakened and discredited by intransigent imperial behavior. These cases either avoided formal, direct foreign occupation (Turkey and Iran) or experienced a milder form of imperialism than did Tunisia, South Yemen, and Algeria. With regard to the latter scenario, imperial occupation policies did not dramatically weaken the social power of traditional elites in Iraq, Jordan, Syria, and Egypt. When these elites demanded independence, the European powers were not intransigent: they established powerful parliaments populated by indigenous elites, and they granted these nations independence relatively rapidly thereafter. Traditional elites retained control over nationalist movements in these cases, preventing the second-generation takeover that drove the creation of single preponderant parties elsewhere in the region. What's more, the parliaments that were created provided indigenous elites with incentives to form competing party organizations to maximize their access to the policy influence and patronage opportunities available in such bodies. Multi- rather than single-party systems were the result.

In Iran, Iraq, Jordan, Syria, and Egypt, multiparty systems saw four or more parties occupying the political stage. The emergence of large numbers of parties in these cases generally can be attributed to electoral systems featuring large district magnitudes (which tend to proliferate the number of parties) combined with the existence of multiple important class, ideological, and social cleavages in society. By contrast, during Turkey's interim transitional period, three opposition parties rose in sequence to confront the ruling Republican People's Party (RPP), establishing Turkey's as a nascent two-party system.[18]

Two historical phenomena produced Turkey's two-party system. First, beginning in the early nineteenth century, a classic center-periphery conflict unfolded in the Turkish political community. For more than a century, politics pitted reformist, centralizing elites tied to the civilian and military bureaucracies of the capital against local provincial elites (primarily wealthy landowners, commercial men, and clerics) who resisted reform and centralization. The protagonists argued about taxation, about how much power was to be concentrated in the central state, about what role the state would play in society and the economy, and about the proper relationship between religion and politics. These questions consistently split the community into the same two camps. While the RPP represented the community's bureaucratic, reformist, centralizing elites, the Progressive Republican Party (PRP), Free Republican Party (FRP), and Democrat Party (DP) mobilized in sequence the voice of the Turkish periphery. Their repeated challenge to the RPP signified the continuing political salience of the center-periphery cleavage in Turkish politics.

Second, an important institutional by-product of this center-periphery conflict provided Turkey's opposition parties with the organizational ability to successfully build a single, unified opposition to the RPP. During the nineteenth century, central elites were forced to grant peripheral elites increased political participation rights in return for the latter's cooperation with key reform efforts. To this end, central elites established a tiered, territory-wide system of provincial administrative councils capped by a parliamentary body in the capital. Over time these institutions fostered vibrant elite networks and important social capital in the countryside that enabled peripheral leaders to act collectively in their battles with the Turkish center. The PRP, FRP, and DP succeeded in launching national parties because they took advantage of these peripheral networks, which linked local elites together both within and across provinces. Provincial elite networks helped opposition parties avoid coordination failures and solve collective action problems as they set out to build national parties capable of humbling the RPP.

Methodology, Research Design, and Case Selection

The book's core claim regarding how party system characteristics shaped the regime-formation experiences of postimperial, Muslim Middle East states is, in the context of comparative research in political science, an argument about critical junctures. Critical junctures are periods of dramatic political change that unfold "in distinct ways in different countries" and that produce "distinct legacies" (Collier and Collier 1991, 29). Here the period of change is the reordering of power relations—dramas wherein political parties were key actors—that became possible in the Middle East when European powers vacated the area. Party system characteristics and parties' interaction varied in distinct, patterned ways across the cases; this variance helps explain the shape of founding political regimes—the legacy of the juncture.

Two phases of comparative historical analysis produced this argument. This research strategy juxtaposes the historical trajectories of "nation-states, institutional complexes, or civilizations . . . to develop, test, and refine causal, explanatory hypotheses about events or structures integral to macro-units such as nation-states" (Skocpol 1979, 36). Comparative historical analysis is an appropriate strategy because the study's dependent variable—regime type—is for each country case the product of conditions, processes, and multiple actors' agency, all playing out over long periods of time. When the task at hand is to uncover historical sequences and causal mechanisms central to the evolution of macrostructural phenomena, no other methodological approach is superior to comparative historical analysis (Skocpol 1979, 36; Stephens 1998, 22).[19]

The first research phase utilized both primary and secondary sources to analyze processes of regime formation in a pair of cases, Turkey and Tunisia, to test the plausibility of extant causal hypotheses as well as to generate new ones. Following Mill's "Method of Difference," this pairing facilitated the examination of divergent regime formation experiences in countries that contained a large number of important similarities. Both countries have experienced stable political administration for centuries. Tunisia has been a distinct political and territorial entity for several hundred years. Similarly, the lands that today constitute Turkey have been part of the same polity for centuries.[20] Neither country's borders were drawn arbitrarily by Western powers—as was the case in many other Middle Eastern countries.[21] In addition, beginning in the late eighteenth century, an increasingly powerful Europe threatened the regional status quo. Turkish and Tunisian political elites' responses to this threat were remarkably similar and included military modernization, centralizing administrative reforms, constitution writing, and the creation of parliaments.

Of the political systems present in the region, Tunisia's is the most comparable to that which was upended in Turkey in 1950 when a competitive regime was founded there. In both countries, hegemonic political parties whose institutional roots lay in battles for national sovereignty constructed westernizing, secularizing, statist, authoritarian one-party regimes. Tunisia's regime proved to be dramatically more robust than Turkey's. While the former has yet to confront an opponent it could not best, the position of the authoritarian ruling party in Turkey was shaky from the start. Robust, rival political parties challenged it early and often, and in 1950 it yielded to competitive party politics. This paired comparison highlighted the causal importance of political parties as actors and of the party number variable in regime-construction processes.

The second, hypothesis-refining, phase of the research drew on secondary sources to broaden the cross-national scope of the project. It examined the experiences of all other states in the region where parties played an important role in shaping founding regimes. This added to the research design numerous additional cases in which, as was the case for Turkey, postindependence politics saw multiple parties competing for influence in institutional environments that included elections and parliaments. Comparing party system dynamics in Turkey to those in Iran, Iraq, Jordan, Syria, and Egypt highlighted the argument's two additional critical variables—the presence or absence of polarization and mobilizational asymmetry—that explain Turkey's unique, competitive regime outcome. Adding cases also facilitated the parallel demonstration of the book's core arguments (Skocpol and Somers 1980, 176). Its claims regarding the regime-formation consequences of the emergence of single preponderant parties are thus shown to order the historical evidence not only in the Tunisian case but also in the South Yemeni and Algerian cases. Similarly, the study shows that polarized, mobilizationally asymmetrical party systems were a death knell for nascent democratic practices in five separate cases.

Three important questions prompted by the research design can now be addressed. First, how valid is the comparison of Turkey, which was never colonized, to a set of cases most of which *were* colonized—many for substantial periods of time? The presence or absence of a Western imperial interlude does not correlate with regime outcomes in this set of cases (see table 2). Like Turkey, Iran was never colonized. Yet Iran did not develop lasting democratic institutions. Of the eight countries that were colonized, some evolved single preponderant parties while others traveled the "multiparty" route to authoritarianism. Important variation in Middle East states' experience with imperialism explains this lack of a direct link between imperialism and later political outcomes (see table 2). The cases differ significantly with respect to the length of time imperial powers stayed, whether or not they were intransigent about leaving, and the kinds of political institutions they put into place. As Turkey is not the sole case in the data set to have escaped imperialism, and because imperialism looked quite different from case to case, thinking about Turkey in the context of this set of referents is justified.

To do so is all the more reasonable because although neither was formally colonized, Turkey and Iran shared a number of important socioeconomic experiences in common with their colonized neighbors. Economies across the Middle East were integrated into global markets late and in a dependent manner as exporters of agricultural or primary products; Turkey and Iran were no exception. The political and military weaknesses of both vis-à-vis Europe forced them to make commercial concessions that allowed cheap, imported, European manufactured goods into local markets, hurting the local artisan and craftsmen classes. The same phenomenon took place in the colonized economies. Finally, indebtedness to European creditors obliged Iran and Turkey (when it was still the Ottoman Empire), as it did Egypt, Tunisia, and Morocco, to cede substantial fiscal sovereignty to European commissions.

A second important question is, how comparable is Turkey, which was situated at the core of the Ottoman Empire, to most other Middle East states, given that the latter constituted this empire's periphery and were politically subjugated to the core? Could divergent experiences of "being Ottoman" skew the analysis? The Middle East as "Ottoman periphery" contained within it quite a lot of variation—variation that again does not correlate with political outcomes (see table 2). South Yemen and Iran never came under Ottoman rule. By the start of the nineteenth century, Tunisia and Egypt were autonomous: elites in Tunis and Cairo no longer took orders from İstanbul regarding domestic or foreign policy. Thus, the preponderant party case set and the multiparty case set each include countries with

TABLE 2. Countries and Colonizers

Country	*Ottoman?*	*Western Colonizer*	*Years Colonized*	*Independence Struggle*	*Indigenous Preindependence Parliaments?*	*Second-Generation Takeover?*
TUNISIA	autonomous	France	1881–1956 (76)	1920–1956 (36)	no	yes
SOUTH YEMEN	no	Britain	1839–1967 (129)	1950–1967 (17)	no	yes
ALGERIA	yes	France	1834–1962 (129)	1926–1962 (36)	no	yes
IRAN	no	n/a	n/a	n/a	yes (1st parl. 1906)	n/a
IRAQ	yes	Britain	1920–1932 (12)	1920–1932 (12)	yes (1st parl. 1924)	no
JORDAN	yes	Britain	1921–1946 (26)	1928–1946 (18)	yes (1st parl. 1929)	no
SYRIA	yes	France	1922–1946 (24)	1922–1946 (24)	yes (1st parl. 1928)	no
EGYPT	autonomous	Britain	1882–1936 (55)	1919–1936 (17)	yes (1st parl. 1923)	(yes)
TURKEY	yes	n/a	n/a	1918–1923 (5)	yes (1st parl. 1876)	n/a

no Ottoman impact, countries with a distant Ottoman impact, and countries with a recent Ottoman impact. Because variation in "Ottoman-ness" does not appear to illuminate variation in either party system characteristics or founding regime types, the fact that Turkey once represented the hub of the Ottoman Empire should not render it too exceptional to be considered together with the other cases included in the research design.

A third, valid case selection concern is that, relative to the other countries analyzed in this study, one could argue that Turkey possessed a more robust, institutionalized state apparatus at independence. In part because Turkey was never colonized and because it represented the core of the Ottoman Empire, well-established civilian bureaucracies functioned alongside a professionalized military, and both had long been staffed and led by indigenous elites. By contrast, in many countries that had been subject to Ottoman and then either British or French rule, states were more rudimentary, were less institutionalized, and had come under indigenous control much more recently. While Turks faced the task of reforming an existing state as actors there struggled over what the rules of the political game would be after 1923, actors in many other cases were struggling after independence to build states in the first place.[22] Does this apples-to-oranges quality of experiences render the comparison problematic?

Two observations help to establish the legitimacy of the comparison. First, the extent to which Turkish "stateness" outpaced that of its neighbors should not be exaggerated. World War I left what remained of the Ottoman Empire in political and economic shambles; in its wake, reformist elites fled İstanbul, established a new capital at Ankara, and proceeded to rebuild the state. Meanwhile, elsewhere in the region imperial powers were building up state apparatuses, including bureaucracies, militaries, and educational systems. While it is true in those cases that, at independence, indigenous elites gained control of the commanding heights of the state for the first time, they were not faced with the task of building states from scratch. Second, if the Turkish state indeed was more institutionalized, this should have made the establishment of authoritarian rule relatively *more* probabilistic there.[23] With a well-developed state apparatus in existence, those actors that first assumed its commanding heights at the independence juncture had access to a formidable institutional tool for maintaining their hegemony over would-be rivals. In cases where state structures were less developed, there should have been less such "hardware" available to *any* actor that was intent on establishing dictatorship.

We must acknowledge that, despite Turkey's comparability to other Middle East cases, it differed from its regional neighbors in important ways *before* it consolidated a competitive founding regime. It had been the "hub" rather than a "spoke" of the Ottoman Empire. It never fell subject to direct Western imperial control. Physically as well as philosophically, it stood closer to democratic experiments in Western Europe than did its regional neighbors. Yet holding up Turkey's experience to that of others in the region is worthwhile because no one has linked these observations to the emergence of competitive political institutions there in a systematic, causal fashion. This book does. Its concluding chapter shows that those characteristics that made Turkey unique in the region prior to the critical independence juncture shaped the characteristics of Turkey's postindependence party system in important respects. These, in turn, put Turkey on a path to competitive politics. By grasping how Turkey's unique qualities relate to party system characteristics, therefore, we gain a nuanced understanding of how those qualities (indirectly) influenced Turkish regime formation.

The Organization of the Study

The chapters that follow advance a two-stage argument (see fig. 1). Part I of the study addresses the factors that gave rise to nascent, postindependence party systems in the Middle East manifesting quite diverse characteristics—characteristics that later would be consequential for founding regime outcomes. Chapter 1 details how single, preponderant, mass-mobilizing parties emerged in Tunisia, South Yemen, and Algeria because nationalist movements passed into the hands of "second-generation" elites after traditional elites' status was undermined by imperial occupation policies and imperial intransigence in the face of early indigenous demands for independence. It also deals with the details of the Moroccan case—one that is slightly aberrant but still can be explained within the framework of the argument.

Chapter 2 demonstrates how multiple parties emerged in Iran, Iraq, Jordan, Syria, and Egypt because traditional elites did not become critically weakened or discredited, and thus nationalist movements never passed into the hands of second-generation elites. Permissive electoral systems worked in tandem with social heterogeneity to ensure that these party systems contained large numbers of parties. Chapter 3 argues that three factors produced Turkey's regionally unique two-party system. These were majoritarian electoral rules, a long legacy of center-periphery conflict that structured politics along bipartisan lines, and robust social networks that enabled dissenting elites in the periphery to solve collective action problems and build substantial opposition parties of national scope with which to challenge the ruling party.

Part II of the study addresses how party system characteristics then shaped founding regime types in the postimperial, Muslim Middle East. Chapter 4 returns to the Tunisian, South Yemeni, and Algerian cases. Building on the insights of chapter 3, it outlines the social networks second-generation elites in those cases drew upon to build preponderant, mass-mobilizing parties successfully. It then establishes why and how, when such parties existed at the critical independence juncture, immediate authoritarian rule was the result. Chapter 4 ends by completing the narrative of the Moroccan case. Chapter 5 establishes how and why polarization and mobilizational asymmetry (between parties interested in defending the political-economic status quo and parties interested in challenging it) led to the establishment of delayed authoritarian rule after interim transitional periods ended in Iran, Iraq, Jordan, Syria, and Egypt. Chapter 6 begins by asserting that because Turkey's party system had just two rather than three or more parties, *de*polarization was more feasible and thus more likely in the Turkish case. It then shows how Turkey's party system became decreasingly polarized and increasingly mobilizationally symmetrical during the interim transition period. The end result was the establishment of a lasting competitive regime.

After recapping the study's primary findings, the concluding chapter reflects on what already distinguished Turkey from much of the rest of the

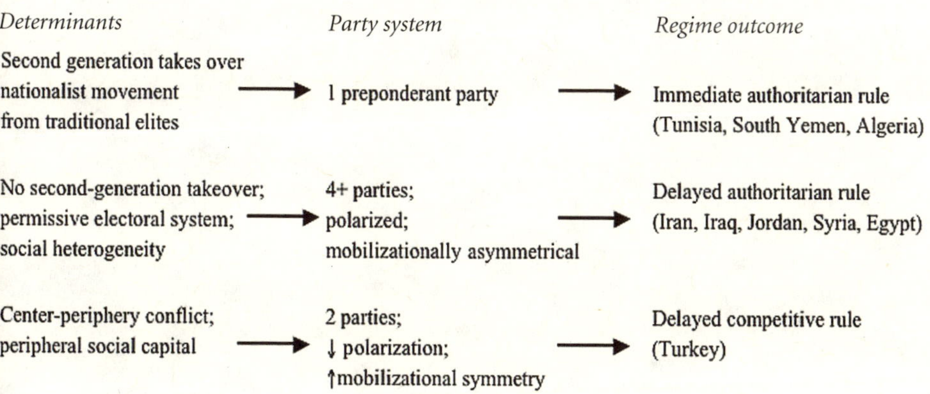

FIG. 1. Party system characteristics and regime outcomes.

region before founding regime formation processes unfolded and the extent to which these qualities can be argued to have contributed to the emergence of a competitive regime there. Turning to practical matters, it next details the lessons and cautions that the study's findings hold for U.S. policymakers who, in the contemporary era, have made democratization a priority. The conclusion ends with discussions of the book's contributions to the broader Middle East politics and comparative politics literatures. The book's argument about the origins of regional regimes provides crucial context for two prominent current accounts of authoritarian rule in the Middle East—those pertaining to rentier income and to imbalanced state-society relations. For comparative politics theorizing more generally, the study's most important theoretical insight is that, although material conflicts may drive politics to a substantial extent, rigorous attention to party system characteristics must complement attention to class-oriented variables if effective, complete accounts of regime formation processes are to be produced.

PART I

Explaining Party System Characteristics

1

The Emergence of the Preponderant Single-Party Systems

The political preponderance of one party at independence distinguishes Tunisia, South Yemen, and Algeria from the other cases analyzed in this study. True, these parties were not the only parties present on the political stage at independence: Tunisia's Neo-Destour and South Yemen's and Algeria's respective National Liberation Fronts had their would-be rivals. They were "preponderant," however, in that they were mass parties organized in all (or nearly all) urban and rural areas: they exerted social control in both the capital and the countryside.[1] By contrast, all other parties either were elite organizations and/or were rural-only, urban-only, or regional parties. The preponderant parties' territorial breadth and social depth rendered their rivals politically irrelevant for the shaping of founding regimes. Chapter 4 will argue that these single preponderant parties were causally pivotal for inspiring and enabling party leaders to rapidly construct (one-party) authoritarian regimes in these three countries. This chapter is devoted to illuminating the dynamics and factors that *produced* single, preponderant, mass-mobilizing parties in Tunisia, South Yemen, and Algeria.

When Middle East elites began demanding independence from their imperial occupiers, the societies they inhabited were in transition from being largely rural ones, with simple class stratifications in which patron-client ties predominated, to ones that were more educated and more urban and that harbored important new social forces. These societies' "traditional" elites included wealthy landowners who were patrons to peasants, tribal leaders who were patrons to tribesmen, and merchants, traders, and the *ulama* (the

Muslim clerical class) who were patrons to the humbler urban strata, including guild members. Industrialization, agricultural commercialization, and the spread of education confronted traditional elites with the emergence of new professional middle-class groups (lawyers, doctors, pharmacists, teachers, civil servants, and so on), a budding urban working class, and, in some cases, an urban subproletariat made up of peasants and tribesmen migrating to cities in search of increased economic opportunity.

Single, preponderant, mass-mobilizing parties in Tunisia, South Yemen, and Algeria resulted from the impact of imperial powers' policies on traditional elites' sociopolitical standing. In these three countries, imperialists' modes of occupation significantly disrupted traditional patron-client relationships, while imperial responses to traditional elites' demands for independence (or lack thereof) discredited the latter in the eyes of newly emergent social forces. Both dynamics critically weakened traditional elites' social power, leading to a situation wherein a new, humbler elite was able to assume control of nationalist movements, building preponderant mass-mobilizing political parties by recruiting to their cause not only traditional and new urban strata but also peasants and tribesmen.

France and Britain took control of Tunisia, South Yemen, and Algeria quite early with respect to the onset of nationalism. Nationalist demands emerged 40, 110, and 90 years respectively after the onset of European control. What's more, France and Britain took control of these lands in an international context that granted them considerable freedom of choice regarding their policies there. The territories they seized after the close of World War I were mandates awarded them by the League of Nations with the expectation that they would protect natives' welfare and prepare them for independence. By contrast, Tunisia, South Yemen, and Algeria fell to European control during the nineteenth century, an era characterized by much more permissive international norms regarding imperialism. These were straightforward colonial possessions not subject to the higher ethical standards of the mandate system (Balfour-Paul 1991, 49). A presumption of Western civilizational superiority justified imperialism (Jackson 1990, 60–61), and blatant practices of imperial exploitation were not looked down upon (Spruyt 2000, 82).

As a result, the European powers had both the time and the latitude they needed to significantly alter the socioeconomic structures they found when they arrived. For example, France turned Tunisia and Algeria into settler colonies, and sizable numbers of citizens from the colonial metropoles relocated to live and work in positions both inside and outside of the colonial administration.[2] The processes by which settlers acquired land often disrupted established patterns of landownership, cultivation, and social relations in the countryside. Imperialists' economic policies—especially the importation of cheap European manufactured goods—harmed merchants' and craftsmen's livelihoods in towns. Policies that secularized governance undermined the *ulama*. All of these developments chipped away at the foundations of traditional patron-client relationships by undermining patrons' abilities to continue to provide for client needs. Traditional elites' power in society began to weaken as a result.

Still, for the most part, across the region traditional elites were the first to establish nationalist political parties and demand independence. The parties they built were elaborated only to a limited extent, however. Typically, they established branches in major cities and towns but refrained from penetrating rural areas and tended to recruit members from the upper and middle classes only. Traditional elites' choice to organize according to such limited parameters was consistent with their position in social and political hierarchies. As the society's ultimate elite, they would not have been disposed to engage actively society's lower strata, nor would they have been comfortable doing so. At the same time, it was not in their interest to mass mobilize, for to do so would have threatened their own positions as patrons by broadening the political horizons of their clients.

In Tunisia, South Yemen, and Algeria, imperial powers were intransigent in the face of these demands for independence. For the purposes of this study, "imperial intransigence" is a function of two aspects of imperialists' responses to early nationalist demands: whether or not the former established politically powerful parliaments populated by indigenous elites, and the amount of time that elapsed between the first indigenous demands for independence and independence itself. France and Britain did not establish influential indigenous parliaments in these three cases; indeed, they made few if any concessions at all to early nationalist demands. Instead, they dragged their feet, and independence would not come for another thirty-six years in Tunisia and Algeria, and for another seventeen years in South Yemen.[3]

When their demands for independence fell on deaf ears, traditional elites in Tunisia, South Yemen, and Algeria found their social power further weakened. This trend was exacerbated by the fact that these early nationalists tended to back down in the face of imperial intransigence. For the most part they neither upped the ante by resorting to such pressure tactics as strikes, demonstrations, and/or violence, nor did they elect to mobilize on a broader basis. Their tactical moderation and their ineffectiveness vis-à-vis the nationalist cause discredited traditional elites in the eyes of new, emerging social forces. It should be noted that some segments of the Algerian and South Yemeni traditional elite did *not* demand independence. In these instances the ultimate societal outcome—the discrediting of those traditional elites in the eyes of new emerging social forces—was the same.

As the years went by, the reins of nationalist movements in these societies passed from the hands of socially weakened and politically discredited traditional elites into the hands of elites from the new emerging social forces—especially lawyers, teachers, civil servants, and students. This "second generation" of nationalist leaders tended to be more radical in its political outlook than were traditional elites. This difference resulted in part from Western-influenced educational opportunities that had been made available to the new elites—opportunities that entailed learning about ideals of sovereignty and self-determination. At the same time, second-generation leaders watched with growing frustration as traditional elites failed to produce results in the nationalist fight. In Tunisia, South Yemen, and Algeria, they edged traditional elites aside, making very different tactical and mobilizational choices as they took independence matters into their own hands. While traditional elites associated only with the urban upper and middle classes and relied primarily on the power of persuasion to gain independence, second-generation nationalists resorted to strikes, demonstrations, and violence, drawing peasants, tribesmen, and urban labor into their ranks.[4]

This passing of the mantle of nationalist movements into the hands of a second generation of elites helps explain the emergence of single, preponderant, mass-mobilizing parties in these societies. Unlike traditional elites, this new class of nationalist leaders was willing, able, and motivated to engage in this more intense and difficult genre of party building. They were *willing* to do so because the effort did not threaten their social standing, as it would have for traditional elites. They were *able* to do so because they tended to come from humbler origins in provincial and rural areas, whereas the traditional nationalist elite had been oriented around national capitals. Their origins meant that second-generation leaders were closer to the masses, enabling them both psychologically and logistically to mobilize the latter. In addition, second-generation leaders could mass mobilize because, as traditional elites' social power declined concomitantly with their ability to provide for their clients, nothing stood in the way of their clients exiting those relationships and following the new leadership. Finally, second-generation leaders felt they *had* to mobilize on a grand scale, for only by organizing the masses in acts of protest (violent and otherwise) could nationalists hope to persuade the imperial powers to leave.

This chapter documents these dynamics in detail for the primary, Tunisian case. It also establishes that parallel developments unfolded as single preponderant parties emerged in the South Yemeni and Algerian cases. Finally, the Moroccan experience is examined. There, traditional elites' social power was *preserved* by imperial occupation policies. Also, the French were less intransigent: while an elective parliament for indigenous elites was not established, traditional elites' nationalist demands were honored quite quickly. Control over the nationalist movement thus never passed fully into the hands of second-generation elites, precluding the emergence of a single, preponderant, mass-mobilizing nationalist party.

Tunisia

France took control of Tunisia in 1883. In the subsequent four decades, French policies substantially altered existing socioeconomic relationships, weakening the social power of traditional elites by reducing their ability to serve their clienteles. One arena where such changes occurred was landowner-peasant relations. More than 180,000 French citizens settled in Tunisia, a process that entailed a change in possession of more than a fifth of the country's arable land from Tunisian to French hands. This meant that tens of thousands of peasants were either evicted or became agricultural workers (Moore 1965, 19). French policies also forced Tunisian elites to hand over 2,000 hectares of public *habous* land annually,[5] which was then sold to settlers. In addition, a 1926 law provided new legal rights to tenants and squatters on *habous* lands that remained in (wealthy) Tunisian hands.

Politically, France's strategy of indirect rule diminished the power and authority of the traditional elite families from whom provincial administrators—the *caid*s—had been drawn. While the *caid*s were maintained, "shadow" French administrators, with whom real power lay, were inserted into the governance system behind the *caid*s. In a similar fashion, traditional patterns of tribal leadership were disrupted as the French began appointing the tribes' leaders (the *sheikh*s), whereas in the past the tribes themselves made the selections; the *sheikh*s then became civil servants in the French administration (Moore 1965, 11–13).[6] As *caids* and *sheikhs* now lacked genuine power, and because they were "often more concerned to ensure their own reappointment than the welfare of their charges," the general population began bringing their concerns directly to French officials (Anderson 1986, 149). In the meantime, Tunisia's indigenous clerical class came on hard times as the French established a secular system of justice that marginalized the jurisdiction of the traditional *shari'a* (Islamic law) courts. Finally, the urban bourgeoisie suffered serious financial losses when cheap manufactured imports were introduced into the economy.

At the same time, French policies helped foster the emergence of new social forces that grew up outside the parameters of the traditional economy and patterns of patron-client ties. Changes in land tenure created a new commercial agricultural proletariat class. Settler activity spurred the development of a modern urban economy wherein especially the construction and public works sectors gave rise to a native industrial proletariat (Moore 1965, 22). French policy, the strains of World War II, and drought triggered significant tribal rural-to-urban migration that led to the emergence of shantytowns around major cities. Finally, the extension of modern, Western educational opportunities to Tunisians created a new intelligentsia of students, teachers, administrators, and members of the liberal professions (doctors, lawyers, pharmacists, and so on). Importantly, this new intelligentsia "accepted the new values of liberal France" (Moore 1965, 15–16).

This was the context in which the first Tunisian nationalist organization to demand independence from France, the Destour Party, emerged in 1920. The Destour viewed the West as an obstacle standing in the way of an Islamic renaissance. It argued that the French had spoiled a nineteenth-century Tunisian "golden age" (Moore 1965, 28). The party demanded a constitution providing for an elected parliament and an accountable government as well as increased Tunisian participation in politics and national administration. Party leaders hailed from Tunisia's propertied classes, as did most of its activists (Anderson 1986, 166). The Destour "included the following: the religious leadership, or ulema; the religio-judicial leadership, or muftis, *caids*, and *aduls* (notaries); prominent merchants; leaders of the most respected crafts; and the informal leaders of various quarters of the cities" (Brown 1964, 41). Indeed, "the Destour was essentially the party of an old indigenous elite" (Moore 1965, 27). It built only a modest organizational base, primarily in northern Tunisia's large towns, opening forty branches and enrolling forty-five thousand members by 1924.

France largely ignored the Destour's demands. Its officials chose not to establish a parliament in which indigenous actors could develop a voice in governance. In 1892, the French had created the legislature-like Consultative Conference. This institution allowed French nationals to express economic preferences and review the budget; they could not influence the full spectrum of protectorate policy. The French expanded the Consultative Conference in 1907 to include a handful of appointed Tunisian members. In 1922, the Grand Council took the place of the conference. The council included twenty-six elected Tunisian members; however, protectorate officials closely controlled Tunisian candidate lists. Again, the council's only function was to examine and approve the protectorate budget; it did not discuss political or constitutional issues. Beyond the matter of a parliament, the French reacted to the Destour with some carefully calculated liberalization measures; on the whole, however, the response was rejection and repression. Tunisia's first nationalist party would have little to show for its efforts as the years passed.

In the face of French intransigence, the Destourian leadership proved unwilling to increase significantly the pressure it was bringing to bear on France. Party leaders took a conservative approach to their task, presenting their demands to French authorities "much as a lawyer would plead his case in court" (Moore 1965, 28–29). As important, Destour leaders chose not to organize on a broader basis by engaging the Tunisian masses directly in their battle. Such a strategy clashed with their interests insofar as to do so would have been to risk further the patron-client relationships they presided over—already under strain due to French occupation policy—by mobilizing their clients politically. It was also not in their nature to engage the masses in this fashion. In the pyramid of traditional Tunisian society, the attitude of those occupying higher echelons toward those below them bordered on contempt (Moore 1965, 13). Tellingly, disdainful of workers' Bedouin origins (Moore 1965, 29), the Destour did not support Tunisia's first autonomous trade union movement in 1925 when the latter came into confrontation with French authorities.

Already socially weakened as a result of French protectorate policies, Tunisia's traditional elite became politically discredited as well. Those that served as arms of the French administration (as *caids*, *sheikhs*, and so on) came to be seen as opportunistic collaborators (Hermassi 1972, 67). Those that ran the Destour sorely disappointed their compatriots. Not only did they fail to obtain meaningful concessions from the French, but they were also unwilling to alter their strategy in the wake of French intransigence. When the Destour betrayed the union movement in 1925, "the leadership lost not merely the support of the urban proletariat but it also lost what

Marx called 'the moral power of the shop'—organized craftsmen and small traders—who began to seek political guidance elsewhere" (Hermassi 1972, 119–20).

Fourteen years after the Destour first sounded the independence call, a breakaway group of Destourians founded the Neo-Destour (ND) Party in 1934. Its founders had grown frustrated with the Destour's legalist, gradualist approach to pushing for independence. In the ND's eyes, the Destour too often seemed "satisfied with verbal protest and the circulation of petitions"—methods that were proving insufficient for forcing the French out (Hermassi 1972, 115). Moreover, the ND felt that the Destour's recruitment effort was too narrow and too limited to traditional urban elites. In a speech at the party congress at which the ND split away, ND leader Habib Bourguiba criticized the Destour for "distrusting and shying away from contact with the people and for toadying to the French government."[7]

The ND would lead Tunisia to independence in 1956. Its founding represented the passing of the mantle of the nationalist movement into the hands of second-generation elites (Moore 1965, 30; Anderson 1986, 167). While the Destour's founders were mainly traditional elites from the capital, Tunis, this second generation comprised young men from upper-, middle-, and lower-class *provincial* backgrounds. In general they had pursued a modern primary and secondary school education in Tunisia, and many of them had traveled to France for university. There they were exposed to ideas about nationalism, self-determination, democracy, and sovereignty; in addition, many adopted the ideologies and organizational methods of leftist French political parties. When they completed their studies, these second-generation elites tended to pursue careers in law, medicine, teaching, or government service in Tunisia. Relative to traditional elites, second-generation elites were more politically radical, a product of their comparative youth, their educational background, and the growing frustration they felt as they watched traditional elites fail to produce results in the nationalist fight.

In building the ND, Tunisian second-generation elites pushed traditional elites aside and took independence matters into their own hands. As the remainder of the case narrative will demonstrate, the ND differed both tactically and mobilizationally from the "old" Destour. While the latter had relied primarily on the power of persuasion to gain independence, ND activists resorted to strikes, demonstrations, and, on occasion, violence. Traditional elites organized mainly in urban areas among the middle and upper classes, but the ND mobilized the masses in the countryside as well as the cities.

The fact that this second generation of elites took control of Tunisia's nationalist movement helps explain why a single, preponderant, mass-mobilizing nationalist party emerged there. The new nationalist leaders differed from their traditionalist predecessors in a number of ways that drove them to engage in more exhaustive party-building endeavors. They were *willing* to mass mobilize because doing so did not threaten their social standing as it would have for traditional elites. They were *able* to do so because they tended to come from humbler origins in provincial and rural areas, whereas the traditional nationalist elite had been oriented around Tunis. Their origins meant that second-generation leaders were closer to the masses, enabling them both psychologically and logistically to mobilize the latter. Anderson phrases it thusly:

> To Bourguiba, contact with the masses meant not only frequent tours through the countryside and constant organizational activity, but also thorough knowledge of their needs. The importance of his origin in the Sahil was evident in his call for the elite to "retrace its steps," something which would lead him and the new generation of leaders, in contrast to their predecessors, into the rural areas. (1986, 168)

In addition, second-generation leaders could mass mobilize because, as traditional elites' status and ability to act as patrons declined, their clients had increasingly little to lose by abandoning their patrons and following the new leadership. Moore tells us, for example, that impoverished artisans of Tunis's *medina* (old city) exited their traditional guild structures to join the ND; similarly, the Zitouna (Tunis's main mosque and center for religious instruction) lost the loyalty of most of its students to the ND, "offering a bold and vigorous leadership unlike that of the old sheikhs" (1965, 35).

Finally, ND leaders felt they *had* to mobilize on a grand scale. Having observed the Destour's experience, second-generation elites concluded that only by organizing the masses in acts of protest (violent and otherwise) would they be able to persuade France to leave. ND leaders believed that a much more confrontational strategy would be required to force France to rethink its opposition to Tunisian independence. They espoused a broad mobilizational approach to the struggle. The party was to be the instrument of mobilization (Hermassi 1972, 123). With it, ND leaders sought to educate the Tunisian masses about the injustices of the protectorate. The party would then organize the people in carefully planned and controlled acts of civil disobedience designed to raise to an intolerably high level the costs to France of maintaining the protectorate.[8] These acts included strikes, boycotts, demonstrations, and, at times, terrorism.[9]

To implement this strategy on a scale sufficiently large to move France to recalculate the costs and benefits of maintaining the protectorate, the ND had to establish an organizational presence nationwide. "The objective of the ND leadership consisted of making their party into a mass organization and then mobilizing the entire Tunisian population, of which it had to be the sole representative" (Kraiem 1985, 37). And this it did. In Moore's words, ND leaders "barnstormed the country whenever they were not in jail or under house arrest" (1965, 34). Party leaders worked to recruit the entire spectrum of Tunisian social groups into their organization, including businessmen, workers, students, peasants, tribal groups, artisans, and merchants.

Their efforts yielded impressive results. The ND's core organizational structure during the independence struggle consisted of three components. The political bureau served as the ND's executive organ: it wielded significant, centralized power and served as the party's nerve center. The political bureau issued directives to the federations, the regional-level ND units. The federations in turn instructed and supervised the branches, the party's grassroots-level units. Table 3 demonstrates the growth over time of the number of ND federations, branches, and members. Importantly, whereas in its early years the ND was most "present" in a few regions (including Tunis, the Sahel, and Bizerte), by the 1950s the party's structures spanned the entire protectorate territory. In the words of one Tunisian historian, "the Neo-Destour wove a veritable spider web which would, little by little, come to span the entire country" (Hamza 1991, 212).

The ND's endeavors also extended beyond this web of party branches and federations. It built a set of satellite institutions that wedded a number of politically important sectors of society to its independence campaign.[10] In 1946 the party created a 40,000-member business union, the Union Tunisienne des Artisans et Commerçants (UTAC). That year the ND also established the Union Générale des Agriculteurs Tunisiens (UGAT) to organize farmers and agricultural laborers.[11] In 1952 the Union Générale des Etudiants Tunisiens (UGET) was established to bind students to the independence movement.[12] ND party militants founded these three organizations and directly issued their marching orders during the independence struggle (Abdallah 1963b, 605; Moore 1964, 86; Meric 1973, 285).

The most important institution allied to the ND was the Tunisian labor union, the Union Générale des Travailleurs Tunisiens (UGTT). Unlike UTAC,

TABLE 3. Growth of the Neo-Destour

Year	*Federations*	*Branches*	*Members*
1937	17	400+	28,000
1944		180	100,000
1950		260	210,000
1952	13	600	200,000–300,000
1955	32	1000	325,000
1957			600,000
1958	41	1800	

SOURCES: Moore 1964 and 1965 for 1937, 1955, 1957, 1958; Hamza 1991 for 1944 and 1950; and AMAE 638/297/121, 182, for 1952.

UGAT, and UGET, the ND did not directly found the UGTT. The union's origins were more autonomous, dating to 1946, when Farhat Hached created it as a Tunisian nationalist alternative to the European-dominated and communist unions that had existed since the 1920s. Still, the ND leadership assisted in the building of the UGTT, and the two institutions worked together closely in the battle for independence.[13] By 1955 the UGTT possessed 100,000 members, 90 percent of whom simultaneously were members of the ND (Hermassi 1972, 155). ND leaders also often served simultaneously in UGTT leadership positions (AMAE 639/298/48-87). The ND "joined forces with, and ultimately dominated the union, as a way of harnessing the latter's unique ability to mobilize the workers" (Murphy 1999, 47–48).

This building of an extensive party apparatus supplemented by important auxiliary organizations gave ND leaders the weapon they needed to accomplish their political goals. They used it to galvanize the population against the French presence. According to ANT and AMAE documents, party leaders hammered nationalist themes home through theatrical productions, in open and clandestine newspapers, and on propaganda tours of the countryside during which leaders made speeches at sporting events, mosque inaugurations, and the like. ND leaders also used the party apparatus to mobilize the populace in demonstrations and acts of civil disobedience that were designed to raise France's costs of continued occupation. Demonstrations included public meetings, parades, and petitions. Civil disobedience most often took the form of strikes and work stoppages that harmed French interests by paralyzing the economy (Ling 1967, 133). However, during periods of particular French intransigence and/or the breakdown of Franco-Tunisian negotiations, the ND resorted to more violent methods. Beginning in 1952, *fellaghas*—guerrilla fighters linked to the party (Abdallah 1963a, 422; Moore 1965, 111; Ling 1967, 167)—attacked French interests with gasoline fires, bombings, and assassinations.

By the mid-1950s this strategy had worked. The "French finally found the political, economic, and moral costs of remaining as rulers in Tunisia too high" (Rudebeck 1967, 32–33). In 1955 France granted "internal autonomy" status to Tunisia. Shortly thereafter, in 1956, Tunisia became fully independent.

The Destour Party had challenged the protectorate from 1920 to 1934 with little success. As a result, ND elites concluded that only a single, mass-mobilizing independence party could bring sufficient pressure to bear on the French to achieve Tunisian independence (Interview D; Moore 1965, 104; Ling 1967, 141). Bourguiba stated this clearly at a 1955 party congress:

> Indeed our reasonable demands have rallied to our side the large majority of the French people. In other words, our strategy has consisted of unifying our ranks and disunifying and weakening the ranks of the colonists. The situation must not be reversed so that we become divided while the French, who were divided, some for us, some against us, come to agree and say: these people don't know what they're doing. (AMAE 639/299/183)[14]

The result was that as Tunisia approached the end of the protectorate period, its nascent party system contained one preponderant party. Historians and social scientists routinely use the terms "hegemony" or "monopoly" to describe the position of the ND (Interview B; Moore 1965, 30; Camau 1978, 37; Hamza 1991, 210–11; Moalla 1992, 165). What's more, in choosing to negotiate specifically with ND leaders about the future status of the protectorate, *France* recognized the ND as Tunisia's premier political institution:

> Although similar political alignments and attitudes were prevalent in Morocco and Algeria, only in Tunisia did the major political party become the recognized *porte-parole* of the nation, even prior to the final confrontation which led to independence. In the Tunisian context, this role was never disputed by the old Destour, the monarchy, or even France itself. (Hermassi 1972, 124)

Those who describe the ND as possessing "monopoly" power in Tunisia at independence qualify the term with adverbs such as "virtual" or "near," however, because on the eve of independence other political parties did exist in the national arena. They held meetings and published pamphlets and newspapers in which they criticized the ND for seeking to monopolize the nationalist movement and for behaving in an authoritarian manner.[15] Two parties in particular are of note for their longevity on the Tunisian political scene,[16] but neither posed a serious challenge to the ND as independence approached.

The first was the "old" Destour, the remnants of the parent party from which the ND had split in 1934. Though in the early 1950s the old Destour was publishing a newspaper, *Indépendence*, Moore tells us that by independence the party was "an antique" (1965, 36). Ling concurs, pointing out that by 1952 the old Destour "had lost most of its following" (1967, 146). Furthermore, because the Destour was an elite party and because it was present only in northern urban areas, it did not represent a threat to the ND—a mass party organized across both urban and rural Tunisia. The second would-be rival to the ND was the Tunisian Communist Party (PCT). Politically and organizationally, it too was no match for the ND in the 1950s.[17] After its creation in 1946, the UGTT rapidly gained the support of the majority of Tunisian workers (Micaud 1964, 134), denying the PCT its most natural constituent base (Camau 1978, 37). Kraiem tells us that by 1949 the PCT was in dire financial straits and was organized to any real extent only in Tunis (1997, 316). In 1950 the PCT possessed 111 branches and 3,728 members (Kraiem 1997, 342) as compared with the ND's 260 branches and 210,000 members.[18]

Thus, while other parties existed, they were organizationally and numerically insignificant relative to the ND. Describing the early 1950s, Hamza sums up the ND's political preponderance this way:

> Neither the old Destour, reduced to a general staff without troops, nor the Communist Party, totally discredited . . . and massively deserted by its Tunisian militants . . . would henceforth be capable of contesting [the ND's] leadership or even to chip away at the immense prestige which the [ND] enjoyed in the eyes of a population which was largely won over to its views and massively enrolled in its ranks. (1991, 212)

With the goal of overcoming France's intransigence in the face of Tunisians' independence demands, the ND had been diligently building and disciplining its ranks for nearly twenty years. In terms of its mass membership, nationwide urban and rural organizational elaboration, and political influence, it far outweighed all other political groups in Tunisia. As independence approached, the ND was the preponderant party in the Tunisian political community.

South Yemen

Geopolitically, South Yemen was divided into two units during the period under examination here: the port city of Aden and its tribal hinterland. Britain occupied Aden in 1839 and, over time, increased and formalized its domination over the South Yemeni hinterland. Sociopolitical control of the tribal hinterland was fragmented across numerous traditional leaders, the sultans. Aden's was a bifurcated population. At the top of the socioeconomic and political hierarchy was a class of long-standing Adeni residents who were primarily merchants, traders, and craftsmen. At the same time, as the British presence dramatically expanded the scope of Aden's economic activities, a sizeable working class emerged that would eventually become unionized. This class was composed largely of migrants coming to Aden both from its hinterland and from North Yemen.

The nationalist impulse appeared in South Yemeni politics comparatively late. The first organization to call for independence was the Aden Association (AA). This group represented Aden's elite merchant, trader, and industrialist classes; the working class was led by middle-class, white-collar Adenis and did not follow the AA's lead (Bujra 1970, 199). Beginning in 1950 under the slogan "Aden for the Adenis," the AA asked that Aden's government become autonomous but remain within the British Commonwealth. The AA's demands applied to Aden only: the port city and its hinterland were not yet an integrated political community, and AA elites did not wish to see integration effected.

Britain was intransigent in the face of these Adeni traditional elites' calls for independence. The British did not create a parliamentary body in which South Yemenis could cultivate a voice in politics. In 1947 a legislative council had been established to advise the governor in Aden, but all of its members were either ex officio or appointed by the governor. Reforms in 1955 and 1959 increased the number of council seats that were elective, but suffrage restrictions meant that only long-established residents of Aden could vote—migrant workers from the South Yemeni hinterland and North Yemen could not. The broader population was so angered by these restrictions that two of the three parties that existed at the time boycotted the elections. Because the legislative council was composed and served the interests only of Aden's traditionalist elite (the AA stood in elections and its members held council seats), that elite became politically discredited. Also contributing to its declining influence was the fact that more than a dozen years would pass with no sign of progress toward independence other than the council reforms. Though the United Kingdom was granting independence to its other Middle East holdings (Iraq in 1932, Egypt in 1936, and Jordan in 1946) relatively readily, for geostrategic reasons it was reluctant to let go of South Yemen. British policy decisions and statements in the 1950s indicated that the United Kingdom had no intention of relinquishing its hold on the colony in the foreseeable future (Halliday 1974, 183).

In the meantime, the sultans of the South Yemeni hinterland were *not* demanding independence. Concerned about preserving their positions and worried that North Yemen might use force to effect Yemeni unification, the sultans sought to join forces in a federation whose security and prosperity would be guaranteed by British material and military support (Kostiner 1984, 41). Indeed, when by the mid-1960s it did finally appear that Britain would be taking its leave, conservative British politicians who opposed the policy accused their government of betraying and abandoning its clients in South Yemen. In an age of intensifying nationalism across the region, the sultans' conservative stand discredited them in the eyes of rising second-generation elites in the hinterland.

This dynamic augmented the already-existing disenchantment of hinterland South Yemenis with their sultans, an outcome that resulted from the interaction between the latter and British imperial officials. The sultans had allowed the United Kingdom to begin building rudimentary state institutions in their territories in return for British financial and military aid. Sultans previously had relied on their subjects for tax revenues and military recruits, a linkage that kept them at least minimally concerned with their subjects' preferences and welfare. As money and arms began flowing in from the outside, the sultans became freer to disregard their subjects. "Increased political rigidity was accompanied by decreased responsibility, and the sultans of South Yemen grew more powerful and less accountable at the same time" (Ismael and Ismael 1986, 10). British policies "resulted in an indelible association between British colonialism and the hated, repressive, semi-feudal social and political structure of the interior in the minds of many Yemenis" (ibid., 14). Local rulers in the hinterland lost legitimacy in the eyes of those they governed.

At the same time, British policies distributed educational opportunities to the general population (rather than just the elite) of South Yemen. The result was the appearance of new, politically engaged and comparatively radical social forces in the political arena. This development, paired with the discrediting of traditional elites both in Aden and the hinterland, led to a situation wherein second-generation elites would take over control of the nationalist movement. In Tunisia, the second-generation takeover that was embodied in the emergence of the ND occurred fourteen years after the traditionalist Destour first sounded the independence call. In South Yemen, thirteen years after the AA's call for Adeni independence, a group of educated middle- and lower-middle-class men (primarily students, teachers, and young functionaries), whose origins were the hinterland tribes, founded the National Liberation Front (NLF) in 1963.

NLF founders' humble roots combined with the fact that they hailed from the hinterland meant that they were well positioned to build a single, preponderant, mass-mobilizing nationalist party. Mass mobilization would only help, not harm, their interests because they were not patrons to clients who needed to be "kept in line." Indeed, the NLF was a leftist party that was calling not only for independence but also for progressive socioeconomic reforms in the context of an augmented state sector—policies that would disrupt traditional relationships. That they were of and from the "ordinary" hinterland population enabled them to organize rural areas effectively. Finally, politically the NLF was disposed toward building a preponderant mass-mobilizing party. The NLF was critical of existing South Yemeni parties' conservatism and gradualism. Given British intransigence, the NLF believed that armed struggle would be necessary to push the United Kingdom out of South Yemen and that urban-only efforts would be insufficient; thus, the party aimed to organize the rural population as well. The NLF felt that only a single, united organization could successfully defeat the British. In a radio broadcast announcing the birth of the party, the NLF stated:

> Our aspiration in the Occupied Yemeni south has now entered a phase which demands a fundamental change in the methods of the struggle to win complete independence and to overcome imperialism. The weakest point is the lack of coordination in the struggle in the Yemeni south as a whole. The major reason for that is the lack of a common command for national action . . . Another reason lies in the circumstance that the majority of political organisations limit their activity to Aden. (quoted in Lackner 1985, 39)

The NLF was determined to "assume sole leadership of the struggle" for South Yemen's independence (Stookey 1982, 62). It would have rapid success in attaining its goals. The NLF's willingness to confront the British militarily won it the support of Aden's workers, who labored under difficult conditions and had long been politically disenfranchised. By 1965 the NLF had wrested control of the important trade union congress away from its erstwhile leaders. In the meantime, the increasing dissatisfaction of hinterland residents with their local leadership helped the NLF win the loyalty of the rural South Yemeni masses, and the party rapidly took control of the countryside. As it built its presence in the capital and in the countryside, the NLF began orchestrating rebellions and armed attacks against British interests. By February 1966 the strategy had worked: the United Kingdom announced it would grant South Yemen independence two years later, in 1968. As it happened, the British withdrew ahead of schedule and the colony achieved independence in November 1967.

In the wake of British withdrawal, no other South Yemeni political group could hope to confront the NLF successfully. The Aden Association had crumbled by the 1960s. The South Arabian League (SAL), founded in 1950, had sought to unite the sultanates of the hinterland with Aden to form an independent South Arabia. However, the leaders of the SAL focused their organizational efforts mainly on rural elites (Ismael and Ismael 1986, 22). When they "belatedly . . . realized the necessity of effective organization among the common people, the latter were already marching to other drums. The league played no significant part either in the liquidation of colonial rule or in the organization of the independent state" (Stookey 1982, 61).

The Adeni trade unions' political wing, the People's Socialist Party (PSP), was founded in 1962 and called for a negotiated South Yemeni independence and unification with North Yemen. Though Bujra describes it as "the most dynamic and highly organized political party in South Arabia" (1970, 200), the PSP was organized only in Aden city, and its ranks steadily fell prey to NLF recruitment efforts. The NLF was the undisputed dominant political force in newly independent South Yemen.

Algeria

Among the cases considered here, the interaction between the imperial power and traditional elites was most dramatic in Algeria. There, French policies did not just weaken but in fact destroyed the sociopolitical standing of traditional elites. France declared Algeria a colony in 1834, approximately ninety years prior to the emergence of modern Algerian nationalism. In the interim, France drastically altered indigenous socioeconomic structures. Its policies depopulated the cities and "virtually annihilated not only the Turks but also the indigenous urban bourgeoisie" (Moore 1970, 42). France undermined the clerical class by confiscating all public *habous* land and establishing a secular judicial system in place of the religious courts. Tribal elites' power was destroyed by policies that restricted tribal residence and movement, relocated tribes to more distant and marginal territories, and allowed land once collectively owned by tribes to be divided into privately held plots. French policies also undercut landowning elites. One key measure gave sharecroppers the legal right to abandon their landlords. Moreover, the French confiscated and/or forced Algerian proprietors to sell great swaths of agricultural land that were subsequently purchased by French settlers. These policies impoverished rural Algerians, yielding a burgeoning unemployed class that flocked both to Algerian cities and to France. Moore characterizes Algeria's traditional elites as having been "worn down or destroyed by the intensive colonial situation" (1970, 44). The result, in Hermassi's words, was a situation wherein "the dispossession and exclusion of the local population combined with the collapse of the population's indigenous institutions made Algerian society into 'a dust of individuals'" (1972, 65, 70).

Having been eviscerated by the French, Algeria's traditional elite did not figure prominently among the nationalist groups that began surfacing in the late 1920s and 1930s. The sole echo was Sheikh Abdelhamid Ben Badis's conservative Association of the Ulama movement, led primarily by educated clerics. Through education and other grassroots efforts, this group sought to rekindle Algerians' interest in Arabic language and culture and to revitalize, purify, and unify an Algerian Islam it believed had been corrupted by the practice of mysticism. The association, however, did not organize broadly or deeply across Algeria. Neither did it demand immediate independence. Instead, it asked for increased political equality and better economic conditions for Algerians. A second "nationalist" group was led by a new, French-educated and Gallicized, liberal, middle-class Algerian elite. Ferhat Abbas headed up this current, which advanced an assimilationist platform that called on France to integrate Algerian Muslims into French society on an equal footing with other French citizens. This group also did not organize on a mass basis. Indeed, its Francophone aesthetic and assimilationist bent meant that it would not and could not engage the

Algerian masses effectively. Both groups became politically discredited among Algerians because of their failure to demand full independence.

At about the same time that the above two movements were emerging, a third, more radical, and truly nationalist organization also took the stage. Messali Hadj, an industrial worker with only a primary school education, founded a left-wing populist movement that demanded immediate independence from France and set about organizing on a mass basis. Hadj's movement—first termed the Algerian People's Party (PPA) and later dubbed the Movement for the Triumph of Democratic Liberties (MTLD)—centered on a redistributional platform calling for land reform and the nationalization of industry. Not surprisingly, it developed support among the urban underclass and peasants. "The PPA-MTLD never seems to have had more than 15,000 members, but it had clearly outdistanced Abbas' rival party by the late forties" (Moore 1970, 84). Though both had emerged essentially at the same time, the momentum of the nationalist movement had shifted to the PPA-MTLD, with its leadership of humble origins.

France was the epitome of intransigence in the face of Algerians' demands for independence. It repressed both Ben Badis's and Hadj's organizations, and did not grant an elective parliament that furnished indigenous elites with a political voice. Instead, Algeria was incorporated into the French body politic. Residents of Algeria elected representatives who served in the French parliament. At first, only settlers had this privilege. While over time the same right was extended to native Algerians, it provided them with no appreciable increase in control over their welfare or political-economic destiny. French intransigence stretched on for three decades, and no appreciable consideration of nationalist demands was forthcoming into the 1950s.

The extinguishing of the traditional elite combined with imperial intransigence meant that the reins of the nationalist movement shifted into the hands of leaders from comparatively humble origins who had the willingness, ability, and motivation to mobilize on a grand scale. In the face of French stonewalling, frustration, anger, and desperation mounted among politically active Algerians—particularly those associated with Hadj's PPA-MTLD. By 1954 a group of its activists had become fed up with French intransigence and with Hadj's failings, among them his commitment to moderate methods of protest. His activists "were becoming impatient with interminable political dialogues, meaningless manifestos, and unfulfilled promises" (Entelis 1986, 48) and believed that violence had to be deployed in the struggle against the French.

This group formed the Front de Libération Nationale (FLN) and launched a violent insurrection against French rule in 1954. While not well organized at the outset, the FLN succeeded, during the course of the war, in rallying hundreds of thousands of Algerians—especially peasants—to the party and its cause. The FLN was driven to engage the masses because it believed that only popular mobilization and the use of violence would effect France's departure from Algeria. That it succeeded in mobilizing the people is not surprising, considering its leaders' origins. Party founders were young, between twenty-seven and thirty-two years of age. More important, they were "of modest semiproletarian origin" (Entelis 1986, 49). All were from peasant or working-class backgrounds. Most had only a primary school education and none had attended university. "All but a handful of these revolutionaries lived in small towns or villages, which put most of them in closer touch with the institutions and attitudes of the rural poor than the typical big-city politician" (Ruedy 1992, 157). Because FLN founders were of modest backgrounds themselves, mass mobilization did not threaten their interests. It was an endeavor that came more naturally and easily to them than it would have to leaders from higher social strata.

At independence, serious intraparty conflicts and elite power struggles rendered the FLN a weak party organization (Ottaway and Ottaway 1970, 12, 83; Entelis 1986, 54; Bennoune 1988, 303), especially relative to its counterparts in Tunisia and South Yemen. Still, relative to other political forces in Algeria, the FLN was preponderant. The disrupted state of Algerian society, the perceived need to present a single cohesive front against the French, and the French forces' virtual lockdown on the Algerian countryside during the second half of the war meant that, at independence, the FLN faced no challengers as the nation's premier political party.

The FLN was not Algeria's sole political organization, however. Algeria had a Communist Party, the Parti Communiste Algérien (PCA). In the years following independence, the PCA did not challenge the FLN for power (Ottaway and Ottaway 1970, 89–91). Algeria also had a nationalist union, the Union Générale des Travailleurs Algériens (UGTA). Much as occurred in Tunisia, by 1963 the UGTA "had lost its fight for autonomy and had been put under the control of undynamic party-appointed leaders" (ibid., 57). In 1969 the UGTA was made into a mass appendage to the party, with its leadership dictated by the FLN. A third challenge to the FLN surfaced in 1963 when independence leaders who felt shut out of evolving power arrangements created the Front des Forces Socialistes (FFS) in the Berber-speaking region of Kabylia. The FFS, however, "remained almost entirely a Kabyle movement and did not even have the backing of all the Kabyle leaders" (ibid., 98). By late 1964 the FLN—thanks to its access to the liberation army it controlled—put an end to the FFS's political challenge, confirming its preponderance on the Algerian political stage.

Morocco

The Moroccan case demonstrated some but not all of the elements that produced single, preponderant, mass-mobilizing nationalist political parties in Tunisia, South Yemen, and Algeria. In the latter cases, European powers had the time, the political latitude, and the will to alter indigenous socioeconomic structures significantly. The result in all three cases was socially weakened traditional elites. France did not colonize Morocco until 1912, and did not fully pacify the countryside for some two subsequent decades. As a result, the French had significantly less time to disrupt indigenous socioeconomic relationships. Moreover, France's approach to domination—in great contrast especially to that taken in Algeria—purposely sought to preserve Morocco's traditional elites. Entelis writes that "traditionally privileged classes were preserved, especially the commercially and culturally dominant Arab bourgeoisie in the cities of Fez and Rabat and the Berber tribal notables of the countryside" (1980, 28). Moore concurs: "The old families . . . acquir[ed] new bases of wealth and prestige in the modern sector to complement and reinforce their traditional statuses" (1970, 44).

Morocco's first nationalist party, Istiqlal, was founded in 1943 by members of the nation's traditional elite—specifically the urban bourgeoisie. However, as the party developed, it came to embody an alliance between traditional urban elites (especially religious notables and commercial businessmen) and rising second-generation elites who were Western educated, younger, more radical, and more inclined to mass mobilize (Gallagher 1959, 2; Zartman 1963, 33; Tessler 1982, 40). As a result of the latter's presence in the partnership, the Istiqlal organized more broadly and deeply across the Moroccan social spectrum relative to the other traditional nationalist parties considered in this chapter. It attracted the support of traditional bourgeois elites, members of the petit bourgeoisie such as craftsmen and shopkeepers, and a significant number of younger, more radical members. The latter helped Istiqlal "organize urban labor and the teeming *bidonvilles* [shantytowns], which acted as more-or-less temporary way stations for the rural unemployed" (Waterbury 1970, 51). The party also incorporated extant student, youth, sports, and charitable groups into its structures (Gallagher 1956, 6). Within just a few years, Istiqlal possessed a broad, nationwide organization and substantial popularity. Istiqlal's primary strength, however, lay in the cities. It did not mobilize the countryside and did not command the loyalty of most elites and nonelites in rural Morocco (Waterbury 1970, 234; Tessler 1982, 45).

What was France's response to Istiqlal's demands? As in Tunisia, South Yemen, and Algeria, France did not establish an influential indigenous parliament in Morocco. The only legislature-like organ created was the politically weak Government Council, a body composed of French settlers and Moroccan appointees who advised the protectorate administration on social and economic issues (Cohen and Hahn, 1966, 37–38). On the other hand, once the Moroccan nationalist movement got under way in 1943, France was relatively quick to make concessions and then relinquished the protectorate altogether in 1956. In Tunisia and South Yemen, fourteen and thirteen years, respectively, elapsed between the founding of traditionalist nationalist organizations and the moment when second-generation elites assumed control of nationalist movements. Morocco was free within thirteen years of Istiqlal's birth.

In Morocco, then, the reins of the nationalist movement never passed fully into the hands of second-generation elites. Traditional elites were not socially weakened by French policies, nor were they politically discredited by what turned out to be only mild French intransigence. At the same time, new, emerging social forces were present in the Moroccan political arena only to a limited extent. These groups tended to be the product of the increasing availability of modern, Western educational opportunities provided by European imperialists. Yet the comparatively short duration of the French stay in Morocco meant that, by the 1940s, sufficient time had not yet elapsed for a robust new generation of Western-educated lawyers, teachers, civil servants, students, and others to seize control of the nationalist movement (Moore 1970, 48; Entelis 1980, 27). Had France been more intransigent, the Istiqlali traditionalists grown politically discredited, and a critical mass of second-generation elites emerged, the result likely would have resembled the outcomes that obtained in Tunisia, South Yemen, and Algeria. Instead, however, "in Morocco . . . there was no time for newcomers to emerge in sufficient numbers to challenge the old families . . . France gave up Morocco before colonial conflict could generate a radical take-over of the nationalist movement" (Moore 1970, 47, 59). Because second-generation elites never took over complete control of the Moroccan nationalist movement, a single, preponderant, mass-mobilizing party did not emerge in that case.

Conclusion

This chapter puts forth arguments explaining how single, preponderant, mass-mobilizing nationalist parties came into existence in Tunisia, South Yemen, and Algeria (but not Morocco). The story of such parties' emergence is set in a context of societal transition and modernization. In the three central cases, traditional elites' power in society was weakened significantly by imperial occupation policies and by imperial intransigence in the face of traditionalists' demands for independence. Such intransigence took the form of refusing to establish elective parliaments in which indigenous elites wielded some measure of political power, in addition to a general refusal over long stretches of time to make concessions in the face of nationalists' demands. Over time, control over nationalist movements thus passed into the hands of second-generation elites—men of comparatively humble, rural social origins who were willing, able, and motivated to mobilize on a mass basis. Chapter 2 will show how very different interactions between imperial powers and traditional elites in Iran, Iraq, Jordan, Syria, and Egypt produced multiparty systems rather than single preponderant parties at the independence juncture.

2

The Emergence of the Multiparty Systems

The preceding chapter analyzed the dynamics that produced single preponderant parties that monopolized the political stage when imperial powers departed Tunisia, South Yemen, and Algeria. This chapter explains why multiparty rather than single preponderant party systems arose in Iran, Iraq, Jordan, Syria, and Egypt. As was the case in Tunisia, South Yemen, and Algeria, in these countries traditional elites began demanding independence from their imperial occupiers early in the twentieth century. These societies also were undergoing similar modernizing transformations that entailed the emergence of new social forces. However, the behavior of imperial powers vis-à-vis traditional elites in these societies differed significantly from what transpired in Tunisia, South Yemen, and Algeria. Traditional elites were not as socially weakened by imperial occupation policies, nor were they as politically discredited during the first wave of nationalist agitation for independence. As a result, traditional elites never lost control of nationalist movements to a rising, "second" generation. The nationalist parties or movements they founded remained limited in mobilizational terms, while other segments of the elite also had important incentives to build parties. The result everywhere was multipartism.

While between 40 and 110 years elapsed between the time when France and Britain took control of Tunisia, South Yemen, and Algeria and the time when indigenous activists first called for independence, nationalist demands emerged almost immediately after foreign control was established in the multiparty cases. In addition, the imperial powers had considerably less policy leverage in these cases than they had in Tunisia, South Yemen, and Algeria. Russian and British intervention in Iran was indirect and never fully subsumed Iranian sovereignty. As for the other cases, as noted in chapter 1, with the exception of Egypt (occupied by Britain in 1882), these were territories awarded to France and Britain by the League of Nations with the expectation that they would protect natives' welfare and prepare them for independence. What's more, these territories were "A class" mandates, identified in the League of Nations' charter as those that "soon would be capable of exercising sovereign statehood" (Jackson 1990, 73). Indeed, referring to the Middle Eastern mandates, the League charter stated that their "existence as independent nations can be provisionally recognized" (quoted in Anghie 2002, 526). In the eyes of the world, Iraq, Jordan, and Syria were on the doorstep of independence.

Thus, relative to the single preponderant party scenarios, European powers did not have sufficient time or policy latitude to radically disrupt existing socioeconomic structures in the multiparty cases. When traditional elites began calling for independence, therefore, unlike in the single preponderant party cases, they were not doing so from an already weakened social position. Their patron-client structures remained largely intact.

Like their (weaker) counterparts in Tunisia, South Yemen, and Algeria, traditional elites in the multiparty cases built nationalist parties or movements that were elaborated organizationally only to a limited extent. However, in the multiparty cases, the colonial powers were not intransigent in the face of traditionalists' calls for independence. Within a few years, Iranian nationalists had forced a weakened monarchy to establish a parliament, and in the other four cases France and Britain established elective parliaments that enabled indigenous elites to wield significant political power. The imperial powers then granted these countries' independence within a comparatively short period of time following the opening of those parliaments (between eight and eighteen years).

The fact that traditional nationalist elites in the multiparty cases had something tangible to show for their efforts—in particular, the establishment of national parliaments—helped buttress their power in these changing societies. Their relative success in eliciting concessions from the imperial powers meant that they did not become politically discredited in the eyes of emerging social forces. More important, the establishment of parliaments meant that nationalist elites now had access to the state and to state resources with which they could continue to provide for their clients. Thus, even if members of the rising, educated middle classes were disillusioned with traditional nationalists and entertained thoughts of challenging the latter for control of nationalist movements, they faced serious recruitment obstacles. Whereas second-generation elites in Tunisia, South Yemen, and Algeria could relatively easily detach peasants, tribesmen, and urban lower classes from weakened patrons who could no longer service their clienteles effectively, traditional elites in the multiparty cases were in a substantially stronger position. As a result, they did not lose control of nationalist movements.

Two elements, then, explain why multiparty rather than single preponderant party systems developed in Iran, Iraq, Jordan, Syria, and Egypt. First, the mantle of nationalist movements never passed into the hands of a second generation of elites—that is, those elites that would have been willing, able, and motivated to mobilize on a mass basis. Second, the existence of influential parliaments populated by indigenous elites inspired other segments of the traditional elite as well as new, emerging social forces to compete with traditionalist nationalist parties for access to those bodies. Numerous groups sought parliamentary representation both for the policy influence and for the spoils and patronage opportunities promised by such a presence. That competition yielded multiparty systems.

The pages that follow document these dynamics for the five core multiparty cases of this study: Iran, Iraq, Jordan, Syria, and Egypt. The chapter concludes by extending the analysis to explain why these five countries evolved plural party systems containing *large* (more than four) numbers of parties. This outcome stands in stark contrast to the two-party system that emerged in Turkey, which, as will be argued in chapter 6, facilitated the establishment of a competitive electoral regime in that country. With the exception of Egypt, large numbers of political parties in these cases were the product of the interaction between permissive electoral systems (with multiple candidates representing a given electoral district in parliaments) and societies that harbored numerous significant economic, ideological, and social cleavages.

Iran

A modern state began to take shape in the late 1700s when the Qajar tribe unified Iranian territory under its control and inaugurated dynastic patrimonial rule that would last into the early twentieth century. By the nineteenth century, the Qajar state was a weak one, however. The dynasty failed to build an effective central state apparatus, and its efforts to establish a standing army likewise came to naught. As a result, the state's authority was tenuous in the provinces. It could not collect taxes effectively and was chronically insolvent. The Qajars maintained their hegemony therefore by manipulating the regional, tribal, ethnic, and religious divisions among Iran's heterogeneous and scattered peoples (Abrahamian 1982, 43).

In contrast to the other cases considered in this chapter, Iran was never formally colonized. But the Qajars' political-military weakness and need for revenues led them to fall prey to the imperial ambitions of Russia and Great Britain to such an extent that by the early 1900s Iran's sovereignty had been seriously compromised (Bausani 1971, 171; Kamrava 1992, 21; Limbert 1995, 45). Nineteenth-century military losses at the hands of Russian forces saw the Qajars waive their right to a navy on the Caspian Sea. They also granted territory, war reparations, and commercial capitulations to Russia. Britain, too, extracted commercial capitulations from Iran (Abrahamian 1982, 51). Iran ceded further sovereignty to these powers by selling concession rights in return for cash. Foreign nationals purchased the right to collect customs, operate ports, build roads and telegraph networks, establish banks, and search for oil. At the turn of the twentieth century, "foreigners held almost total control of Iran's administration. The British had oil rights in the south; a Belgian . . . was minister of customs and de facto minister of finance; and Russian officers commanded the Persian Cossack Brigade, the only effective armed force in the country" (Limbert 1987, 79).

The twentieth century would bring worse impositions before it would bring independence. In 1907 an Anglo-Russian agreement formally divided Iran into Russian, Neutral, and British zones of influence. British, Russian, German, and Turkish forces occupied Iran during World War I. When the war ended, Britain stood as the dominant foreign power in Iran as reflected by the Anglo-Persian Treaty of 1919. This treaty "would have made Iran a virtual British protectorate" (Arjomand 1988, 60) by giving Britain the right to supply and rebuild Iran's army, build a railroad, and pursue customs and other administrative reforms—all financed by British loans. Finally, following a period of independence from foreign intervention between 1921 and 1941, during which time the 1919 Anglo-Persian Treaty was abrogated, British and Soviet forces occupied Iran during World War II to prevent Iran from siding with the Axis powers.

This chapter argues that plural nascent party systems emerged in the cases in which the leadership of nationalist movements did not pass into the hands of second-generation elites and indigenous preindependence parliaments motivated intra-elite competition for access to the policy influence and patronage those parliaments made available. In Iran, because imperial intervention was informal, neither Russia nor the United Kingdom created a parliamentary body as part of its political presence. A powerful indigenous parliament did arise in Iran, however, when in the early twentieth century key nationalist social groups—angry at the Qajars' sovereignty-harming concessions—demanded the creation of a legislature that could check the Qajar shahs' unlimited decision-making authority. The movement to establish an Iranian parliament began in 1905 and came to fruition in 1906.[1] That parliament became the focus for pluralistic political competition among numerous segments of the Iranian elite (both traditional and new) who were looking for policy influence and patronage opportunities; traditional conservative elites dominated that body and used their access to state largesse to serve their clienteles.

From 1906 to 1953, a battle for political authority ensued between the legislature and a series of shahs. The opening rounds went to parliament. Iran's first national assembly convened in October 1906 and drafted a fundamental law that assigned considerable powers to parliament. A dying shah signed the law in December. In 1907 parliament drafted a supplement to this law, further concentrating power in the legislature and making cabinets responsible to it. The new shah refused ratification at first, but then relented in October 1907 in the face of mass demonstrations. In 1908 the shah bombed parliament, touching off a civil war that pitted constitutionalists against royalists. The constitutionalists won, and Iran's second and third national assemblies convened in 1909 and 1914, respectively.

During WWI, political chaos and foreign occupation eclipsed the constitutional conflict. Afterward, however, the conflict revived, with the Iranian monarchy regaining the upper hand. Through a series of shrewd political alliances and the support of the military, between 1921 and 1926, Cossack Colonel Reza Khan gradually consolidated personal control over the country and made himself king, bringing an end to the Qajar dynasty. From 1926 to 1941 he ruled Iran as an autocrat. Reza Shah abrogated the 1919 Anglo-Persian Treaty and built a modern, centralized state apparatus that was capable of collecting taxes and that boasted a powerful army. He also pursued secularizing legal and cultural reforms in the mold of Turkey's Mustafa Kemal Atatürk. Reza Shah did not achieve these ends through liberal politics, however. While he maintained the facade of the institution, and Iranians elected eight parliaments during his reign, Reza Shah used the military and the interior ministry to orchestrate election outcomes in a manner that suited him. Under his rule, parliament became a rubber-stamp body (Arjomand 1988, 64), "a decorative garb covering the nakedness of military rule" (Abrahamian 1982, 138).

An exogenous shock altered the playing field, however, turning the political tide back in favor of a strong and independent parliament. In 1941 allied forces occupied Iran, deposed Reza Shah, placed his young son Mohammad Reza on the throne, and lifted restrictions on political activity. At the outset, the new monarch was weak (Limbert 1987, 88). His weakness translated into newfound strength for parliament. The monarch's power waned considerably, while that of parliament and the prime minister waxed to the point of becoming dominant over the shah (Kamrava 1992, 57). Indeed, Kamrava describes the Iranian regime during the period 1941–1953 as a constitutional monarchy (1992, 57).

Importantly, as in all of the cases considered in this chapter, the revitalized parliament that began reasserting itself in 1941 was the site of competition among multiple political forces. Those years were "a time of vigorous, open debate and competition among numerous parties led by strong-willed and ambitious politicians" (Limbert 1987, 88). Between 1941 and 1953, Iranians elected four parliaments. Conservative parliamentarians dominated Iranian politics during those years. These hailed largely from the nation's large-landholding, tribal, merchant, and state elites, and looked upon membership in parliament as a mechanism for accessing the state patronage resources they needed to maintain their own positions (Azimi 1989).

Iraq

Britain acquired the League of Nations mandate for Iraq in 1920. Iraqi opposition to this turn of events was almost immediate, with a significant revolt against British control breaking out in that same year. In contrast to its response to the emergence of South Yemeni nationalism, Britain would not be intransigent in Iraq. In part due to the impact of the revolt (Marr 2004, 24), and in part because the terms of the mandate obligated Britain to establish constitutional government there in preparation for eventual Iraqi independence, in 1922 Britain established a system of indirect governance that afforded Iraqi elites significant political power. Put in place was a constitutional monarchy in which all of the primary actors were Iraqi while British advisors operated behind the scenes. While the Iraqi king had substantial authority, an indigenous parliament also wielded considerable influence. Cabinet ministers were both individually and collectively responsible to parliament, and a parliamentary vote of no-confidence could bring down the government.

Iraqi nationalists would not be satisfied with this arrangement, however. Between 1922 and 1932 at the urging of Iraqi nationalist elites, Iraq and Britain repeatedly renegotiated the treaty that governed their relationship—in Iraq's favor. The rapidity with which Iraqi nationalists were able to extract gains from Britain—the first Iraqi parliament sat in 1924 and independence came a mere eight years later—meant that traditional elites in that state would not become politically discredited. At the same time, imperial policies augmented rather than weakened the social power of traditional elites. The British routinely awarded land, property rights, and other privileges to tribal leaders in the countryside in return for performing local governance functions and tolerating the mandate. Marr describes the mandate parliaments as "increasingly filled with tribal leaders and urban wealthy, willing to trade acquiescence to the mandate for privileges such as grants of land" (1995, 93). For Iraqi elites, parliament held out not only the promise of policy influence but also the possibility of patronage resources that could be used to provide for clients.

Together, British policies that buttressed traditional elites' social power, the lack of British intransigence in the face of nationalist demands, and parliament's political attractions helped ensure that a single, preponderant, mass-mobilizing party never emerged in Iraq. Instead, Marr tells us that "one feature of the period was political pluralism and sometimes intense competition for power at the top" (1985, 46). Citing Batatu (1978), Fernea and Louis note that "in the 1920s and 1930s the socially-dominant landed classes vied with each other for power, prestige, and property" (1991, xxi). In the early 1920s, three political parties were established: the National Party, the People's Party, and the Progressive Party. All three sought independence, but they differed as to the means through which they believed it should be pursued (Khadduri 1960, 29). In 1930 these parties regrouped into two main formations, the *'Ahd* and the National Brotherhood parties. Iraq thus reached independence with a plural political arena rather than one dominated by a single preponderant party.

Jordan

In 1923, Britain acquired the League of Nations mandate for the Kingdom of Transjordan. There, nationalist resistance to foreign control surfaced almost as rapidly as it had in the Iraqi case. Within just four years, Transjordanian nationalists—both traditional notables and urban intellectuals—created the Hizb al-Sha'b (Party of the People). It demanded that a representative legislature be established and that the kingdom become independent. Again, Britain was not intransigent in Jordan and agreed in 1928 to establish an indigenous legislative body, the first of which sat in 1929.[2] Members of Jordan's traditional elite—primarily tribal leaders and prominent landholders—dominated these legislative councils, which in subsequent years played a significant role in agitating for Jordanian independence. Thus, first-generation nationalists acquitted themselves relatively well in Jordan, obtaining a parliament almost immediately and independence eighteen years later, in 1946.

At the same time, Jordan's traditional elite benefited from the operation of the legislative council. A 1928 Organic Law created the institution, specifying that it would comprise six appointed members and sixteen indirectly elected members, all of whom were Jordanians. Formally, the council possessed limited political authority relative to the king, the executive branch, and the British. While council members' policy influence may have been limited, the evidence suggests that, for the traditional elite, the council nonetheless held out the possibility of accessing state resources for patronage purposes. Lamenting the fact that all members who served in the council's five sessions hailed from the same thirty-six prominent families, Abu Jaber writes that "the new institutions . . . were manipulated by the traditional aristocratic elite to maintain their influence and prestige" (1969, 227). Serving in parliament evidently helped these tribal and large-landholding elites maintain their power in society.

The nature of British control would mean that when Jordan gained its independence in 1946, it did not possess a single, preponderant, mass-mobilizing nationalist party. British policies did not weaken traditional elites' social power. This fact is illustrated particularly starkly by the fact that Jordan's Hashemite King Abdullah, with British consent, "'courted the tribal shaykhs, endow[ing] them with various economic and political benefits and grant[ing] them a large measure of internal autonomy. In return, the Hashemites gained the zealous collective loyalty of the tribes . . . who . . . became the regime's political mainstay" (Bar 1995, 221–22). What's more, the lack of British intransigence in the face of nationalists' first calls for independence meant that the traditional elite did not become politically discredited. The elected legislature that then evolved helped this elite maintain its status, while it also encouraged Jordanian elites to compete with one another for access to and influence within the council. Indeed, between 1927 and 1947, a total of six "parties" emerged. More akin to caucuses, these parties lacked both ideological distinctiveness and extra-council organizations. Instead, they represented shifting and highly personalized relationships and alliances of members associated with one or another major council personality (Aruri 1972, 78–79). As chapter 5 will demonstrate, when Jordan's body politic expanded after 1948 to include West Bank Palestinians, multiparty competition would become more structured.

Syria

In 1922, the League of Nations recognized France as the mandatory power in Syria. France immediately faced Syrian nationalist opposition to its presence there. At first this took the form of isolated demonstrations and attacks on French positions. These were followed by a widespread revolt beginning in 1925, which France used considerable force—including twice bombing Damascus—to suppress. These events persuaded France that some accommodation would have to be made with Syria. Subsequently, the nationalist process unfolded primarily in the form of persuasion and bargaining through iterated rounds of negotiation, punctuated with the occasional resort to nonviolent pressure tactics such as strikes and demonstrations.

The National Bloc was the nationalist party that took the lead in pressing for Syria's independence in the late 1920s, '30s, and '40s. The party was composed primarily of large urban absentee landowners and merchants. Its demands were "reasoned and pragmatic," and included "a liberal constitution, representative government, a treaty normalizing relations between Syria and France, positions in the administration and judiciary, and certain economic measures which would benefit the class interests of the Bloc leadership" (Khoury 1987, 265). The National Bloc did not organize on a mass basis (in particular it avoided organizing the countryside); it also published virtually no specific social or economic platform. Both moves would have risked bloc members' position in society: "to most nationalist landlords, the constitutional route to independence and power was much safer and more attractive than one dependent on the mobilization of the masses" (ibid., 265).

The French were not intransigent in the face of Syrian demands for independence.[3] In response to nationalist agitation, in 1928 France permitted the election of a constituent assembly that was to draft a Syrian constitution. After watering down the document's most nationalist provisions, the French promulgated this constitution in 1930, and in 1932 a new chamber of deputies was elected. It was with these deputies that France (unsuccessfully) attempted to reach an agreement over the future shape of the mandate. Parliamentary elections were held a third time in 1936 after a Syrian delegation traveled to France and signed an agreement providing for a French-Syrian alliance on the basis of full Syrian independence. France never ratified that agreement but would proclaim Syria's independence in 1941 and restore the constitution in 1943. That year, elections took place for a government that would lead Syria into full independence in 1946. The National Bloc played a key role in pushing for all of these developments.

French policies did not critically weaken the social power of Syria's traditional elite prior to its assumption of control over the nationalist movement. Most notably, France's presence did not alter the socioeconomic structures that regulated landholding and undergirded agricultural production (Tibawi 1969, 355; Khoury 1987, 63). France's lack of intransigence in the face of Syrian nationalists' independence demands helped traditional elites sustain their power and influence. Though halting, progress toward independence was forthcoming—as with the 1928 assembly, the 1936 agreement, and the 1941 declaration. Syrian nationalists could boast tangible results of their efforts and therefore never became politically discredited as their peers in Tunisia and Algeria had. In addition, the ability of the National Bloc and other segments of the traditional elite to participate in governance via seats in parliament—or service in the cabinets that controlled policy during periods when parliament was dissolved—allowed them crucial access to the state resources they needed to maintain their clienteles.[4] This development, too, buttressed the social power of the traditional elite.

Syria arrived at independence with a plural domestic political chessboard, then, for two reasons. First, its traditional elite retained both social power and political credibility through independence; as a result, the mantle of Syria's nationalist movement never passed into the hands of a more radical, second-generation leadership inclined toward mass mobilization tactics. Second, the fact that France permitted traditional elites some substantial measure of participation in government moved rival Syrian elites to compete for access to those institutions. Parliamentary seats held out the possibility of obtaining patronage as well as exercising real policy influence—whether through constitution writing, negotiating with the French, or presiding over Syria's transition to independent statehood. As a result, "there was fierce competition among Nationalists for access to the French" (Khoury 1987, 301). Indeed, the National Bloc did not possess majorities in the 1928 and 1932 parliaments. National Bloc members negotiated the 1936 agreement with France, and the prestige the party derived from this gave it a parliamentary majority in 1936. The party won a majority in 1943 as well. Still, in the late 1930s and early 1940s divisions emerged within the National Bloc, and other parties arose to challenge its dominance as well.[5]

Egypt

The Egyptian case is actually a hybrid of the dynamics that produced single, preponderant, mass-mobilizing parties and those that produced multiparty systems. The opening acts of the story demonstrate important parallels with what took place in Tunisia, South Yemen, and Algeria. Britain established its control over Egypt in 1882, prior to the emergence of the post-WWI mandate "ethic" in the international community. Nationalist groups opposing British control surfaced but were not broadly organized and were largely ineffective. After thirty-seven years of occupation and twenty-eight years of agitation for independence, the Wafd—a party more akin to the preponderant mass-mobilizing organizations described in chapter 1—emerged to demand independence. The closing acts of the story, however, parallel what took place in the multiparty cases that are the subject of this chapter. Once the mass-mobilizing Wafd demanded independence, the British were not intransigent: they granted Egyptians an influential parliamentary body in 1923 and granted independence some twelve years later, in 1936. That parliament offered Egyptian elites the opportunity to access state resources for distribution to their clienteles, an activity that the Wafd immediately embraced. Others did as well, however, yielding a multiparty system functioning in postindependence Egypt.

In the years following the establishment of British control, three groups arose to confront foreign occupation, but none organized itself broadly and deeply across the country. The first two nationalist movements construed the confrontation in religious terms—that European occupation represented a Christian assault on the Muslim world—and in their rhetorics were loyal to the Ottoman sultan, who was still technically sovereign over Egypt. Mustafa Kamil's nationalist movement began in 1895, published the newspaper *al-Liwa'* from 1900 to 1907, and founded the National Party in 1907. It sought to end the British occupation immediately (by mass-based force if necessary), abolish the capitulations Egypt's economy labored under, and establish constitutional government. Kamil's movement mainly mobilized Egypt's student population, resulting in numerous strikes and demonstrations. However, the movement "never had grass roots support or even rural backing" (al-Sayyid-Marsot 1977, 46). Sheikh Ali Yusuf's movement published *al-Mu'ayyad* from 1890 to 1913 and in 1907 founded the Constitutional Reform Party. More conservative than Kamil, Yusuf received financial support for his campaigns from the Khedive, whose hereditary autocratic rule over Egypt he supported. Vatikiotis notes that "the party had no real following in the country" (1991, 229–30).

The third nationalist grouping of this era was Ahmad Lutfi al-Sayyid's Hizb al-Umma (Party of the Nation), which was founded in 1907 and published *al-Jarida* from 1907 to 1915. Led by a new, Western-educated bureaucratic class, in contrast to the above groups, the party did not relish Ottoman sovereignty over Egypt, and it conceived of the confrontation with Britain in secular rather than religious terms. Hizb al-Umma saw the United Kingdom much less as an outright enemy and more as a formidable force that Egyptians needed to learn from, cooperate with, and then negotiate with to achieve independence. However, it too never organized extensively; it was more "a spontaneous grouping of educated secularists" (Vatikiotis 1991, 227).

Not surprisingly, none of these groups made appreciable headway in ending British control. Indeed, the trend seemed to go in the opposite direction. While Britain's status in Egypt had for decades been unofficial and ambiguous in light of Egypt's ongoing legal connection to the Ottoman Empire, with the strains of WWI approaching, Britain declared Egypt a protectorate in 1914. Britain's use of Egypt during the war intensified both her presence there as well as indigenous opposition to that presence; it also drove home the point that, to date, Egypt's nationalist groups had failed.

This was the context for the emergence of the Wafd Party in 1918. It sought to secure Egypt's independence by petitioning the powers assembled at the Paris Peace Conference. The Wafd explicitly sought to mobilize on a much broader basis than its predecessors had, for only by demonstrating the extent of the popular support it engendered did it feel it would be able to sway the British. Initially it circulated petitions throughout the country, with signatures indicating citizens' support for the Wafd and its independence campaign. This effort yielded 100,000 signatures (approximately 10 percent of the male population) in ten days (Terry 1982, 86–87). The extent of Egyptian anger at the British and of Egyptian support for the Wafd also became clear in March 1919, when British authorities exiled four Wafd leaders and then suppressed an ensuing pro-Wafd demonstration. These actions touched off widespread and long-lasting nationwide protests and upheaval.

The Wafd would go on to build a national grassroots organization, including in the countryside, and was the only Egyptian party to do so. "The Wafd . . . rank and file rapidly grew to include almost the entire nation" (al-Sayyid-Marsot 1977, 49).

In 1922 in response to Wafdist-led nationalist agitation, Britain terminated the protectorate. Technically, Egypt was independent, but because Britain maintained troops there and retained control over Egypt's army, foreign affairs, and the Suez Canal, "the reality was continued British control" (Baynard 1995, 305). Still, in 1923 the British permitted the emergence of an elected Egyptian parliament, a step that—as in all of the other cases considered in this chapter—spurred the emergence of multiple competing parties as rival elites jockeyed for access to the assembly. Egyptians elected their first parliament in 1924 and between 1924 and 1936, six parliamentary elections took place. During this period, rivalries between the Wafd and a number of other political parties developed as Egyptian elites competed for the policy influence and patronage possibilities that came with a seat in parliament. The Wafd tended to win elections in landslide fashion; when it led cabinets, it used its position to distribute patronage to its clienteles (Terry 1982, 160; Vatikiotis 1991, 280, 282). Other parties sought to do the same. Twelve years after the first Egyptian parliament opened for business, with the 1936 Anglo-Egyptian Treaty, Egypt gained a fuller independence and a seat at the League of Nations.

At this point it is important to elaborate on the origins and orientation of the Wafd, for these help to clarify the ways in which the Wafd resembled the single, preponderant, mass-mobilizing parties discussed in chapter 1 as well as the crucial ways in which it *differed* from those parties. Three key parallels are worth mentioning. First, the Wafd resembled the mass parties in that, in certain respects, its leadership had a second-generation "feel": its founders and many of its followers had Western educations, which radicalized their views relative to those of their elders. Second, the Wafd's leaders had deep ties to rural areas that helped them to mobilize the countryside. Third, the emergence of the Wafd represented the passing of political initiative and the nationalist movement into the hands of a new elite in Egypt.

Yet while in Tunisia, South Yemen, and Algeria the second generation of nationalist leaders was distinguishable from the first primarily in class terms, this was not the case in Egypt. The key distinction between the old and new elites in this case was an ethnic one: the latter was an indigenous Egyptian elite that sought to wrest control of the country from the Turco-Albanian ruling elite that was a legacy of Ottoman control (al-Sayyid-

Marsot 1977, 46). The Wafd thus signified the presence of a new elite at the helm of Egyptian politics, but this was nonetheless a quite wealthy, propertied elite that owed its status in large part to the British. For while the Turco-Albanian ruling elite had once constituted the largest landholding group in Egypt, British policies had rendered Egyptian agricultural life particularly profitable and facilitated the emergence of a new, indigenous, wealthy, landowning class. That class sent its sons to school in urban areas, where many became lawyers, doctors, and civil servants; it also used its newfound wealth to branch out into industry, commerce, and finance.[6] This was the class that produced the Wafd leadership, the "first movers" of which were the aristocracy and the bourgeoisie (Terry 1982, 72).

The distinction with the single preponderant party cases is significant. The rise of the Wafd did not represent a *social* revolution as it did in Tunisia, South Yemen, and Algeria. Wafd leaders derived considerable status and influence from their property and other material holdings, resources with which they could underwrite sustained political influence. It was not in the Wafd's interests to mobilize Egypt's masses as intensively and continuously as occurred in the single preponderant party cases. Assuming that continuous, intense mobilization could well lead to a situation wherein the masses began demanding policies designed to lift up those at the bottom of the socioeconomic pyramid in Egypt, to do so would have been to threaten their own positions as landowners, industrialists, financiers, and so on. So while the Wafd found it had to mobilize the masses to a certain extent to extract key political concessions from the British, it did not do so in the more encompassing ways that led to the creation of single, preponderant, mass-mobilizing parties in Tunisia, South Yemen, and Algeria.

Why the Large Number of Parties in These Multiparty Cases?

This chapter has argued that multiparty systems emerged in Iran, Iraq, Jordan, Syria, and Egypt because nationalist movements did not come to be controlled by second-generation elites and because, prior to independence, all five possessed parliaments in which indigenous elites wielded significant political power. It has not, however, explained why these five cases developed systems of *five or more* political parties (see table 1). Chapters 3 and 6 will demonstrate that developments in Turkey yielded a *two-party* political arena, an outcome that was important for facilitating the emergence of competitive electoral politics there. Because, by contrast, the presence of comparatively large numbers of actors in the multiparty arenas of Iran, Iraq,

Jordan, Syria, and Egypt would render the task of consolidating competitive political norms more difficult, it is important to understand the determinants of party number in these cases.

In the early years of the political science debate over the determinants of party system characteristics, Duverger set the pace for its institutionalist partisans by noting that majoritarian electoral rules favored two-party systems (1954). Lipset and Rokkan countered for the sociological camp by tracing divergences in European party systems to the differential outcomes of a set of founding national conflicts and social cleavages that predated mass suffrage, including center-local, state-church, and rural-urban (1967). The two traditions have grappled with each other ever since.

Cox offers a thoughtful and systematic synthesis of these two approaches (1997). Electoral laws affect the processes by which social cleavages translate into the number of viable competitors for office at the district level. Small district magnitudes and majoritarian rules for translating votes into seats will place an upper bound of two on the number of locally viable candidates. Large district magnitudes and proportional rules impose a larger upper bound, and, in socially diverse settings, the result tends to be a much larger number of locally viable candidates. Social structure and electoral structure then interact again at the national level to determine how district-level candidacies are linked together to form national party systems. For Cox, "social structure" refers to the existence of groups (labor, religious, ethnic, and so on) with the organizational cohesiveness to solve the coordination problems involved in building national parties; "electoral structure" includes rules for the selection of presidents and prime ministers as well as for the distribution of upper tier seats and campaign finance.

Following the literature, explaining the emergence of large numbers of political parties in Iran, Iraq, Jordan, Syria, and Egypt is relatively straightforward. In Cox's words, "systems should have many parties only when there are many cleavages combined with a permissive electoral system" (1997, 274). Electoral systems in all but one of these cases indeed were permissive, particularly with regard to district magnitude, a crucial institutional variable influencing the formation of parties (Ordeshook and Shvetsova 1994, 105). Iraq's 1924 and 1946 electoral laws provided for multimember districts; in a few districts, quotas for Christian and Jewish deputies were mandated. Iran's 1906 and 1909 laws established in some cases extremely large district magnitudes.[7] Jordan's 1947 electoral law (as amended in 1949 to reflect the political incorporation of the West Bank) provided for sixteen electoral districts. Five of these selected a single deputy, but eleven elected between two and five deputies. In each district the law dictated how many deputies were to be Muslim (and, of these, how many were to be Circassian) and how many were to be Christian. Syria's 1949 law provided for multimember districts and mandated quotas for the election of non-Muslim deputies according to what proportion of the local population non-Muslims constituted.[8]

At the same time, all of these countries harbored multiple significant cleavages within their citizenries. First, as chapter 5 will elaborate, substantial economic cleavages characterized these societies. In Iran, Iraq, Jordan, Syria, and Egypt, groups clashed over how national economies were to be organized—over the state's proper oversight role, the delineation of property rights, and redistribution and welfare schemes. These battles reflected significant differentiation within populations with respect to how subpopulations related to the mode of production and what each therefore felt was in—or inimical to—its interests. That notable economic differentiation existed is not surprising: at this time Middle Eastern states were embarked on the "modernizing" transition from predominantly rural, agriculture-based economies to significantly urbanized, industrial ones. This transformation saw new social classes—industrialists, workers, urban professional and bureaucratic classes, and so on—growing up alongside extant landholding and peasant groups. Increasing variation in class structures manifested itself in party system structure. Owners of factors of production (landlords, industrialists, and others) tended to cleave to conservative parties while workers, peasants, and many among rising urban professional and bureaucratic classes gave their allegiance to the more radical challenger parties.

Second, as chapter 5 also will elaborate, significant ideological cleavages characterized the political arenas of these multiparty cases. This phenomenon owed much to the structure of international politics at the time, as well as to the history of state formation in the region. Cold War ideological divides manifested in Middle East party systems in the form of Socialist and Communist parties that were pitted against parties committed to the defense of capitalist structures. In addition, the fact that the Arab states of the Levant region—Lebanon, Syria, Iraq, Jordan, and Israel/Palestine—had acquired form and borders not through indigenous processes of political contestation but rather as a result of French and British actions following World War I meant that many saw these state creations as illegitimate. Particularly during the 1950s, ideologies of Arab nationalism swirled about the region, generating calls for various schemes of political unification. Not all subscribed to these views, however, and party systems in Syria, Iraq, and Jordan thus encompassed groups that were committed to the territorial status quo and groups that adamantly opposed it.

Finally, in all but one case,[9] ethnic, religious, and regional social cleavages were reflected in party systems. In Syria, while class cleavages and economic conflict probably were most influential,[10] regional and religious divisions were not irrelevant to party system structure. While the Nationalist and People's parties had divergent public policy interests (Heydemann 1999), many attribute a regional dynamic to their mutual hostility, as the Nationalists were based in Damascus and the People's Party in Aleppo (Seale 1965, 28–30). In terms of religious heterogeneity, while a majority of Syrians are Sunni Muslim, other Islamic and Christian sects also make up the population. The Muslim Brotherhood found its main constituency among urban Sunnis (Picard 1980, 148), with strong early support coming from Aleppo in particular (Batatu 1982, 16). Members of the minority sects meanwhile often joined the Ba'th and Communist parties (Picard 1980, 148; Khader 1984, 4, 19; Ma'oz 1972, 399; Van Dusen 1972, 131), presumably because these challengers advocated secular states in which minorities felt they ran less of a risk of discrimination. The Ba'th in particular grew to have a distinct Alawite (and rural) cast in terms of its membership recruitment (Ma'oz 1972, 402; Batatu 1999, 142). Finally, ethnicity figured in party system dynamics to the extent that Communist Party leader Khalid Bakdash's "appeal remained strongest among his fellow Kurds" (Van Dusen 1972, 129).

While economic and ideological cleavages animated Iraqi party politics to a great extent, again, social divides mattered as well (Eppel 1998b, 242, and 1999, 421). The Iraqi population is largely Sunni Kurd in the north and east, Sunni Arab in the center, and Shi'ite Arab in the south. While Nuri al-Sa'id's conservative Constitutional Union Party was dominated by Sunnis, the Socialist Nation Party founded by Sa'id rival (and Shi'ite Muslim) Salih Jabr drew significant support from Iraqi Shi'ites (Tripp 2000, 129; Grassmuck 1960, 398, 408; Eppel 1998b, 244). Longrigg tells us that Jabr's party also explicitly sought Kurdish support (1953, 363). Marr reports that Istiqlal was a largely Sunni party, while the National Democratic Party appealed especially to Shi'ites and other minorities (2004, 63). The Communist Party garnered support from a variety of minority groups—including Jews, Christians, and Shi'ites (Marr 2004, 63; Sluglett and Farouk-Sluglett 1993, 81). For a variety of reasons, Kurds as well gravitated to the Communist Party (Zubaida 1991, 198; Haj 1997, 117; Longrigg 1953, 336, 353; Tripp 2000, 115).

Regional and national divides also coincided in Jordan. The key social cleavage was a by-product of Jordan's annexation in 1950 of the West Bank region of the former Palestinian mandate. Jordan subsequently granted citizenship to the 800,000 Palestinians it now governed. These new citizens were significantly more urbanized, educated, and politically mobilized relative to their Transjordanian compatriots. Hostility emerged between the two communities: Palestinians viewed Transjordanians as backward while Transjordanians bristled as often better-skilled Palestinians beat them out for important positions in government and the private sector (Patai 1958, 51–52). Moreover, Palestinians were reluctant citizens and harbored numerous grievances against the Hashemite regime. They objected to the annexation, to their political underrepresentation in parliament (they constituted approximately two-thirds of the population but had only 50 percent of the seats), to socioeconomic discrimination against the West Bank in terms of public policy, and to the government's handling of Israeli border incursions. Not surprisingly, although no party was *exclusively* a "West Bank" or "East Bank" formation, an East-West divide did shape Jordan's party system (Abidi 1965, 208–9; Vatikiotis 1967, 109; Cohen 1982, 244, 251).

Religious divides also affected the Jordanian party system, with the Ba'th attracting many Christian followers because of its secularist bent and the Communist Party attracting mostly Christian followers for the same reason (Salibi 1993, 174). Not surprisingly, Jordan's Muslim Brotherhood harbored significant enmity toward the Ba'th (Cohen 1982, 189–90). Cohen also notes that the Liberation Party had little influence in those West Bank cities that were home to large Christian populations (216–17).

Finally, Iran's vast and often inaccessible territory was home to numerous tribal confederations as well as ethnic, linguistic, and religious pluralism. Particularly germane for its nascent party system was the fact that two great powers—Britain and Russia—exercised significant political influence in the south and the north of the country, respectively. "The two imperial powers . . . used policies of divide and rule, whereby they established liaisons with different tribal authorities in their respective zones of influence, and exploited their ethnic, religious, and political differences, not only against each other but also against Tehran" (Saikal 1980, 15). As a result, caucus groupings in the Iranian parliament often were characterized by regional and tribal bonds that corresponded to foreign allegiances (Abrahamian 1982, 178–81, 200–201). In addition, just as minority communities tended to lean toward secularist parties in the cases described above, Iran's Azeri-speaking population and Christian communities were particularly prominent in the communist Tudeh Party (ibid., 384).

Conclusion

While single, preponderant, mass-mobilizing parties dominated Tunisian, South Yemeni, and Algerian postindependence politics, the nascent party systems analyzed in this chapter contained five or more political parties. Their pluralism was a product of the fact that nationalist movements did not come to be controlled by second-generation elites with the willingness, ability, and motivation to mobilize the masses on the scale seen in the cases discussed in chapter 1. Imperial policies did not dramatically weaken the social power of traditional elites in these cases. When these elites demanded independence, the European powers were not intransigent: they established powerful parliaments populated by indigenous elites, and they granted these nations' independence relatively rapidly thereafter. Moreover, the parliaments that were created provided indigenous elites with incentives to form competing party organizations to maximize their access to the policy influence and patronage opportunities such parliaments made available. Excepting the Egyptian case, these countries' political arenas were populated by comparatively *large* numbers of parties due to the interaction between permissive electoral structures and the presence of significant economic, ideological, and social cleavages among their citizenries.

3

The Emergence of Bipartism in Turkey

Building on the arguments presented in chapters 1 and 2 regarding the determinants of the numbers of parties in regional party systems, this chapter demonstrates that the emergence of an influential, elective, preindependence parliament in the Turkish political arena moved rival elites to build competing party organizations to access that increasingly powerful body. At the same time, because they were never colonized, Turks never fought an extended independence battle against an intransigent imperial power[1]—a battle, that is, that could have seen mass mobilization-inclined, second-generation elites take control of the nationalist movement as occurred in Tunisia, South Yemen, and Algeria. These two factors ensured that Turkey would arrive at the independence juncture with a plural nascent party system rather than a single preponderant party.

Yet this party system contained just *two* parties, while the multiparty cases considered in chapter 2 contained five or more. Chapter 6 will argue that this distinction is causally important for explaining the emergence of competitive politics in Turkey because bipartism facilitated depolarization in the political arena during the interim transitional period. Accounting for Turkey's regionally unique two-party system, therefore, becomes a critical analytical task. Economic, ideological, and social heterogeneity married with permissive electoral structures yielded large numbers of parties in Iran, Iraq, Jordan, Syria, and Egypt. Turkish elections followed majoritarian electoral rules, wherein the candidate or party that wins the most votes in a given electoral district *monopolizes* that district's representation in parliament.[2] Conventional theorizing has long said that a two-party system should be the national result of such rules because voters will choose not to "waste" votes on small parties that have no reasonable hope of obtaining a plurality. Empirically, however, majoritarian electoral rules and two-party systems do not correlate well: most nations employing majoritarian rules today enjoy multiparty competition rather than bipartism, with third parties often securing substantial parliamentary presences (Cox 1997, 26).

Cox explains why this should be the case. He demonstrates that majoritarian rules should produce bipartism at the *district* level. National bipartism is another story. Under majoritarian rules, national party systems theoretically could contain up to 2D parties where D is the number of electoral districts. In practice there will be many fewer than 2D national parties, because politicians will seek to coordinate their activities and link together under a common party label for the pursuit of mutually shared goals (Aldrich 1995). However, the extent to which politicians in majoritarian systems come together under a common party label can vary from country to country, producing dissimilar national party systems despite identical electoral structures.

By the late 1940s as political liberalization began in Turkey, opposition elites had strong incentives to join under a common party label. The ruling Republican People's Party (RPP) had been in power for two decades and was organized in nearly every Turkish province. Given majoritarian rules, in order to win enough parliamentary seats to be the majority party, form a cabinet, and control policy, any new party would have to organize broadly and deeply across every Turkish province and go toe-to-toe with the ruling party successfully in a majority of those provinces. By 1950 the opposition Democrat Party (DP) had achieved this feat. What's more, its predecessors—the Progressive Republican Party in 1924 and the Free Republican Party in 1930—had threatened to do the same before they were suppressed by the RPP.

Alone, however, the incentives to build a strong, unified opposition party did not assure the outcome. They can't explain why, on repeated occasions, only *one* set of dissenting elites at a time attempted to build national parties to rival the RPP. Neither can they explain why dissenting elites ultimately were successful in mounting a challenge to the hegemonic RPP. After all, Cox discusses the very real empirical possibility of coordination failure, noting that "differences in the ability of political forces to coordinate often contribute to the maintenance of dominant-party systems" (1997, 249). Coordination failure in the Turkish case could have taken at least two forms:

two or more opposition parties might have come onto the scene, splitting the opposition vote and thus failing to fell the RPP; or, a single opposition party might have launched but failed to elaborate a national organization that was sufficiently extensive to fell the RPP.

Why did only one rival party set out to challenge RPP hegemony? The question is important because it addresses why the first form of coordination failure was avoided and, therefore, why Turkey's party system did not come to contain three or more parties. This chapter shows that, for a century prior to Turkey's postindependence transitional period, the Turkish political community cleaved along one and only one axis: center versus periphery. "Central" elites associated with the civilian and military bureaucracies of the imperial capital, İstanbul, sought to concentrate power in a more centralized imperial state, a state that in their view had a significant role to play in society and the economy. "Peripheral" elites, local leaders in provincial towns and villages, tended to come from commercial, agricultural, and/or religious backgrounds. Their political orientations were conservative. They resisted centralization and instead advocated checks and balances and a decentralized state that played a minimal socioeconomic role. These questions consistently split the community into the same two camps, and no other potentially cross-cutting cleavage issues existed. When party-building began, these competing visions helped mold the emerging party system into a two-party format.

The pages that follow also explain why opponents of the ruling RPP did not experience the second type of coordination failure, instead ultimately *succeeding* in launching a national party capable of taking on the RPP. Opposition elites in the periphery were capable of acting unitarily on a national scale to challenge the center because, beginning in the mid-nineteenth century, a territory-wide system of provincial administrative councils fostered crucial elite networks in the countryside. These networks were vibrant, they linked local elites together both within and across provinces, and they encompassed all of Turkish territory. The opposition put them to use for party-building purposes. Provincial elite networks helped the RPP's opponents solve collective action problems as they set out (repeatedly) to build a national party capable of humbling the RPP. Whereas center-periphery conflict also played out in Iran, Morocco, Egypt, and Tunisia, in no other case did a comparable set of institutions tie local leaders together across the periphery, enabling them to act collectively as one in their conflicts with the center.

The finding that such networks played a crucial role in opposition party-building endeavors amplifies important observations that have been made recently in the parties' literature. Aldrich wrote that "a political party is a collective enterprise, subject to significant collective action problems in forming . . . it" (1995, 58). Kalyvas echoes this view: "The existence of a group of individuals with common interests does not necessarily produce collective action on behalf of this interest. Therefore, the leap from common interests to collective action has to be accounted for" (1996, 11). In other words, in Turkey, the existence of discontent with RPP rule combined with majoritarian electoral rules is insufficient to explain the emergence of a single, successful national opposition party—and, hence, a two-party system.

Building a political party entails coordinating the actions of a large number of individuals, at the top levels of leadership as well as at the "middle management" and the mass-mobilization levels. In short, political party formation requires overcoming collective action problems. Assuming that successful party formation entails the provision of public goods[3] (for example, policy changes, independence, or political liberalization), citizens will wish to "free-ride," letting others bear the costs of organization, knowing the benefits will eventually be enjoyed by all. The specific challenge is to reduce participants' expectations that their party-building colleagues will defect from commitments made to the envisioned collective endeavor. Scholars have specified several circumstances that reduce actors' expectations that others will defect, opening the way for coordinated action.[4] These include a small number of players, the existence of players who do not discount the future too heavily, the availability of information about players' past behavior, the existence of credible sanctions against defection, and the availability of selective incentives accruing only to those who contribute to the collective endeavor.

Preexisting social networks embody nearly all of these traits. They entail a small or manageable number of players who have dealt with and expect to continue to deal with one another in an iterative fashion. As a result, members have good information about others' past behavior, do not discount the future too heavily, and can be sanctioned for defecting from the new collective action attempt. As preexisting social networks supply many of the conditions under which collective action is theoretically more feasible, scholars of parties, not surprisingly, have found networks to be crucial organizational resources for would-be party builders (Cox 1997; Rosenstone and Hansen 1993; Duverger 1954; La Palombara and Weiner 1966; Aldrich 1995; Kalyvas 1996; Berman 1997). In accounting for the development of a two-party political system in Turkey, this study joins with these works in highlighting the importance of preexisting social networks where prospects for party building are concerned.

The chapter now turns to detailing the above dynamics, doing so through an analysis of crucial political developments in the late Ottoman Empire. The narrative opens at the turn of the nineteenth century, and it documents the emergence of Turkish bipartism through the eve of the establishment of the Turkish Republic in the early 1920s.

Center Confronts Periphery in the Late Ottoman Empire

At the close of the eighteenth century, a class of powerful regional strongmen called *âyan* mediated the power of the central Ottoman state over its subjects in the periphery, or provinces.[5] The *âyan* typically were wealthy, prominent, town-dwelling landowners. They were local community leaders, and their position as such derived from their possession of governmental tax farms. Tax farming had been practiced in the Ottoman Empire since the end of the sixteenth century. The central government auctioned off to the highest bidders the right to collect taxes in designated areas of the empire. Purchasers of tax farms would collect from the peasants in their locales sums in excess of what they had paid for the farm, keeping the difference for themselves. Tax farming provided the central government—which did not possess a sufficiently elaborate state apparatus to collect taxes directly—with assured, "prepaid" tax income that was not dependent on the quality of the harvest or other sources of fiscal uncertainty.

The position of the *âyan* highlighted the weakness of central government authority in the provinces. They commanded personal provincial armies that İstanbul relied upon to defend the empire in wartime (İnalcık 1964, 48). The *âyan* were the provinces' wealthiest residents, and İstanbul needed the revenues the *âyan* could supply through their ability to purchase tax farms. *Âyan* also played a dominant role in local governance, overseeing the civil and financial administration of towns in the periphery (Özbudun 1976, 31). In short, the *âyan* were *the* local authority figures. Importantly, though certain rapacious *âyan* exploited peasants by levying extraordinary tax sums, *âyan*-peasant relations were often good, and peasants' allegiances lay with the *âyan* rather than with representatives of the central state (Karpat 1966, 79). Many *âyan* successfully positioned themselves as the people's protectors, blunting the impact of the central government on their lives and their incomes (İnalcık 1964, 47–48). The web of relationships tying *âyan* to local populations meant that the center's social and political control over the periphery was thin indeed.

Power in the late-eighteenth-century Ottoman Empire thus was bifurcated along a center-periphery axis. "The leadership cadres among the empire's Muslim population . . . consisted essentially of two major groups: the *âyans* . . . and the bureaucratic-military elements associated with the government" (Karpat 1972, 251). The former were the dominant elites of the periphery; the latter, the elites of the center. This state of affairs was jeopardized, however, by a series of eighteenth-century military defeats at the hands of tactically, technologically, and organizationally superior European armies. Distressed, Ottoman sultans began searching for ways to reverse the empire's evident relative decline. They concluded that because the existing armed forces were incapable of defending the empire, a new, modern military force trained and equipped according to European standards had to be created. Increased tax revenue would be required to pay for this force. The only way to generate more revenue was for the empire to collect taxes directly. With tax farming, the *âyan* pocketed a considerable amount of revenue—revenue the central government now desperately needed. Of course, reforming tax collection practices in the empire would mean challenging the status and power of the provincial *âyan*.

Selim III (1789–1807) was the first sultan to attempt to restructure center-periphery relations with a view toward strengthening the empire. He ordered the creation of a new, modern army, and he issued directives aimed at increasing the power of the central state relative to the provincial *âyan*, reforming the tax-farming system, and bringing more tax revenue to İstanbul. Not surprisingly, this agenda earned Selim several enemies. The *'ulema* (the official religious dignitary class) resented the mimicry of European military organization entailed in building the new army. The new army threatened the prestige and the livelihoods of the Janissaries, the traditional Ottoman infantrymen. The *âyan* objected to Selim's efforts to undermine their position. Selim could not prevail over these interests. In 1807 the İstanbul Janissary garrison rioted, deposed Selim, installed his cousin Mustapha (IV) as sultan, abolished the new army, and established a conservative, antireform regime in coalition with the *'ulema*.

Though the *âyan* were not anxious to see İstanbul's power grow at their expense, some among them realized that if the empire was to survive, some reforms would have to be effected. Meanwhile, the *âyan* were no friends of the Janissaries, whose provincial garrisons represented a challenge to the *âyans*' local authority. Thus a good number of *âyan* opposed the Janissary-

'ulema antireform government in İstanbul. Opposition to this government began to coalesce around prominent Rumelian *âyan* Bayraktar Mustafa Paşa. Together with survivors of Selim III's fallen reformist regime, Mustafa Paşa led forces under his command on a march on İstanbul in 1808. The forces gained control of the city within a week, deposing Mustapha and installing Mahmut II (1808–1839)—a known supporter of reform—as sultan. Mustafa Paşa himself became grand vizier (the equivalent of a prime minister).

Mustafa Paşa proceeded to convene in İstanbul an unprecedented assembly of top central government officials and provincial *âyan* from around the empire. His goal was to obtain his fellow *âyans*' support for badly needed reforms, including the reconstitution of Selim III's new army. In return for their support for reforms and their pledge to obey and defend the sultan's authority, the central government offered the *âyan* recognition of a set of political and economic rights and privileges as well as limits on the powers of central state officials over local administration (Karpat 1966, 80). This agreement was put in writing in the *Sened-i İttifak* (Document of Agreement), which historians concur signaled the high point of *âyan* power in Ottoman history (Zürcher 1994, 30–31; İnalcık 1964, 52–53).

The events surrounding the convocation of the 1808 assembly that produced the *Sened-i İttifak* made it clear that the center would not be able to extract the resources it sought from its subjects in the provinces without offering political concessions to peripheral elites. The gathering represented the beginning of a trend in which central imperial elites consulted increasingly frequently and substantively with peripheral leaders—a trend that would culminate with the creation of a parliament. The assembly also demonstrated that central elites would not be able to tax, conscript, and administer effectively in the periphery by circumventing local elites; rather, the latter would have to be given a stake in new governing arrangements.

Co-opting Local Leaders: The Provincial Administrative Council System

Âyan reformer Mustafa Paşa did not serve as grand vizier for long. Later in 1808, the Janissaries again revolted in protest of the reconstitution of the new army, and again established a conservative regime in İstanbul. Importantly, however, Mahmut II was allowed to remain on the throne due to a lack of available successors and on the condition that he disband the new army (something he did, but only temporarily). Mahmut II was a reformer, but he had learned important lessons from the fates of Selim III and Mustafa

Paşa about how power relationships would have to be altered if taxation and other governance reforms were to succeed. From 1812 to 1820, using a number of different strategies (bribery, hostage taking, divide-and-conquer methods, and use of the new army), he destroyed the military might of most of the *âyan*. In 1826 Mahmut II physically eliminated the politically disruptive Janissaries by ordering their massacre on an occasion when they had (again) amassed to revolt. He also set up reserve regiments of the new army in the provinces, under the command of men answerable to İstanbul, further broadening the coercive reach of the center over the periphery.

Establishing the center's coercive monopoly did not mean that the center could tax, conscript in, and otherwise govern the periphery effectively, however. Many *âyan* retained possession of their land. In the meantime, agricultural commercialization and the integration of the empire into the world economy had created in Anatolia and Rumelia an influential new freehold landlord class (Lewis 1968, 450; also Karpat 1972, 260). This class, together with other propertied local figures, including merchants, traders, artisans, moneylenders, and religious figures, constituted an important layer of peripheral elites standing between the center and its subjects. These "notables" (as the bulk of the historical literature refers to them) typically were city dwellers.[6] Their influence, however, extended to outlying rural areas through a variety of patron-client ties (landlord-tenant, creditor-borrower, marketer-food producer, and so on). Notables would wield the local social, economic, and political power to frustrate the center's reform efforts, a fact that forced the center to create new institutions that gradually brought the notables into governance processes increasingly formally and substantively.

Beginning in the late 1830s, Mahmut II and his successor, Sultan Abdülmecit (1839–1861), carried out significant administrative reform,[7] the centerpiece of which was replacing tax farming with direct taxation. Before direct taxation was implemented, the lines of provincial administration were reorganized. Within each province, the boundaries of the counties (*sancak*s or *liva*s) were redrawn to render them into administrative units of roughly equal wealth and population. The counties were subdivided into districts (*kaza*) and the districts into subdistricts (*nahiye*). Clear lines of authority were designated between the leaders of each of these levels of administration. Finally, a salaried bureaucrat dispatched from İstanbul to collect taxes, called a *muhassıl*, was assigned to each county. It was through these *muhassıls* that tax farming by local notables was to be replaced with direct taxation by the center.

To assist the *muhassıls* in their tax-collecting duties, administrative councils at the county and district levels were established in 1840. Thirteen individuals sat on the county councils. Seven were representatives of the central government. These were the *muhassıl*, two treasury scribes, the county police chief, the county's local religious judge (*kadi*), its local Muslim dignitary (*mufti*), and the leader of its Christian community (Shaw 1969, 60–61). The remaining six seats on the council were occupied by local notables who were chosen by their peers via indirect, two-stage elections.[8] These six elected members were compensated, in part for the opportunity cost of their time and also "apparently, to make them much more amenable to the desires of the state than might otherwise have been the case" (ibid., 70). The district councils had five members: the *muhassıl*'s local deputy (*vekil*), the local judge (*kadi*), the local police chief, and two (indirectly) elected, compensated local notables.

The creation of these councils aimed at bringing local notables into a cooperative alliance with the *muhassıls* for the task of tax collection. It was thought that the centrally appointed *muhassıls* would be able to collect the requisite amount of taxes only by gaining access to notables' local knowledge and networks of influence (Davison 1966, 99; Thompson 1993, 461–62). Indeed, advising the *muhassıls* and their district-level deputies as to how tax burdens should be distributed locally was the main task assigned to these councils (Shaw 1969, 64). The councils also possessed the judicial powers to hear and decide cases dealing with instances of alleged injustices committed by local administrative or police officials. By January 1841 there were 49 county councils and 580 district councils functioning in all parts of the empire; by 1844, "district and county councils were operating almost everywhere" (ibid., 66–80).

Yet the performance of the administrative council system in its early years disappointed İstanbul as tax revenues accruing to the center actually fell. The central government did not possess enough administrative staff to act as *muhassıls* and was often forced to fill these positions with local notables. The latter used their positions simply to continue in their old tax-farming ways. In cases where the *muhassıl* was a bureaucrat dispatched from İstanbul, local notables elected to administrative councils failed to facilitate the central government's agenda. These notables did not help the *muhassıls* penetrate their local networks of authority. Instead, local elites "hung back and watched the new *muhassıls* . . . fail due to their lack of local connections and knowledge and to the huge areas assigned them for collection" (Shaw and Shaw 1977, 96). Notables seized on the council system not as a mechanism for becoming clients of the center (as the latter had hoped would occur) but rather as a vehicle for preserving their autonomy and voicing local grievances (Thompson 1993, 464). Given the still-precarious nature of the central government's presence and authority in the periphery, notables came to control administrative councils because the center depended on them so heavily to implement reforms (Hourani 1966, 62).

Over the course of the next three decades, İstanbul tinkered with the council system to better harness the institutions to the goals of the center. Reformers at the center repeatedly rewrote provincial governance laws, struggling to strike a balance between the authority of the centrally appointed governors and that of the councils, whose local notable members' interests often clashed with those of the governors. The central government attempted to put an end both to administrative abuses by governors and to corruption among those local notable council members who used their official positions for narrow, self-serving ends (Shaw 1969). It did so by dispatching as provincial bureaucrats more competent and diligent individuals trained at new secular civil service schools in İstanbul, by granting councils more authority to hold centrally appointed bureaucrats accountable, and by sending inspectors to the provinces to check up on both sides. In time, the central government succeeded in engineering the administrative council system in such a way that the councils assisted the central government in collecting taxes and in improving the quality of provincial government.

By the end of this reform period (1876), the administrative council system had expanded considerably in terms of its administrative scope and responsibilities. Whereas at the outset councils had been established in county and district seats only, by 1876 councils also functioned in provincial capitals and at the subdistrict level, while each town and village possessed its own municipal body headed by local elders. To cap the system, annual provincial general assemblies were instituted in 1864. These were attended by four elected representatives from each county, who together considered proposals submitted by the county and district councils. They then sent requests concerning local matters and desired legislation to the central government.[9] Originally the councils had been charged with two tasks only: advising centrally dispatched officials on how tax burdens should be distributed locally, and investigating allegations of official abuse. As early as 1844 İstanbul directed the councils to deliberate on measures that would "improve the state and benefit the security of people" (quoted in Shaw 1969, 83). By 1876 administrative councils were dealing with such matters as improving local infrastructure, education, agriculture, transportation systems, and public safety.

By 1876 the councils also had gained a significant amount of authority. Changes to the provincial administration law made in 1864 subjected officials dispatched from İstanbul to the authority of local administrative councils at the province, county, district, and subdistrict levels to a much greater extent than they had ever been before. Though provincial governors could raise tax levels, "only the general council could decide on how these taxes could be apportioned" (Shaw 1969, 116). In addition, in the case of alleged abuse by county or district administrators, whereas the early councils could put forward punishment recommendations to İstanbul, by 1876 the councils had the authority to investigate accusations and to try officials locally, punishing or dismissing the officials as they saw fit (ibid., 106–7). Shaw points out that "the fact that the councils were in a position to subject their executive counterparts to such punishment enabled them to control the latter, and hold them responsible for their actions" (ibid., 107).

During the middle third of the nineteenth century, then, central Ottoman elites accomplished their reform goals by formally enlisting the political cooperation of notable elites in the provinces. The center achieved this cooperation by constructing a tiered, territory-wide system of administrative councils. Over time, this system evolved into one that offered peripheral elites considerable participation in the governance process. In return for the ability to extract more resources from the provinces, the center granted provincial elites significant new political rights and roles.

The Councils, Parliamentary Development, and Provincial Elite Integration

Participation on the administrative councils imparted a variety of governance skills to local elites. Those who served on administrative councils accumulated important experience drafting reports on local issues of concern and pursuing and advocating their interests at the various levels (subdistrict, district, county, and province) of council jurisdiction. Notables who served as council members also gained practice at debating, negotiating, and finding collaborative solutions to local problems, both with one another and with council members who had been dispatched to the provinces by İstanbul to represent the central government. In addition, local elites on administrative councils became familiar with the many different policy arenas the councils delved into, including infrastructural improvement, education, the administration of justice, and agricultural affairs.

The provincial administrative council system also created robust networks among notable elites in each province. Three mechanisms built and reinforced these networks. First, council elections facilitated provincewide elite circulation and consultation. Shaw's description of voting procedures (1969) is worth quoting at length:

> Within each *kaza* [district] the notables of each village chose their own electors by lot . . . The village electors then chose candidates for the *kaza* council from among the village notables . . . The electors and candidates from all the villages then gathered in the *kaza* capital, where the former examined, interviewed, and discussed each of the latter, gradually cutting down their number until the required two were left to occupy the *kaza* council seats. The same process was followed by the *kaza* councils to choose electors from among themselves, and candidates and members for the councils of the *sancaks* [counties] in whose jurisdiction they were located . . . [this system] was indirect and complicated, but it did assure all the candidates a full hearing, and it made it possible for a large number of community leaders to be heard in the process by which the council members were elected. (63–64)[10]

Second, the council system's tiered nature meant that issues of concern and project proposals formulated at the district level normally had to be vetted at the county and province levels before action was taken. Similarly, decisions taken at the provincial level had to be communicated to and implemented through lower-level councils. Whether business traveled up or down the council system "ladder," it kept elites in contact. Finally, the provincial general assemblies provided occasions when elites from all parts of a province gathered, exchanged, and deliberated.

The development of these networks generated organizational capacity among provincial elites. Putnam argues that networks of civic engagement such as those spawned by the council system create social capital, or features of social organization that facilitate coordinated action (1993, 167). Networks allow information about individuals' reputations, past behavior, and trustworthiness to be communicated. They also "allow trust to become transitive and spread" as members vouch for one another (ibid., 169). Networks make interactions more connected and iterative, and they establish shared norms and traditions of reciprocity among participants. All of these functions facilitate collective action by reducing actors' incentives to defect from shared endeavors and by helping actors' commitments to one another appear credible.

There is considerable evidence to suggest that the Ottoman provincial administrative council system improved local elites' ability to act collectively. Shaw describes the councils as having "stimulat[ed] local pride and local enterprise" and tells us that between 1864 and 1876, most provincial schools were built and financed through local fund-raising efforts undertaken by the councils (1969, 109). During these years, "with the central government falling into increasing financial difficulties, most . . . roads, streets, canals, lighting systems, and the like were introduced as the result of the impetus and financial support provided by the members of the councils" (ibid., 121–22).

Furthermore, research on the operation of the Damascus administrative council from 1844 to 1845 suggests that patterns of local politicking were altered within even the first few years that these new institutions functioned. Thompson argues that before the councils were created, local elites endured a relatively dependent political status and were factionalized, competing with one another for access to the provincial governor. When the councils were instituted in 1840, the local elites elected to them became more autonomous. Subsequently, these elites ceased to represent solely their own personal networks and instead developed broader local affiliations; factionalism disappeared and, over time, local elites developed "a consciousness of class, a horizontal affiliation supplanting their primarily vertical factional ties" (1993, 469–71). By granting local notables a share of effective local power and by building new networks among them, the provincial administrative council system improved the ability of elites in the Ottoman periphery to act collectively in pursuit of their political interests.

Tanzimat-era reforms built peripheral elite networks and organizational capacity not just within provinces but also across provinces, thanks to a series of parliament-like gatherings when top Ottoman officials summoned provincial elites to İstanbul for consultations. The first such occasion was the 1845 Extraordinary Assembly of Provincial Notables. Each province elected and sent two notables to the capital, where central government officials solicited their opinions on the state of the reforms. Notables were also asked what the legislative preferences of the periphery were in such matters as taxation, infrastructure, and agricultural affairs (Davison 1966, 100). The notable delegates spent more than two months in İstanbul, during which time they reported on provincial conditions in audiences with the sultan and with top Ottoman officials in charge of implementing *Tanzimat* reforms. Central officials evidently took provincial notables' input seriously, basing a significant portion of future reform projects and legislation on notables' recommendations (Shaw 1970, 62–63; Shaw 1969, 84–85).

A related central government objective for the 1845 assembly was to "enable the delegates from different provinces to meet one another and to exchange information on local problems and experiences in applying the *Tanzimat*" (Shaw 1970, 62–63). Later in the reform period, provincial leaders had more opportunities to work with one another as they interacted with the center. In 1868 the *Şura-yı devlet* (Council of State) was established as the empire's main legislative body. Provincial notables occupied between a quarter and a third of the seats on the first council (Davison 1966, 103–4; Shaw 1970, 76–78). Each year as part of its official workload, the council met with three or four representatives from each province's general assembly to discuss the provinces' legislative and public works requests. Council business thus facilitated provincial elite network building.

The First Ottoman Parliament, 1876–1878

The first Ottoman parliament convened following the promulgation of the Ottoman constitution in 1876.[11] The constitution reflected continuing domestic efforts to optimally manage center-periphery conflict and to increase subjects' contentment and prosperity.[12] Subjects' contentment was important in order to decrease nationalistic and separatist impulses; their prosperity was key to the goal of increasing tax flows to a center that was strapped for cash. As efforts in the 1860s and 1870s to augment the authority and policy-making role of the provincial administrative councils demonstrate, an important segment of the reformist wing of the central administration believed that a key foundation for Ottoman renewal was increased levels of consultation between local actors and central state officials.[13] The constitution created a representative national legislature to further facilitate such consultation.

The reformers who fashioned the constitution were interested in increased levels of political consultation—but they were not democrats. They created a legislature that was weak relative to the Ottoman executive (that is, the bureaucracy and the sultan's officials). Its upper house, the senate, was composed of men appointed by the sultan for life terms. It could veto laws passed by the (elected) lower house, the chamber of deputies. The sultan appointed the grand vizier and all other ministers, who were responsible to the sultan, not parliament; parliament did not have the power to bring down a cabinet. The parliament also was very circumscribed in its ability to initiate legislation. The sultan could open, close, and dissolve parliament as he saw fit. A third to half of the chamber was composed of provincial representatives who were chosen through indirect (two-stage) elections. To be eligible to serve in the chamber, candidates had to be residents of the localities in which they were elected. The electors were the members of the province-, county-, and district-level administrative councils. These elections therefore sent local notables to İstanbul to serve in the new parliament (Akşin 1971, 168). Most of these notables were former administrative council members.

During the brief life of the first Ottoman parliament, these notables, who tended to come from landowning, commercial, or religious backgrounds, repeatedly challenged the policy preferences of those members of the chamber who were drawn from the civil and military bureaucracies of the capital (Özbudun 1976, 37). For example, representatives from the provinces disclosed and criticized the exploitation, theft, and bad behavior demonstrated by central Ottoman state officials at all levels, from the sultan to provincial tax collectors (Akşin 1971, 168). Furthermore, chamber debates reveal that the primary divisive issue for deputies concerned the role of the state: central government officials' instincts were to expand its scope, while peripheral representatives sought to constrain the growth of the state and promote the free functioning of private enterprise (Karpat 1959, 82). Elsewhere, Karpat tells us that "in stating their practical demands [the deputies from the countryside] were precise and factual, and openly revolutionary in criticizing the bureaucracy," and that the provincial notables' demands included press freedoms and the subjection of the Ottoman executive to more substantive control by an elected, representative parliament (1972, 268–69).[14]

Scholars agree that peripheral deputies acquitted themselves quite ably (Zürcher 1994, 80; Devereux 1963; Tekeli 1983, 1800; Turan 1994, 110; Tanör 1990, 142). They succeeded in thwarting the promulgation of a bill designed to give the government tight control and censorship over the press. The chamber also revised an 1864 law regulating provincial administration so as to reduce the power of İstanbul-appointed officials over the proceedings of the local administrative councils and to prevent İstanbul from receiving a disproportionate amount of tax revenues relative to smaller provincial towns. In large part due to the activism of provincial notable deputies, the chamber became a vehicle for criticizing the government's decisions and policies. Indeed, it was the deputies' willingness to challenge Ottoman ministers that prompted the sultan to prorogue the parliament indefinitely in 1878.

The first Ottoman parliament highlighted two important aspects of late Ottoman political development. First, two political tendencies confronted one another in the political arena. On one side of the divide stood "central" elites based in İstanbul who served in the Ottoman civilian and military bureaucracies and who advocated a larger, more interventionist role for the state. On the other were "peripheral" elites—local notables in the provinces—who wanted to limit the power and scope of the bureaucracy and who sought ways to hold accountable a state that they had experienced as autocratic and arbitrary. Second, important networks and substantial organizational capacity had emerged among local provincial notables. Despite significant constitutional constraints on their authority, the members of the chamber who hailed from the periphery acted effectively in defense of common interests. Their legislative victories reveal an integrated peripheral political elite rather than a fragmented one susceptible to manipulation and division by the center. Peripheral elites acted collectively in the parliamentary arena; their ability to do so stemmed from the networks they developed while serving in the administrative councils and proto-parliamentary bodies created by the *Tanzimat* reforms.

The Second Ottoman Constitutional Period and the Rise of Party Politics

The prorogation of the parliament in 1878 ushered in a thirty-year period of increasingly centralized, despotic rule under the leadership of Sultan Abdülhamit II. Despite this trend away from consultation between İstanbul and the periphery in a forum such as parliament, the kinds of institutions that had fostered provincial elite networks and organizational capacity continued to function. For one, the provincial administrative council system remained intact. In addition, chambers of commerce and agriculture were established in every provincial capital in 1880. These chambers consisted of the leading merchants and farmers in each province. They played promotional and advisory roles, preparing reports for İstanbul that contained recommendations for furthering local agricultural and trade endeavors.

Beginning in 1887, in reaction to the authoritarian trend of Ottoman politics, a political party called the Committee for Union and Progress (CUP) began to set up branches in the European (Rumelian) provinces of the empire. The CUP was composed generally of relatively low ranking bureaucrats and army officers, as well as teachers and students connected with a new crop of modern secular schools built during the *Tanzimat* era to produce civil servants and military officers capable of combating Ottoman decline. CUP members saw ruin at the end of the despotic political path the empire was on. They advocated the reopening of parliament to effect increased levels of consultation in Ottoman government. By 1908, CUP sympathies ran strong among the ranks of key Ottoman army units that were stationed in the empire's European provinces. With their backing, on July 23 the CUP forced the sultan to reinstate the constitution, which had been suppressed and ignored for three decades. Elections to form a new parliament were held in November, and on December 17, 1908, the Ottoman parliament was reopened.

This began what is known as the Second Constitutional Period, so called because the years 1908 through 1918 saw the Turkish political community experiment for a second time with integrating a legislative body into governance procedures. Importantly, these years witnessed continued center-periphery political conflict. Because of the reopening and subsequent constitutional strengthening of parliament, the conflict now began to take the form of party politics. From its base in the empire's European provinces, the CUP gradually took over the reins of the central imperial administration in İstanbul and in the Anatolian provincial capitals. However, because the CUP's social reach in many parts of Anatolia was thin, the party was forced to send many provincial notable elites whose political views differed fundamentally from its own to İstanbul as members of parliament under its banner. The CUP quickly found it could not control these deputies' voting decisions. Within a few years many of these deputies left the CUP and helped found a substantial opposition party. This party's platform espoused many of the political preferences of the periphery, and its branch organizations were built by provincial elite networks.

Although the CUP began life as a secret society and took power in 1908 by force, the backgrounds of its activists and the political views it advocated as it strengthened its hold on the imperial administration are such that it should be considered the "new" Ottoman "center" for the purposes of the argument developed here. As stated earlier, CUP members typically came from the bureaucracy, the army, and the new civil service schools in the capital. These institutions served as venues where like-minded individuals met, networked, developed mutual trust, and organized.[15] Their livelihoods and life experiences were intimately connected with the life of the Ottoman state—a state that they knew was in geopolitical jeopardy. The politics of the dominant CUP faction was one of centralization, reform, and increased state power.

As part of its 1908 intervention, the CUP pressed the sultan to reconstitute parliament because it needed to develop a power base from which to challenge the hegemony of the sultan and the Ottoman executive bodies. The CUP had ample reason to feel insecure. Its members were young in a society that accorded respect and deference to age. In addition, although many were well educated, none had substantial administrative or governing experience (Ahmad 1969, 16–18). Moreover, their organizational base was limited to the empire's European provinces. They had little to no footing beyond this geographical area, nor were they well organized in İstanbul (ibid., 42–43). For this reason the CUP immediately sent emissaries to the empire's Anatolian provinces to explain who they were and what they stood for, as well as to organize support for their cause in parliamentary elections scheduled for November 1908 (Kabasakal 1991, 62; Zürcher 1984, 44). The emissaries began establishing local CUP branch offices tasked with identifying candidates for parliament to run on the CUP's ticket and making sure that these men were elected (Ahmad 1969, 27–28).

Yet CUP officials arrived in these provinces as social and political outsiders. They had been secularly educated in İstanbul; they hailed from urban areas and from "officialdom" (that is, the Ottoman civilian and military bureaucracies); and they advocated centralizing and secularizing reform. In more rural Anatolia the CUP found it could not call the political shots alone and often was forced to choose parliamentary candidates from the local notable class (Zürcher 1994, 99; Özbudun 1976, 40–41; Ahmad 1969, 27–28)—whose backgrounds and outlooks differed substantially from its own. Thus to establish branches outside of its European stronghold, the CUP had to work with peripheral elites. The latter tended to be conservative, against administrative centralization, and against secularization. Because of the political skills and networks peripheral elites had developed in previous decades, they would be effective actors—and troublesome for the CUP—when they arrived in İstanbul for parliamentary service.

When parliament opened for business in December 1908, the CUP was able to amend the 1876 Ottoman constitution in ways that significantly strengthened parliament vis-à-vis the executive. The sultan now could appoint only the grand vizier and the Şeyhülislam (the empire's highest-ranking religious figure). The grand vizier obtained the right to appoint cabinet ministers. Importantly, he and his cabinet were made accountable to parliament, not the sultan. For the first time, parliamentary votes of no confidence could bring down cabinets. Parliament also acquired the right to initiate legislation and to conclude treaties. The "core" CUP MPs and the local notable MPs who had been elected on the CUP ticket shared the conviction that the pre-1908 Ottoman governance structure was too despotic. Both groups agreed that an elected parliament should temper the authority of the executive branch. As a result, passage of these constitutional amendments was not problematic. Nevertheless, the differences in the backgrounds and political viewpoints of these two groups soon surfaced.

In June 1909 the CUP leadership sought to amend the constitution to allow MPs to hold other government offices below the ministerial level simultaneously. Although parliament was packed with deputies elected on CUP lists, and although no opposition parties yet sat in the body, the core CUP leadership failed to muster the two-thirds majority needed to amend the constitution. Clearly, CUP emissaries to the non-European provinces had not been able to recruit a set of MPs who either shared their political preferences or felt any imperative to submit to CUP pressure to conform. CUP leaders did attempt to tame the dissenting deputies, calling for unity, discipline, and the performance of "duty" (Ahmad 1969, 54). These calls went unheeded.

Instead, opposition parties began to organize, both inside and outside of parliament, to challenge the CUP's agenda. These included the *Mutedil Hürriyetperveran Fırkası* (Party of Moderate Liberals), formed in late 1909, and the *Ahâli Fırkası* (People's Party) and *Osmanlı Sosyalist Fırkası* (Ottoman Socialist Party), both established in 1910.[16] These parties made parliamentary management very trying for the core CUP leadership. They questioned ministers on policy issues, voiced their own views forcefully in parliamentary debates and in the press, and voted against CUP-backed legislation. These parties did not, however, loom as significant political threats yet—either they did not possess any extra-parliamentary organization to speak of, or their views did not resonate strongly with politically tuned-in citizens. This state of affairs changed in late 1911, however, when, along with other anti-CUP individuals and organizations, these three parties banded together to create a new, more influential opposition presence: the *Hürriyet ve İtilâf Fırkası* (Party of Freedom and Understanding).

The emergence of the *Hürriyet ve İtilâf Fırkası* (HİF) was important for two reasons. First, it constituted a serious political challenge to the CUP because it began to organize, opening branches across Rumelia and Anatolia for the purpose of competing against the CUP in upcoming elections.

By May 1912, the party had established forty-eight branches in İstanbul and ninety-one in the provinces, including in more than a dozen major Anatolian towns.[17] Second, it constituted a conservative, peripheral political challenge to the CUP. While the CUP—angry at the secessions that were shrinking the empire—began to espouse (ethnic) Turkish nationalism, the HİF made more traditional ideological appeals to Ottomanism as the tie that should bind the peoples of what was left of the empire. The HİF opposed CUP efforts to centralize Ottoman politics and increase the state's role in economic affairs, advocating decentralization and emphasizing the importance of individual enterprise instead. The HİF also opposed the CUP's secularizing tendencies. The CUP-HİF confrontation thus embodied the long-standing center-periphery cleavage in late Ottoman politics—a conflict that now took the form of two-party competition thanks to the emergence of an influential parliamentary body.

Given the preferences of peripheral politicians and the skills that they had developed during the nineteenth century, the HİF's rapid organizational progress in the Anatolian countryside is not surprising. Notable elites in the provinces had long resented and resisted İstanbul's attempts to extend its control more directly over the countryside, a project that the CUP too had taken up. As many notables' social status and livelihoods derived from their religious training, the CUP's emphasis on secularizing the public sphere was unwelcome in the periphery. Finally, local elites had gained political skills and built networks in the countryside through their participation on provincial administrative councils. They had the ability and wherewithal to organize, and were a tremendous resource for the HİF as it worked to establish the party nationwide.[18]

In December 1911, only a month after the HİF was founded, its candidate beat his CUP opponent in an İstanbul by-election. By this time the CUP had secured control over the Ottoman provincial administration by placing its people in provincial governorships as well as at the heads of the county- and district-level administrations (Ahmad 1969, 101). But it had penetrated Anatolian provincial political society only to a limited extent. Although the CUP possessed "a significant network of local branches . . . this network never covered even all the major cities or penetrated below the sub-province (*sancak*) level" (Payaslıoğlu 1964, 428). Cognizant of its tenuous hold on the periphery, the CUP was jolted by the by-election loss, and its response was to resort to authoritarian means to keep its hold on power. It used repression and intimidation tactics to influence 1912 election outcomes in its favor (as a result, these have come to be known as "the

Big Stick" elections). Yet Ahmad tell us that even in the assembly constituted by these heavy-handed elections, the CUP still was unsure of successfully moving its legislation through parliament (1969, 105).

The CUP accordingly chose to reduce the authority of a parliament it found it could not control, handing power back to the executive branch (ibid.). The core CUP leadership was well aware that peripheral notable leaders' policy agendas were diametrically opposed to its own and that, if given sufficient political space, those leaders likely could organize substantial political support in the provinces, threatening the CUP's hold on power (Özbudun 1976, 40–41). In the meantime, internationally these were difficult, turbulent years for the Ottoman Empire as World War I unfolded on the heels of the Balkan Wars. This combination of internal and external factors resulted in the breakdown of competitive parliamentary government. The CUP established authoritarian rule over the empire that lasted until the Ottoman defeat at war's end in 1918.

Elite Networks in the Periphery and the Turkish War of Independence

In 1918 WWI's victorious powers began to occupy the lands that today constitute Turkey with the intention of partitioning the territory among several interests. Left to their own devices, as outlined in the 1920 Treaty of Sèvres, the entente powers would have created an Armenian republic, Greek territory, and French and Italian spheres of influence, leaving a tiny Ottoman state in northern Anatolia with İstanbul as its capital. But the entente was not left to its own devices. Though the Ottoman administration in İstanbul cooperated with the entente, Turks in both Rumelia and Anatolia began organizing to defend their land.

Local organizations called Defense of Rights societies constituted the early building blocks of the Turkish independence war effort. These appeared first in Rumelia and in the western and eastern Anatolian regions most threatened by foreign occupation. At least a dozen major societies emerged, including in İzmir, Manisa, Kars, Edirne, Erzurum, Elaziğ, Trabzon, and Sivas. They sought to use Woodrow Wilson's self-determination principle to their benefit in the international arena. They held congresses to proclaim the Turkish-ness of their localities, to demonstrate that their governance processes were representative, and to publicly petition the entente powers that their sovereignty not be destroyed (Zürcher 1984, 88–92).[19] Many operated as de facto regional governments, collecting taxes and organizing local militias to back up their preferences with force.

Between 1918 and 1920 these societies came together to form an integrated national structure. At a July 1919 conference in Erzurum, delegates of the societies in the eastern provinces established an executive apparatus to coordinate their efforts. In September 1919 the Sivas Congress united all of the societies into a single organization and appointed an executive body charged with directing its activities. When İstanbul was occupied in March 1920, the governing structure worked out at Sivas—in which elected representatives from the provinces selected an executive committee—formed the basis of a new parliament, the Grand National Assembly, based in Ankara. From 1920 to 1923 this parliament oversaw the independence war. It was over the course of these events that Mustafa Kemal (Atatürk) established himself as the leader of the Turkish independence movement.

Central CUP bureaucrats, military officers, and intellectuals played an important role in these developments. During WWI, CUP officials anticipated the possible need for a strategic retreat to the Anatolian interior, and they made human resources and materiel preparations for this eventuality. The Defense of Rights societies tended to begin life as CUP initiatives (Zürcher 1984, 88), growing directly out of the party's provincial branches (Rustow 1964, 377; Karpat 1964, 270). The CUP created the *Teşkilat-ı Mahsusa* and the *Karakol*, organizations tasked with smuggling weapons, supplies, money, and men into Anatolia to provision national self-defense efforts. Units of the Ottoman army that had survived occupation intact and that remained autonomous helped fight the war. Finally, the political and military leadership of Mustafa Kemal—an army officer and CUP member—was pivotal to the Turks' eventual victory.

However, that victory hinged on cooperation between centrist CUP bureaucratic, military, and intellectual elites and networks of local notable elites in the provinces (Özbudun 1976, 43; Owen and Pamuk 1998, 13). If most Defense of Rights societies were CUP initiatives, local elites were key participants in the societies' activities (Tanör 1990, 145; Rustow 1959, 542; Zürcher 1984). Indeed, without the cooperation of local elites, the CUP could not have defeated its enemies. The extractive task required to sustain the war was enormous. Prior to a pivotal battle in 1921, for example, "the government requisitioned one-third of all foodstuffs and farm animals and all available arms and munitions in the countryside" (Zürcher 1994, 162). It was provincial leaders who, by drawing on their local networks of influence, mustered the men, materiel, and money needed to fight the war (Yerasimos 1987, 68). "The effort to organize a war of national independence had been led by officers of the Ottoman Army, but grassroots support for the movement had been mobilized by the local notables" (Turan 1994, 114).

The congresses held, the fighting forces organized, and the resources mobilized by the Defense of Rights societies constitute further evidence of the robustness of local elite networks produced by nineteenth-century Ottoman political and administrative reforms. The organizational capacity of peripheral actors was crucial to the winning of the Turkish independence war. During that period, peripheral elites did not act in isolation but rather in alliance with central CUP bureaucratic, military, and intellectual leaders. With the survival of their political community at stake, Turkey's two main elite groups (center and periphery)—normally at loggerheads—worked together.

Conclusion

The origins of Turkey's regionally unique two-party system, then, lie in center-periphery conflict, which began at the turn of the nineteenth century. This conflict arose when political-military threats from its European neighbors forced the Ottoman Empire to build a new, modern army. Raising the revenue required to fund the new army presented central Ottoman civilian and military officials with a dilemma. To channel increased tax revenue to the center, they would have to alter the fiscal status quo, which long had enabled powerful tax-farming provincial elites to pocket substantial sums. Peripheral elites would not give up their tax farms without a fight. At the same time, the central imperial government could not govern effectively in the provinces without tapping peripheral elites' local knowledge and authority. Instead, the center was forced to seek ways of harnessing peripheral elites to the larger fiscal project. During the nineteenth century, the central government extended new, participatory political rights and roles to peripheral elites in exchange for their acceptance of a larger central government presence in the provinces, including direct taxation.

Two related institutional innovations that facilitated this exchange had important ramifications for the shape of Turkey's emerging party system. First, increased levels of center-periphery consultation gradually led to the creation of a powerful elective Ottoman parliament. During the 1908–1912 period, the existence of this parliament moved rival elites to begin building competing party organizations to maximize their respective political voices in that body. Chapter 6 will show that such a parliament would remain a more-or-less constant feature of Turkish politics, and its emergence helps explain why Turkey's nascent party system was a plural one rather than one that was dominated by a single preponderant party. Given their diverging views on state centralization, the state's proper role in economic affairs, and secularization, CUP-HİF competition in 1911 and 1912 strongly suggests that the long-standing center-versus-periphery cleavage in the Turkish political community now had moved into the parliamentary arena, setting the stage for a nascent two-party political system.

Second, the tiered, territory-wide practice of center-periphery consultation that was embodied in the provincial administrative council system helped ensure that peripheral elites would be able to organize effectively enough to challenge the center in substantial ways. For central elites, concentrated and connected to one another in the imperial bureaucracies, political organization was a relatively straightforward task. Peripheral elites, by contrast, scattered across a vast territory, might easily have failed to join forces successfully. They did not, however, because the council system fostered robust networks among peripheral elites both within and across provinces, integrating them and facilitating their ability to act collectively in the face of central government encroachments. In the case of the HİF, the peripheral opposition put these networks to use for party-building purposes. Chapter 6 will show that provincial elite networks continued to help peripheral actors solve collective action problems as they set out (repeatedly) to build a national party capable of humbling the center—thus working against a preponderant party system *dominated* by the center.

Turkey was not unique in the region in manifesting center-periphery conflict during the nineteenth century. Iran, Morocco, Egypt, and Tunisia also came under political-military threat from Europe and/or Russia early in the century. These threats drove central decision makers to attempt to build stronger states and more modern armies, tasks that in turn required them to raise more tax revenue. Though the same dynamics that drove reform in (what would become) Turkey also pitted center against periphery in these four countries, in none of them did center-periphery conflict produce two-party systems. This divergence in outcomes can be attributed to the fact that only in the Turkish case did give-and-take between center and periphery result in institutional innovations that generated periphery-integrating elite networks that facilitated the periphery's ability to act collectively against the center. These institutions in turn seem to have developed because of at least two key factors. First, in the Turkish case, the center sustained reform initiatives for nearly a century despite significant opposition (and outright rebellion in the earliest phase). Second, late

Ottoman politics evinced a balance of power between center and periphery that necessitated the building of consultative institutions if reform was to succeed.

Compared to the Turkish case, central elites in Iran, Morocco, and Tunisia were not persistent about reform and backed down in the face of early opposition. Since little changed in status-quo center-periphery relations, there was no need to create institutions to *manage* change. Only in Egypt was the center persistent about reform. There, however, the center overpowered the periphery and did not need to nurture consultative institutions for reforms to succeed. In none of these four cases where comparable center-periphery conflict unfolded, therefore, were institutions built that could have integrated peripheries and fostered two-party systems as occurred in the Turkish case. Moreover, in Egypt, Tunisia, and Morocco, colonialism then altered political landscapes in ways that made it unlikely that center-periphery conflict would be the primary structuring force when indigenous party systems eventually evolved.

For early-nineteenth-century Iran, multiple military defeats at the hands of Russia demonstrated to the ruling Qajar dynasty that national survival would depend on strengthening the central state, exerting more control over the periphery, increasing tax revenues, and modernizing the army. The dynasty failed, however, to bring about these changes. Only halting reform attempts were made, during the premierships of Amir Kabir (1848–1851) and Mirza Hussein Khan (1870–1880). Vested interests blocked these attempts. Tax collection and financial administration remained problematic throughout the century (Kamrava 1992, 13), and the central government increasingly turned to foreign loans and the selling of concessions to raise revenues. Tellingly, upon the death of the Qajars' most reform-minded Shah, Naser al-Din (1848–1896), "the treasury he left behind was practically empty" (ibid., 19).

Unlike the Ottomans, then, the Qajars did not create a territory-wide system of local governing institutions to manage new center-periphery relationships. They did not convene assemblies of peripheral representatives in the capital. Instead, the Qajars pursued a divide-and-conquer approach to governing the periphery, fostering dissension among Iran's many tribes and religious and ethnic groups (Kamrava 1992, 13; Limbert 1987, 77–78). The result as Iran entered the twentieth century was a politically fragmented periphery. As chapter 5 will demonstrate, Iran's postindependence party system reflected this fragmentation, with conservative rural elites split across at least three parliamentary caucuses whose support bases were regional.

In Morocco, defeats at the hands of France and Spain beginning in the 1840s provoked decision makers at the core of the sultan's governing apparatus to try to develop a modern army. However, their efforts were minimal and did not include reforms to alter the method by which the sultan and his men taxed the periphery. Collecting taxes from the settled tribes of Morocco's watered coastal plains was relatively unproblematic, for this population was threatened by marauding nomadic tribes and needed protection. For Morocco's mountain and desert regions, however, the sultan retained the services of tax-exempt tribal warriors to forcibly tax the nomadic tribes who constantly sought to escape his authority. These tribes "were too internally divided to concert their actions against the government" (Waterbury 1970, 18). The sultan thus focused his tax-collecting attention on one section of the periphery at a time. At no point did he create a set of civil institutions to perform this function simultaneously, territory-wide. Again, the result in Morocco was a politically fragmented periphery, a condition that helps explain why center-periphery conflict did not translate into a two-party system. The French occupation then quelled this conflict and altered the domestic landscape such that issues other than center-periphery battles structured Morocco's postindependence party system.

The French invasion of Egypt in 1798 demonstrated the vulnerability of this autonomous Ottoman province, moving an Albanian-born Ottoman military officer named Muhammad Ali to initiate reforms that closely mirrored those that İstanbul had undertaken. Ali sought to strengthen the central state and build a modern army; in addition, he looked to improve agricultural production and industrialize Egypt to generate sufficient revenue to fund his modernization campaign. One main stumbling block lay in Muhammad Ali's reform path: tax-farming elites in the provinces who pocketed significant sums, which the center now coveted. But these elites were weaker relative to the center than were their counterparts in Anatolia (Vatikiotis 1991, 65).[20] Muhammad Ali was able to end tax farming, assert central state control over all of Egypt's agricultural land, and establish direct central administration over the periphery relatively effortlessly. Thus in Egypt reform efforts were sustained, but they were sustained in no small part because the center was capable of quickly outmaneuvering the periphery. Muhammad Ali had the power to dictate terms; he did not need to create local governing institutions with which to co-opt provincial elites. A long colonial interlude (1882–1936) then further altered the political playing field prior to the emergence of Egypt's postindependence party system.

France's colonization of Algeria beginning in the 1830s sounded the reform alarm in Tunisia. Elites in Tunis subsequently began to attempt to build a modern army and reform the governance apparatus. In Tunisia, however, reform was not sustained. The reform agenda's crescendo came in 1861 with the promulgation of a constitution that, while it created a (weak, appointed) legislative body in Tunis, was perceived in the countryside as increasing the power of the central state. A significant tax hike a few years later occasioned a widespread revolt. In its aftermath, the Tunisian Bey rescinded the constitution and backed away from reform. French colonial control began in 1881 and lasted seven decades, during which time, as chapter 1 illustrated, the dynamics of indigenous Tunisian politics shifted dramatically and led to the emergence of a single preponderant party.

PART II

The Impact of Party Systems on Regime Formation

4

Preponderant Single Parties and Immediate Authoritarian Rule

Chapters 1 through 3 put forth a set of arguments accounting for the divergent forms party systems in the Middle East acquired as the independence juncture neared. Part II of this study turns to an analysis of party systems and their characteristics as independent variables that shaped founding regimes in the region after independence was achieved. Chapter 4 argues that the emergence of single, preponderant, mass-mobilizing parties in Tunisia, South Yemen, and Algeria helps to explain why party leaders sought to monopolize political power and set up authoritarian one-party regimes after independence *as well as* why party leaders were able to do so quickly and effectively.

With their eclipse of the traditional elites, these preponderant, mass-mobilizing, nationalist parties to an important extent embodied an aspect of social revolution in these societies. As nationalist dramas played out, second-generation elites traveled a tremendous distance from humble, distinctly second-class social origins to immense status and prestige as triumphant independence winners. They wished to retain that status after independence. Relative to traditional elites, however, they did not have extensive material wealth or property with which they could assure themselves continued political dominance.

What they did have was an organization that had attached the nation's masses to their leadership. To maintain their newfound status, they would have to sustain those attachments. Crafting a political economy in which the state played a large role in economic affairs and embarked on redistributive public policies after independence was an obvious way to achieve that goal. So was an unfettered ability to make state jobs available to political loyalists. Had second-generation elites presided over the installation of competitive regimes at independence, they would have opened the door for traditional elites—who would likely have advocated more liberal political economies—to get back into the political game and to limit their ability to distribute state patronage to their party clientele. Monopolizing state power was thus imperative if second-generation elites were to maintain their newfound status. This explains the preferences of these elites in all three cases for building authoritarian one-party regimes after independence.

Fortunately for second-generation elites, therefore, the existence of single preponderant parties facilitated the prompt establishment of stable, one-party authoritarian rule at independence. Single preponderant parties constituted extremely effective tools with which elites could construct authoritarian rule. In Tunisia, South Yemen, and Algeria, party leaders used them to suppress their would-be rivals, to take control of the state apparatus, and to craft the new political rules of the game in their favor.

The case discussions that follow substantiate these claims. Each also attends to another important, logically prior analytical task. In light of the insights gained from the Turkish case—particularly, the lesson that substantial collective action problems are inherent in all party-building endeavors—it is important to understand how the single preponderant parties that emerged in Tunisia, South Yemen, and Algeria solved these problems. Chapter 1 argued that such parties arose because nationalist movements came to be controlled by second-generation elites with the willingness, ability, and motivation to mass mobilize. This chapter probes the "ability" part of this formula in more in-depth fashion, because the "nuts and bolts" of party-building processes were causally pivotal to the emergence of preponderant, mass-mobilizing parties and their subsequent utility for the rapid construction of authoritarian one-party regimes in these cases.

A few general observations may be made regarding the relative ease of party building in Tunisia, South Yemen, and Algeria as compared to Turkey. In one respect, party building should have been more difficult in these cases for the simple reason that the endeavor had to be carried out in the context of colonial control, repression, and harassment. In Tunisia, South Yemen, and Algeria, imperial powers were not pleased about the emergence of nationalist parties and put numerous obstacles in the way of their growth. To be a party activist often meant to risk surveillance, arrest, jail time, and/or exile. Such a circumstance exacerbates the free-rider problem that lies at the heart of achieving collective action. If a would-be activist faces high potential personal costs from contributing to a party-building enterprise, s/he is more likely to hold back, allowing others to bear those costs while waiting to enjoy the public good (independence) that s/he hopes will be forthcoming as a result. In this respect, therefore, party builders in Tunisia, South Yemen, and Algeria faced larger challenges than did their Turkish counterparts when it came to motivating their compatriots to join in their endeavors.

In three other respects, however, party building in these cases theoretically should have been *easier* than in the Turkish case. First, party building in Tunisia, South Yemen, and Algeria involved a smaller number of potential players than in Turkey. All three countries had smaller populations than Turkey, with those of Tunisia and South Yemen standing out as particularly tiny by comparison (see table 4). Moreover, both Tunisia and South Yemen were much, much smaller countries than Turkey in terms of total land area. While Algeria is quite a bit larger than Turkey, if arable land is used as an indicator of where populations that are most available for political recruitment are settled, Algeria appears to be a much smaller political community than Turkey. Thus, relative to their counterparts in Turkey, party builders in these three countries faced a less daunting scenario: a smaller total population as audience, a smaller elite to attempt to recruit and incorporate, and a smaller terrain to cover in terms of branch building, campaigning, and so on.

Theorists of collective action emphasize a second element that facilitates coordinated action: the existence of players who don't discount the future heavily—that is, who value future events quite intensely relative to the present. Such players are more likely to keep commitments made to comrades in a collective endeavor to preserve their reputations and assure others' reciprocity going forward—especially if the endeavor is expected to produce a brighter, more rewarding future. With respect to the latter, those citizens in Tunisia, South Yemen, and Algeria whom party-building entrepreneurs sought to recruit likely discounted the future less heavily than did their Turkish counterparts. While Turkish opposition parties sought to wrest control of government from a homegrown dictatorial political party, nationalist parties in these three cases fought for independence from European powers. The latter prospect should have been a comparatively more dramatic and attractive goal for potential recruits. To take nothing away from many Turks' eagerness to challenge the RPP and pluralize their system of governance, political independence from Britain or France must

TABLE 4. Data Relevant to Party Building in Turkey, Tunisia, South Yemen, and Algeria

Country	*Population at Time of Founding Regime (millions)*	*Total Land Area (sq. km.)*	*Arable Land (sq. km.)*
TURKEY	21.48	780,582	269,300
TUNISIA	3.86	164,107	
SOUTH YEMEN	0.84	287,684	
ALGERIA	10.80	2,381,764	76,454

SOURCES: Total land area figures are taken from Drysdale and Blake 1985, 15. Arable land figures were calculated by combining total land area with figures on percent arable land published in the *CIA World Factbook* (www.cia.gov). Population data for Turkey (1950), Tunisia (1955), and Algeria (1960) are taken from Population Division of the Department of Economic and Social Affairs of the United Nations Secretariat 2005. Figure for South Yemen is for the mid-1950s and is derived from Dresch 2000, 76.

have loomed as a more weighty, future-altering prospect for citizens of Tunisia, South Yemen, and Algeria.

Finally, party builders in Tunisia, South Yemen, and Algeria arguably had more potential selective incentives (that is, benefits that accrue *only* to direct participants in the collective endeavor) to offer to those citizens who chose to contribute to their respective nationalist endeavors. Opposition party leaders in Turkey sought to assume cabinet control. If successful, they would be able to offer a portion of their party faithful jobs in existing ministries and the other bureaucracies of the extant Turkish state administration. Nationalist parties in these three cases, by contrast, sought to evict their European masters and engineer a whole new state administration. This project carried with it not just the opportunity to layer party faithful into existing institutions but also to create whole new institutions staffed by party members. In other words, the potential fruits of victory should have been comparatively more extensive and substantial for the party faithful in Tunisia, South Yemen, and Algeria—a factor that facilitated party building in these three cases.[1]

These, then, were general factors structuring collective action dilemmas in the colonial contexts. Still, as the following case narratives will demonstrate, preexisting social networks that could be tapped for party-building projects were central to the emergence of the single, preponderant mass-mobilizing parties.

Tunisia

In Tunisia, Neo-Destour (ND) founders capitalized on several key social networks when building their party. At the elite level, a secondary school called Es-Sadiqia College played a pivotal role in forging close bonds among the men who would fill out much of the ranks of the ND's top leadership (Moore 1964, 81; Hermassi 1972, 112, 121). Created in 1875 by Tunisian reformers to provide a modern, bilingual education to its students, Es-Sadiqia, by the 1910s and 1920s, was attracting the sons of middle- and lower-class families from the Sahel provinces. A great many of these went on to pursue university educations in France, where they not only strengthened their ties to one another, but also absorbed the ideologies and organizational tactics of French left-wing political parties. These were the men who went on to found and develop the ND party in Tunisia. "United by a common socialization and committed to an enlightened view of modernization, they began immediately to enact their perspectives through mass mobilization" (Hermassi 1972, 121).

To flesh out the party organization and to attract grassroots members and material support, these elites drew on several other organizational resources. Significant sums of money flowed to the party from the traditional markets—the souks—of Tunisia's major towns (Moore 1964, 82). Souk artisans and merchants were distressed at the competition for their goods that emanated from untaxed European imports and thus had a special interest in backing an organization they believed would evict the French. Much of the lower, local-level ranks of the party leadership were filled by graduates of another key educational institution, the Zitouna (Moore 1965, 35). This was a university that offered a traditional Muslim religious and legal education, whose students were "naturally a revolutionary group, coming from the disinherited classes of Tunisian society . . . [to whom] few jobs were open" (Moore 1964, 83). For recruitment purposes, ND leaders took advantage of the fact that they themselves tended to come from and maintain close ties with rural areas of the country (Hermassi 1972, 126). They also used Tunisian Sufi Muslim brotherhoods' community centers—zawiyas—to further their cause, using zawiya lodges as meeting places and appealing to their members for support.[2] Finally, a crucial source of recruits and political support for the party came from Tunisia's labor union (Rivlin 1952, 175; Moore 1964, 74). While indigenous attempts at labor organizing date back to the 1920s, as noted in chapter 1, Tunisia's main union, the UGTT, was founded in 1946 and by the 1950s had 100,000 members, most of whom also joined the ND.

At independence, having succeeded in building a single, preponderant, mass-mobilizing party, and intent on defending their newfound political status by sustaining the masses' attachments to the party, Tunisia's second-generation (ND) elites sought to craft the new rules of the political game in a way that would give them a monopoly over state power and policy. As it turns out, their party apparatus constituted an extremely effective tool with which to construct dictatorship. ND leader Habib Bourguiba capitalized on the party's preponderant position in two key ways as he established Tunisia's one-party authoritarian founding regime. He used the party's mass organization to snuff out would-be rivals quickly and effectively, and he layered party members into all key positions in the state administration. Both moves gave him ample political muscle as he laid the constitutional foundations of one-party authoritarian rule.

BOURGUIBA, THE ND, AND THE SILENCING OF WOULD-BE RIVALS

As Bourguiba set out to build ND-led authoritarian rule in Tunisia, he fielded organized challenges from two corners. The first stemmed from a rivalry between himself and Salah Ben Youssef for control of the party—a rivalry that dated back at least to 1949.[3] Ben Youssef had served as the ND's secretary-general for many years while Bourguiba was exiled abroad. During that time Ben Youssef played a key role in enlarging the party and building its satellite organizations. In the early 1950s, however, while Ben Youssef was living in Cairo, Bourguiba returned to Tunisia, reestablished his personal dominance over the party apparatus, and became the main Tunisian interlocutor in negotiations with France over the future status of the protectorate. In June 1955 Bourguiba and the French reached an agreement that would grant Tunisia internal autonomy, but not full independence.

Ben Youssef seized upon this accord as a means of challenging Bourguiba for leadership of the ND. He condemned Bourguiba and the accord as detrimental to Tunisian interests and called for immediate, full independence. Ben Youssef hoped to turn the ND rank and file against Bourguiba and become leader of the party himself. Though Ben Youssef's call for immediate independence resonated with parts of an impatient population, through a combination of charisma and savvy Bourguiba and his allies in the party retained the support of the ND apparatus nationwide. "The core of the neo-Destour party remained unified. It received the backing of the Sahel, which was the stronghold of the movement, of the professions, and of the majority of the students" (Hermassi 1972, 155). Bourguiba also carefully courted and secured the backing of the UGTT (Camau 1978, 42). In October 1955 French authorities estimated that 1,360 ND cells remained loyal to Bourguiba while only 180 had sided with Ben Youssef (AMAE 639/298/196a). At its November 1955 congress, the ND formally endorsed Bourguiba and the internal autonomy accord.

Snubbed, Ben Youssef subsequently took his campaign outside the ND and attempted to create a rival party by appealing to the now politically marginalized traditional elites in Tunisian society, which he calculated would be least comfortable with the prospect of ND rule (Moore 1965; Ling 1967; Hermassi 1972, 156). Not only did these elites resent the eclipse of their influence, which was signified by the second-generation elite's takeover of the reins of the nationalist movement, but also the ND perspective was substantially more Western, secular, and progressive than that of Tunisia's more conservative, traditional elements. Using pan-Arab and Islamic slogans, Ben Youssef courted wealthy landowners (earning the endorsement of UGAT), the religious elite, the elite families of Tunis that had long cooperated with the French administration, the commercial elite on the island of Djerba, the tribal population, and disaffected urban youth. In late 1955 the conflict turned violent, with terrorism erupting in urban areas and guerilla warfare emerging in the countryside.

Ben Youssef failed in this endeavor as well, for two key reasons. First, the French took Bourguiba's side (Interview A; Interview C). France would go on to grant Tunisia complete independence just two hundred days after the internal autonomy accord was signed. Explaining this short interval, Silvera wrote that France was "always animated by the concern to consolidate the position of Mr. Bourguiba" (1960, 30). Facing mounting pressure to take leave of the protectorate, the French had found in Bourguiba a reasonably moderate, pragmatic, and sympathetic interlocutor willing to achieve Tunisian independence by means of a lengthy, step-wise negotiation. Moreover, he clearly expressed his intention to maintain good relations with France in the postindependence era. By contrast, Salah Ben Youssef now presented himself as a comparatively extreme, impatient, and hostile figure whose professed affinity for pan-Arab nationalism suggested to France that an independent Tunisia under his control would be an ally of Egypt and parts east—not France. With French approval, Tunisia's police forces cracked down on the Youssefists between January and June 1956, putting an end to the violent conflict.

By itself, however, France's backing of Bourguiba would not necessarily have sufficed to ensure Ben Youssef's downfall. Also decisive for the outcome of the conflict was the fact that Ben Youssef was attempting to build a vehicle with which to challenge the ND *in the presence of the* ND, and it would be an impossible task. Those whom Ben Youssef courted had the material resources to sponsor him,[4] but they could not muster the wherewithal to overcome the active opposition of a mass, territory-wide ND party organization loyal to Bourguiba.

The ND apparatus played a key role in neutralizing Ben Youssef's campaign. ND activists heckled Ben Youssef at certain of his speeches, rallied the masses to Bourguiba's side at others, and in some cases, physically blocked Ben Youssef's access to certain regions (Moore 1965, 64–65). For example, when Ben Youssef attempted in 1955 to tour northern Tunisia looking for support, "the local party apparatus, vigorously urged on by the political bureau in Tunis, literally shut him out of the region and compelled him to retreat in hardly honorable circumstances" (AMAE 639/298/198a). Bourguiba also set up an organization of the decommissioned ND *fellagha* guerillas, called the "Comité des résistants," to counter Ben Youssef's bid for the loyalty of these combatants and to deploy them in the fight against Ben Youssef (AMAE 639/298/194b, 195a).

The second challenge to the hegemony of Bourguiba and the ND came from Tunisia's nationalist union, the UGTT, which sought to play an augmented and autonomous political role in the postindependence era.[5] As was noted above, UGTT support had been crucial to Bourguiba's success in facing down Ben Youssef. In return for this support, the ND had included progressive social and economic policy language in the resolution generated by its 1955 congress (Hermassi 1972, 156). Shortly after independence under the leadership of Ahmed Ben Salah, the UGTT demanded that the government implement socialist reforms and sought to become the nation's premier political organization by suggesting that the ND merge with it (Moore 1964, 100).

This challenge was a serious one because the UGTT possessed a large, powerful, and prestigious organization boasting some 150,000 members. It will be recalled, however, that most of these were also members of the ND party. Moreover, in addition to the authority relationships inherent in the ND apparatus, Bourguiba had a new weapon with which to meet this challenge. As ruler of a now independent Tunisia, he possessed immense patronage powers of appointment and recompense. This allowed him to defuse the UGTT threat by exploiting personal rivalries within the union's leadership.

In October 1956 Bourguiba encouraged veteran UGTT leader Habib Achour, who was jealous of Ben Salah (Moore 1964, 100), to pull the regional union he controlled out of the UGTT and to establish a rival organization, the Union des Travailleurs Tunisiens (UTT). "The new union . . . called for the development of a professional trade-unionism completely divorced from politics and the resignation of Ben Salah as the preconditions of reunification of the labor movement" (ibid.). Meanwhile, while Ben Salah was abroad, Bourguiba publicly criticized him and appointed Ahmed Tlili—a veteran unionist but also a loyal member of the ND's political bureau—as UGTT secretary-general. In December 1956 Ben Salah resigned as head of the UGTT, and the UTT subsequently rejoined a now politically weakened UGTT. "The party had reasserted control over the UGTT" and "Bourguiba had one less autonomous center of power with which to contend" (Moore 1965, 88).

BOURGUIBA, THE ND, AND THE TAKEOVER OF POLITICS AND THE STATE

At the same time that Bourguiba used the ND to help thwart organized challenges to his party-based political hegemony, he also used the party to support his initiatives as he laid the formal, constitutional foundations for one-party authoritarian rule. He did so by seeing to it that his ND party cadres took over the state administration and that they monopolized the constituent assembly charged with drafting a constitution. With loyal ND elites placed in all key positions,[6] Bourguiba had the political support he needed to legislate the details of his dictatorship.

Independence occasioned the departure from Tunisia of thousands of French nationals, many of whom had worked in the protectorate administration. It was predominantly cadres from the ND and its affiliated national organizations (UTAC, UGET, and so on) that took over vacant state bureaucratic posts (Moore 1965, 141–42). "The leadership of the Neo-Destour was sufficiently broad-minded to recruit or keep capable nonparty men in the civil service, although loyal party members got the best jobs" (Moore 1964, 92). In addition, the ND's youth organizations provided most of the personnel for independent Tunisia's police forces. The boundaries between party and state thus became quite blurry, at all levels of government (Moore 1965, 105; Rudebeck 1967, 52; Murphy 1999, 51). Bourguiba himself would serve for three decades as president of the Tunisian republic and as president of the ND. From the outset at independence, cabinet members in his governments often simultaneously held important leadership positions in the ND (Moore 1964, 98n). In addition, Rudebeck tells us that "party organs often perform[ed] typically 'governmental' or 'administrative' functions" (1967, 52–53).

The ND's presence was preponderant not only in the state administration but also in the assembly that drafted Tunisia's constitution. Elections for this assembly were held in March 1956. Straight majority list electoral rules privileged the ND, by far the nation's most popular and best organized political party. Apparently, however, this advantage did not render the ND complacent. Two former members of the Tunisian Communist Party (PCT) who participated in the 1956 election noted that ND activists harassed, intimidated, and disrupted PCT leaders as they campaigned (Interview E; Interview F).[7] Though the PCT fielded candidate lists in twelve of the eighteen constituencies,[8] the ND's lists, which included representatives of its affiliated national organizations, swept the elections.

Loyal ND elites' commanding presence in the state administration and in the constituent assembly provided Bourguiba with pivotal political support as he set about creating rules of the game that bolstered his (and the party's) hegemonic position in Tunisian politics. The first step in this rule-making process unfolded in 1956 and 1957. It consisted of passing legislation that struck at the power bases of three important but unorganized sources of conservative opposition to Bourguiba: the elite families of Tunis that had served the French administration, the religious establishment, and prominent landholders. Bourguiba's government passed legislation empowering the state to try Tunisians who were alleged to have collaborated with the French.[9] To target the power base of the religious elite, it secularized the laws governing marriage and divorce and brought the Zitouna, Tunisia's central institution of religious scholarship, under the control of the education ministry.[10] Bourguiba's government also eliminated the private *habous* category of land tenure, "depriv[ing] the religious establishment of its independent financial base" (Anderson 1986, 234). This measure hurt Bourguiba's main (often absentee) landholding opponents as well, because many were beneficiaries of the wealth generated by these lands. In another move to chasten his landowning opponents, Bourguiba dissolved the UGAT for having sided with Ben Youssef and saw to it that a new, more politically docile union, the Union Nationale des Agriculteurs Tunisiens (UNAT), was formed in its place and took over its offices.

The second step in this rule-making process involved specifying the content of the Tunisian constitution. It followed the first step both chronologically and out of political necessity, because while Bourguiba looked to establish a presidential republic, many of his conservative opponents had envisioned creating a constitutional monarchy that preserved (at least symbolically) the position of Tunisia's traditional monarch, the Bey. Having succeeded in undercutting the power bases of these opponents, Bourguiba moved on to the task of fashioning the constitution he wanted. In July 1957 the constituent assembly abolished the monarchy, declared Tunisia a republic, and named Bourguiba president for the interim period until a final constitution was adopted. Importantly, this measure granted Bourguiba broad executive and legislative authority. In Silvera's words, "The resolution specified that Habib Bourguiba would exercise the presidency . . . with the old [b]ey's absolute powers" (1966, 7). This arrangement strongly foreshadowed the provisions of the forthcoming constitution.

From this date forward to the promulgation of the Tunisian constitution in 1959, the constituent assembly "was essentially the obedient instrument of President Bourguiba's politics" (Silvera 1960, 58). Packed with delegates who had been nominated as candidates in 1956 by Bourguiba himself, the constituent assembly unsurprisingly supported Bourguiba's vision. In early 1959 Bourguiba began to intervene personally in the work of the assembly to finalize and promulgate the constitution. Silvera commented a year later that "the Constitution of June 1, 1959, which the assembly passed only affirmed president Bourguiba's personal conceptions and is destined to support his initiatives" (ibid., 58).

Tunisia's constitution supported Bourguiba's initiatives because its provisions granted Bourguiba, as president, enormous political power.[11] The president appointed the members of his cabinet, who were responsible only to him. He was empowered to make all key civilian and military appointments. The legislature, by contrast, was extremely weak. Presidential draft laws had priority over those of deputies. In practice this meant that the legislature acted only on presidential bills and never itself initiated legislation. In theory the legislature had the right to veto laws with a two-thirds margin. But such an action was politically unthinkable for assembly members, all of whom hailed from either the ND or its affiliated national organizations[12] and owed their positions to Bourguiba's grace. As president, Bourguiba possessed substantial emergency powers and could issue laws by decree when the legislature was out of session. The judiciary also did not constitute a check on the president: judges were removable, and no supreme court was established to monitor the constitutionality of laws.

Bourguiba established a third key set of rules of the game in 1958, after the assembly had named him president and granted him essentially absolute executive and legislative authority. He remained president of the ND, and in that year overhauled party operations, centralizing and maximizing his control over the party. Bourguiba streamlined the ND, reducing the number of branches from 1,800 to 1,000 (one for each of Tunisia's lowest administrative units, called *sheikhat*) and replacing the forty-one federations with fourteen regional offices (one for each governorate). Whereas in the past the federations' leaders had been elected by the branches, the new regional offices were headed up by commissioners who were appointed from Tunis by the ND's political bureau, itself appointed and dominated by Bourguiba. After 1958 the political bureau closely controlled the regional offices, and the regional offices in turn had increased authority over the branches relative to what the federations had wielded (Moore 1965, 113).

An academic observer of the Tunisian scene commented in 1963 that "he who controls the party controls the country" (Abdallah 1963a, 385). Indeed, control over a preponderant single party was pivotal to Habib Bourguiba as he fashioned Tunisia's authoritarian founding regime. He used the party as an instrument of intimidation, snuffing out organized political challenges both from Salah Ben Youssef and from the UGTT. He also placed ND loyalists in positions throughout the state and security apparatuses as well as in nearly every seat in Tunisia's constituent assembly. This gave the president key political support as he laid down the rules of the game that gave shape to independent Tunisia's single-party dictatorship—rules that weakened his latent conservative opposition, enshrined in the constitution an authoritarian presidential republic, and centralized the president's control over ND operations.

South Yemen

The details of the building of South Yemen's NLF exhibit some parallels with but also some divergences from the Tunisian pattern. Beginning with the latter, external forces and technology constituted key seeds from which the NLF grew up. In the 1950s, clandestine cells of a pan-Arab party called the Arab Nationalist Movement (ANM) had been established in South Yemen, both in Aden and its hinterland. These provided local elites with a readymade ideology and organizational framework upon which to build a mass-mobilizing South Yemeni nationalist party. Dresch characterizes the ANM in South Yemen as the "nucleus" of the NLF (2000, 91). In addition, at the outset, Egypt's President Gamal Abdel Nasser provided important political, moral, diplomatic, and material support for the party.[13] The spread of cheap, portable transistor radios further facilitated NLF growth. This medium broadcast the NLF's message far and wide across South Yemen, reaching the masses in urban areas and also, more importantly, in what once were isolated and remote, poorer rural areas (Gavin 1975, 333; Ismael and Ismael 1986, 15; Dresch 2000, 77).

As was the case in Tunisia, however, both organized labor and new educational institutions constituted important preexisting social networks upon which the NLF drew in its party-building endeavors. Labor trends in South Yemen contributed to NLF growth in two ways. First, in the 1940s and 1950s, thousands of workers from the hinterland began migrating to Aden for periods of between one and three years before returning home with cash and luxury goods; while in Aden, they maintained close ties with their home tribes and villages (Bujra 1970, 193). Many migrant workers became attached to ANM cells in Aden, and then served as a conduit through which nationalist ideas percolating in Aden were spread to the countryside (Halliday 1974, 203). Second, driven by this influx of migrant workers and modeled after Britain's own domestic labor tradition, formal labor union organizing began in Aden in the 1950s. Over time, the Aden Trade Unions Congress (ATUC) emerged as the main body representing South Yemeni labor. In the mid-1960s, the NLF won the support of the ATUC's rank and file, a crucial mass constituency.

New crops of South Yemeni students provided both a constituency and leadership for the NLF. The British administration committed significant resources to school building in both Aden and its hinterland. By the 1950s more than a hundred primary schools, a dozen secondary schools, a handful of teacher training institutes, and a university had been established. At the outset, many schools were staffed with non-Yemeni Arab teachers who propagated Arab nationalist, anti-British ideologies to their students. The rural primary schools provided sons of poorer families in the hinterland with an avenue for advancement that thousands embraced. Many went on to secondary and university educations in Aden. There they were steeped in the NLF's message, which they took home with them when returning to the hinterland.[14] A core ANM branch was located at Aden College, an institution that produced several key NLF leaders. The NLF organized broadly in primary and secondary schools across South Yemen, a network that at the time encompassed more than forty thousand students and a thousand teachers. "Most of the student associations and notably the Aden's College Association . . . were NLF controlled" (Kostiner 1984, 101–2).

Finally, the NLF also succeeded in winning over the rank and file of a third key set of actors: the Federal Army of South Yemen. This was important for two reasons. First, many of these rank and file had been recruited from the hinterland tribes (Bidwell 1983, 88; Kostiner 1984, 101). As was the case with migrant labor and the emerging student population, these army men served as another conduit that spread NLF ideology and support into the countryside. At the same time, because it was a key instrument of coercion, the Federal Army's declaration of its allegiance to the NLF in the fall of 1967 was a crucial development in the NLF's campaign for political preponderance.

Despite the NLF's important organizational accomplishments and dominant position, the transfer of power at independence was not seamless. Just as the Ben Youssef–Bourguiba conflict had threatened to rip apart the ND and plunge Tunisia into civil war, the NLF experienced serious internal fracturing as independence neared. As the NLF's power had grown in the 1960s, the PSP and the SAL teamed up to form a conservative countergroup (called OLOS) to the NLF. A long-standing moderate-radical rift hitherto internal to the NLF then erupted. The party's top leadership—who were backed by Egypt, spent most of the struggle years abroad, and were more moderate than the NLF's middle-rank leaders fighting on the ground in South Yemen—attempted to merge the NLF with OLOS to form FLOSY (Front for the Liberation of Occupied South Yemen). The NLF's more radical internal field leadership opposed and resisted this move, and the conflict between FLOSY and the core NLF cadres took independent South Yemen to the verge of civil war.

In Tunisia, Bourguiba prevailed in his conflict with Ben Youssef because the former retained the loyalty of the vast majority of the ND. The party apparatus became a key weapon in Bourguiba's hands as he blocked Ben Youssef's attempts to countermobilize against the ND. The NLF triumphed over FLOSY for similar reasons. Unlike FLOSY, the NLF had mass support in the countryside as well as in the unions, schools, and security forces in Aden (Halliday 1974, 222–23). The NLF could portray itself as the more authentic movement, free of ties to external powers; it also had greater internal discipline and more extensive combat experience than FLOSY (Ismael and Ismael 1986). "Because of the evident control it exerted over most of South Yemen, it was with the National Front that Britain negotiated the final transfer of power at Geneva" (ibid., 28–29). The NLF's organizational superiority and political-military preponderance allowed it to defeat its conservative rival. As was the case in Tunisia, one-party authoritarian rule was the result. After sorting out a second moderate-radical rift within the party, the again triumphant radical core of the NLF in 1969 "set out ruthlessly to strengthen its hold both on the institutions of the state and on South Yemeni society as a whole" (Gause 1995, 157).

Algeria

In many ways the Algerian case is the exception that proves the "rule" that successful party building hinges on the availability of preexisting social networks whose social capital can be drawn on by party leaders. As chapter 1 indicated, of the three preponderant single parties considered in this study, Algeria's FLN—the party that fought a bloody, eight-year war of independence against France—was by far the least coherent and cohesive. While there was tremendous incentive in Algeria for indigenous elites to develop an encompassing, mass-mobilizing political party to push the French out, and while elites attempted to do just that, they were far less successful than their Tunisian and South Yemeni counterparts when it came to building a powerful party institution. The explanation for this lies in the impact on social capital formation of both the French colonial presence and the way in which the independence war unfolded in Algeria.

As noted in chapter 1, when nationalist resistance to French occupation emerged in Algeria, it did so in a fragmented fashion, with three ideologically divergent currents vying for supremacy beginning in the 1930s and with none making significant headway. Ferhat Abbas led the assimilationist current in Algerian society; he was skeptical that such a thing as "the Algerian nation" existed and petitioned France to integrate Algerian Muslims into French society on an equal footing with other French citizens. Sheikh Abdelhamid Ben Badis headed up the second, conservative current that sought through education and other grassroots efforts to rekindle Algerians' interest in Arabic language and culture and to revitalize, purify, and unify Algerian Islam. Messali Hadj led the third, radical, left-wing populist current that demanded immediate independence from France. In the early 1950s Algerian nationalism still was characterized by these three very different strands of thought and action.

Scholars attribute this nationalist incoherence to a set of French imperial policies that largely destroyed traditional Algerian society (Hermassi 1972, 132–34; Entelis 1986, 36). French policy dismantled the traditional economy, forced extensive population relocations, shut down Islamic institutions, and weakened the indigenous educational system. These actions impoverished and atomized Algerian society while undermining Algerian culture, and the result was an indigenous population that had, in the words of Algerian intellectual Mostefa Lacheraf, lost "the essential support and the impetus for any genuine collective evolution" (Hermassi 1972, 133). Ruedy argues that the new social groups and classes that emerged as traditional society disintegrated did so in isolation from one another, "with few established patterns of communication amongst them horizontally or vertically"; as a result, nationalist Algerian elites were seriously handicapped when it came to building political consensus and/or organization (1992, 115). In other words, Algeria lacked the kinds of substantial nationwide social networks that facilitated the building of powerful parties in Turkey, Tunisia, and South Yemen.

It was largely out of frustration with this situation that a group of individuals from the clandestine paramilitary wing of Messali Hadj's party formed the FLN and launched the independence war—simultaneously. The war began when the FLN was barely born, let alone organized. At the time, the party could boast fewer than three thousand supporters with only several hundred weapons. Party leaders were aware of the desperate nature of their gambit: their hope was that recruits and organizational strengthening of the party would come during the war itself. "What [the FLN founders] hoped for was a psychological shock which would awaken the masses, from disillusion to apathy, to hope and, eventually, action. [One founder] term[ed] the whole operation 'a gamble'" (Gordon 1966, 57).

The war would indeed yield recruits, but not an organizationally sound political party. Initial FLN successes, the attraction—in the eyes of Algeria's impoverished and desperate populace—of an armed confrontation with the French, and the ferocity of French retaliation against the insurrection brought hundreds of thousands of recruits (mostly peasants) to the party and its army. However, in significant part because of France's response to the FLN's challenge, the party-army developed in an uncoordinated fashion and became riven with internecine competition and feuding (Gordon 1966, 62). French tactics isolated the various wings of the FLN from one another and, to an extent, from the Algerian populace. The FLN had divided Algeria into six regions, called *wilayas*, for military purposes. The French worked to cut communications among these *wilayas*. Much of the FLN's fighting apparatus, the ALN, or National Liberation Army, developed in neighboring Tunisia and Morocco. The French sealed those borders with impressive fortifications, further dividing the FLN's military apparatus and effort. French forces surrounded and isolated key ALN bases inside Algeria, and relocated up to two million civilians in a bid to cut off local support for the insurrection. Finally, France used psychological warfare "to play upon and intensify . . . internal divisions" in the party (Moore 1970, 88).

"The extremely decentralized organization of the FLN that was necessitated by the war . . . contributed to the formation of factions . . . By the end of the war, the leadership of the FLN was divided among a multitude of groups that were more or less independent of each other" (Ottaway and Ottaway 1970, 14). France left Tunisia and Britain left South Yemen due in significant part to the domestic strength and activism of the ND and NLF respectively. By contrast, at the end of the Algerian independence war, the FLN was eviscerated as an organization (Moore 1970, 24; Connelly 2001, 234; Naylor 2000, 41). Algeria won independence not because the FLN had mustered sufficient "facts on the ground" to convince the French to depart but instead because of international pressure exerted on France that resulted from the horrible excesses of the war and from effective FLN lobbying of the international community (Ottaway and Ottaway 1970, 14; Entelis 1986, 52; Connelly 2001).

At independence the FLN threatened to fracture into several components: its armed wing, the Armée de Libération Nationale (ALN); its provisional government, the Gouvernement Provisoire de la République Algérienne (GPRA); and the six regional FLN commands. At the end of the day the ALN was the strongest, most cohesive, and most politically powerful institution in the political arena (Ottaway and Ottaway 1970, 24; Entelis 1986, 53; Ruedy 1992, 181). Because it was more cohesive, and because it had superior recourse to coercive means, the army—after a violent confrontation with the GPRA and some of the regional commands—succeeded in installing the government of its choice under the leadership of Ahmed Ben Bella in 1962.

A political regime then developed in which the army, the bureaucracy, and the FLN have been the backbone of politics. Much like Bourguiba, Ben Bella saw to it that the new rules of the game established a strong one-party authoritarian presidential system in which he, as president, headed the state, the government, and the military—and in which the FLN was enshrined as the nation's sole political party. ALN commander Colonel Houari Boumedienne unseated Ben Bella in a bloodless coup in 1965 and proceeded to suspend both the constitution and the weak Algerian national assembly. These changes did not substantially alter the rules of the game; rather, they enhanced the authoritarian nature of the one-party regime. Boumedienne became president, prime minister, and minister of defense, and "the state exercised all powers: executive, legislative, and judiciary" (Bennoune 1988, 8). In 1975 and 1976 Boumedienne presided over a process whereby Algeria gained a new constitution and national legislature. Still, these "new" rules maintained the FLN's monopoly as the sole legitimate political party in Algeria (Entelis and Arone 1995, 400).

Conclusion

This chapter accomplished two tasks. First, given the insight from the Turkish case that party building poses substantial collective action problems to political entrepreneurs, it returned briefly to the story of the emergence of single preponderant parties in Tunisia, South Yemen, and Algeria (the focus of chapter 1) to identify the preexisting social networks that helped nationalist leaders solve collective action problems and successfully build impressive, mass-mobilizing nationalist parties. The content of those cases lends further support to the theoretical intuition that there should be a correlation between party-building success and stocks of social capital embodied in such networks, for the society most ravaged and atomized by colonial policy—Algeria—also yielded the weakest and most fragmented preponderant party.

Second, through a detailed examination of the Tunisian case and shorter, parallel discussions of the South Yemeni and Algerian cases, the preceding pages demonstrated how the development of these parties shaped their leaders' preferences for and capacity to establish authoritarian one-party rule at independence. The men who led their nations to independence sought to create authoritarian one-party regimes to sustain their newfound sociopolitical prestige. The parties they had built proved to be quite useful tools for carrying out those preferences: they helped nationalist elites eliminate would-be rivals and apply the necessary political muscle to craft new rules of the political game that were to their liking.

Coda: Founding Regime Formation in Morocco

As discussed in chapter 1, because second-generation elites never took over complete control of the Moroccan nationalist movement, a single, preponderant, mass-mobilizing party did not emerge in that case. The story of Morocco's passage from independence to a founding regime revolves around the political maneuverings of Istiqlal and Morocco's King Mohamed V. The king was an authentic, popular, and revered figure. He was a member of a three-century-old dynasty that Moroccan Muslims had long accepted as their legitimate sovereign. At the start of the protectorate, the French pledged to preserve indigenous institutions and rule through the king. When the king became too pronationalist, the French exiled him in 1953. This instantly boosted the monarch's political stock as a symbol of Moroccan sovereignty and pride, and the nationalist movement subsequently focused its demands around his return. On the eve of independence, Morocco's king was a force to be reckoned with. Recognizing this, the Franco-Moroccan independence agreement of 1956 placed all sovereign authority, including control of the army, in the king's hands.

Yet the king did not have a blank check with which to shape Morocco's postindependence political regime. In part due to Istiqlal's popularity and extensive urban organization, the king's power in fact "depended inversely on that of the Istiqlal" (Cohen and Hahn 1966, 117). At independence in 1956, Moroccan politics featured a confrontation between two significant political actors, Istiqlal and the king. Each wanted to establish its own political hegemony and saw the other as the most salient obstacle to its success. As a result, unlike Tunisia, South Yemen, and Algeria, Morocco did not see a founding regime established immediately at independence. Neither major actor was able to dictate the rules of the game at that point.[15] Instead, for the next several years, Istiqlal and the king maneuvered to improve their respective relative political positions.

The climax of the Istiqlal-king confrontation occurred in late 1958. In the first two cabinets appointed by the king, Istiqlal had been forced to share power with a smaller party, the PDI, and with independent politicians. But in May 1958 the king allowed Istiqlal to form an all-Istiqlal cabinet. At this point Istiqlal appeared to be nearing political hegemony: it controlled the premiership and the defense ministry along with all other cabinet positions; it had also begun to infiltrate the civil service and the police (Zartman 1973, 248–49). Yet due to a budding internal schism, Istiqlal would not be able to convert its popularity and control of the cabinet into curbs on the king's power.

Late in the year, attacks by dissidents from Istiqlal's younger, radical leftist camp—that is, the second-generation elites of the party—felled this cabinet. They faulted the party's leadership for being excessively conservative and insufficiently supportive of Morocco's populist and working classes. They also wished to see a constitutional monarchy established immediately and criticized party leaders for their willingness to allow the king to retain key political prerogatives such as control over the army and the right to appoint and revoke members of the government. These developments led in September 1959 to the creation of a new political party, the Union Nationale des Forces Populaires (UNFP), by the dissidents.

Istiqlal's split bolstered the king's position immensely. For the most part, the split had resulted from dynamics internal to the party. However, the king also subtly encouraged the growing rift between factions of the party—a party that represented an obstacle in his bid for political hegemony (Waterbury 1970, 171; Schaar 1973, 230). In the aftermath of the split, the king "observed that the bickering caused public dissatisfaction with the politicians and provided him with reasons for placing himself still further above the political struggle" (Cohen and Hahn 1966, 128).

In the years that followed, ensuring that the political stage possessed a number of mutually antagonistic parties vulnerable to monarchical manipulation became the king's prime strategy for maintaining his hegemony. To do this, he held out the prospect of elections and the formation of a parliament. This prospect drove a number of other parties to organize. Importantly, rural notables created the Mouvement Populaire (MP) beginning in 1959 to thwart the possibility of an Istiqlal- and/or UNFP-dominated parliament. In March 1963 on the eve of parliamentary elections, the PDI, a group of independents, and the MP formed an electoral coalition of urban and rural anti-Istiqlal elites called the Front pour la Défense des Institutions Constitutionnelles (FDIC). Importantly, both the MP and the FDIC supported the king's political position and came into being with palace support.

By 1965, a political regime had emerged in Morocco in which the monarch dictated the rules and parameters of politics, alternately widening and narrowing the scope of partisan contestation according to changing circumstances. In the years after independence, the establishment of monarchical hegemony had been possible because Istiqlal was not a preponderant party, and because Istiqlal split into two rival parties. The split left the king in a strengthened political position, and the fact that Istiqlal did not command the loyalty of rural Morocco meant that key social forces were available for the king to mobilize in self-serving ways. The king worked to foster the emergence of numerous political parties dependent on his patronage, which he proceeded to play off one another to consolidate his position as final arbiter in the political system (Moore 1966, 34; Zartman 1973, 251; Schaar 1973, 230; Tessler, Entelis, and White 1995, 384).

5

Polarization, Mobilizational Asymmetry, and Delayed Authoritarian Rule

This chapter opens the book's analysis of regime formation dynamics in the six cases in which founding regimes took hold only after interim transitional periods had transpired. These were countries in which *multiple* political parties were present in the public arena at independence. No single actor could dictate and enforce the rules of a stable founding regime at that juncture. Instead, during transitional periods, the rules of the game were in flux as these parties and other actors jockeyed for position and for political advantage. Though regime rules were fluid, at the outset competitive elections and parliaments to a significant extent determined who would wield policy-making power. All six of these states thus had an opportunity to strengthen and consolidate the practice of competitive politics. Only Turkey did so; its story is the subject of chapter 6. This chapter explains why nascent competitive politics gradually gave way to authoritarian rule over the course of transitional periods in Iran, Iraq, Jordan, Syria, and Egypt.

This chapter argues that two characteristics shared by all five party systems—polarization and mobilizational asymmetry—are significant for explaining why nascent competitive politics deteriorated, allowing for the eventual establishment of authoritarian founding regimes. Nascent competitive institutions in these countries were fragile. Such institutions generate uncertainty about who will come to power and command the strategic heights of national politics. Democratic rules survive only if, from the outset, no important actors have significant incentives to defect from them. For nascent competitive politics to be consolidated, all rival elites must be prepared to live with the fact that no guarantees exist as to who will wield policy-making power. More generally, elites must be convinced that they will be able to defend their interests effectively in a democratic context.

These conditions for the survival of competitive politics were not met in Iran, Iraq, Jordan, Syria, or Egypt. Party systems in all five cases were polarized. This study adopts Waldner's (1999) definition of "intense elite conflict" to characterize political arenas as polarized when their attendant elite factions advocate policies that threaten one or more factions' ability to reproduce their elite status over the long term (29). Waldner's study focuses on intense elite conflict over economic issues, and his definitional discussion specifies that such conflict is present when one or more elite subgroups reaches the judgment that they are threatened with the loss of their ability to compete for economic surplus over the long term. This phenomenon was present as a source of political conflict in all of the cases considered here. In Iran, Iraq, Jordan, Syria, and Egypt, party systems contained radical leftist challenger parties whose political agendas included land reform and/or the nationalization of industry. For the many conservative politicians who came from landholding, commercial, and industrial backgrounds—and for whom material wealth produced political influence (Kaylani 1972, 11)—such policies augured the loss of their status both as economic and political elites.

In addition, three other important policy conflicts consistent with Waldner's general definition of elite conflict (here: polarization) were present in these countries. First, during interim transitional periods, political parties in Iraq, Jordan, and Syria did not agree on what the appropriate borders of the political community should be. Disagreement on this fundamental issue stemmed from the perceived artificiality of the process by which Britain and France drew borders in the region after WWI, from powerful Arab nationalist ideological currents touting various unification schemes for the region, and from the power ambitions of the actors involved. Debates over borders were polarizing because, for those conservative elites in positions of political-economic influence, proposals for border changes and new sovereignty schemes generated high levels of uncertainty as to who would exercise such influence under new arrangements, and how the new political community would determine who would wield power.

Second, in Iraq and Jordan, parties were at distinct odds over whether or not those countries' political and economic ties to the United Kingdom should be maintained. The United Kingdom had been the mandatory power in Iraq and Jordan and had played a central role in creating those states' institutional and political-economic frameworks. In both countries, Britain created monarchies, selected the (initial) monarchs, and oversaw the process by which the commanding heights of politics were occupied by conservative landholding and tribal elites. Iraq and Jordan gained their independence in 1932 and 1946, respectively, but continued to maintain strong ties to the former mandatory power. The United Kingdom retained military basing rights in and provided crucial financial assistance to both states. Iraq received significant British military aid, equipment, and assistance, while British officers commanded the Arab Legion, Jordan's national army. Thus when challenger parties sought to cut these states' ties to Britain, conservative elites faced the prospect that crucial political, fiscal, and coercive pillars of their elite status would be destroyed.

Third, in Jordan and Egypt a key dynamic underlying the breakdown of nascent democratic bargains was the fact that parties were at odds over basic questions of regime type. In Jordan, three of five challenger parties objected to the institution of the monarchy. Clearly—both for the monarch himself and for those conservative elites who historically had supported him and received patronage benefits in return for that support—such policy proposals did not augur well for the maintenance of their elite status. In Egypt the rift over regime type took a different form. There a secularly oriented conservative establishment was confronted with an increasingly powerful Muslim Brotherhood party that advocated the reorganization of politics according to Islamic precepts. What that meant in practice was far from clear, but secular status-quo elites could safely assume that under an Islamist regime they would not meet the criteria for maintaining their privileged positions at the peaks of the political establishment.

Table 5 summarizes the types of polarization that constituted the primary lines of political conflict in each of the five country cases discussed in this chapter.

Polarization meant that the prospect of challenger parties gaining cabinet control was tremendously threatening for conservative party leaderships' confidence in their ability to maintain their elite status. The policy substance that rival party elites brought to the democratic table in these countries was provocative and reduced the chances that parties would allow democratic rules to determine policy outcomes indefinitely.

At the same time that these party systems were characterized by polarization, they were also characterized by what this study terms "mobilizational asymmetry." This refers to the existence of significant gaps in

TABLE 5. Sources of Polarization in Iran, Iraq, Jordan, Syria, and Egypt

Primary Polarizing Issues	*Property Rights*	*Borders*	*Foreign Allegiances*	*Regime Type*
IRAN	*			
IRAQ	*	*	*	
JORDAN	*	*	*	*
SYRIA	*	*		
EGYPT	*			*

contending parties' respective abilities to get out the vote in competitive elections. In Iran, Iraq, Jordan, Syria, and Egypt, party systems pitted conservative actors interested in defending the political-economic status quo against radical challenger forces interested in overturning this status quo. In every case, conservative actors were significantly less well equipped to compete effectively in a democratic context over the long term than were their radical challengers. Conservative forces either failed to organize into party form at all or formed nonideological parties whose political support rested on a limited base of patron-client ties. Challenger forces, meanwhile, were building modern party organizations and were articulating strident ideological platforms.[1] Through organization and ideological exhortation, challenger forces were establishing the capacity to reach a much broader potential constituency over time than were conservative actors, who necessarily relied on personalistic, face-to-face ties and interactions to generate votes.

These diverging trends in mobilizational capacity were of particular concern for conservative actors because, in all five countries, politics was entering into an era of increasingly liberal suffrage norms.[2] When elections first were introduced into the political process in Iran, Iraq, Jordan, Syria, and Egypt in the nineteenth and early twentieth centuries, they were indirect, unfolding in two stages (with primary electors selecting secondary electors, who would then choose parliamentary representatives), and/or used property and/or literacy restrictions to restrict the scope of the electorate. Both mechanisms worked to conservatives' advantage by minimizing the masses' direct impact on election outcomes. However, during interim transitional periods, Iraq (1952), Jordan (1947), and Syria (1949) instituted universal male suffrage[3] *and* direct, single-stage elections. Egypt did so in 1935, just prior to the start of its interim transitional period, and Iran implemented these reforms—which enhanced the masses' impact on elections—in the years following World War I. With their ideological appeals to mass interests and their organizational structures designed to encourage mass participation in the political process, challenger parties stood to profit disproportionately from this change.

The presence of mobilizational asymmetry in party systems thus drove conservative actors to conclude that, over the long term, they would not be able to maintain their elite status democratically. They feared that challenger forces eventually would outpoll them, and thus they were not willing to risk letting elections and parliamentary politics determine the course of policy. Conservative forces did not remain faithful to nascent democratic bargains. Instead, they defected, turning to other, nondemocratic arenas such as armies and monarchs for political support (see table 6). These defections moved the radical challenger parties to defect as well. They cultivated support from armies, foreign powers, and the streets. In this manner, a vicious cycle of political behavior unfolded that undermined democratic norms and paved the way for the establishment of authoritarian regimes.

Iran

Between 1941 and 1953, Iranians elected four parliaments. The conservative parliamentarians that dominated politics during that period hailed from that nation's large-landholding, tribal, merchant, and state elites. They tended not to form political parties. Instead, for electoral purposes they relied on patron-client networks in their (largely rural) home districts, while looking upon membership in parliament as a mechanism for accessing state patronage resources needed to maintain their own positions (Azimi 1989). Most conservative deputies were elected to parliament as independents; they then entered into a fluid kaleidoscope of caucuses once parliament had assembled.[4] Those conservative parties that did form were personalist in nature, tended not to last long, and/or limited their activities to a specific region (Abrahamian 1982, 187). All conservatives agreed on the need to defend the socioeconomic status quo (Azimi 1989, 27). They often divided, however, on the question of Iran's foreign allegiances, with various forces advocating ties to the United Kingdom, the United States, or the U.S.S.R., as well as to neutrality. Iran's conservative elites generally have been char-

TABLE 6. The Polarized and Mobilizationally Asymmetrical Party Systems

	CONSERVATIVE PATRON-CLIENT PARTIES		*IDEOLOGICAL MASS-MOBILIZING CHALLENGERS*	
Country	*Names*	*Alternative Arenas*	*Names*	*Alternative Arenas*
IRAN	Independents	Monarch Army U.K. U.S.S.R. U.S.	Tudeh/Communists Iran Party	Streets
IRAQ	Constitutional Union Socialist Nation Most independents	Monarch	Istiqlal National Democrats Communists Ba'th	Streets Army
JORDAN	Community Arab Constitutionalists Most independents	Monarch Army	Communists Ba'th National Socialists Muslim Brotherhood Liberation	Streets Saudi Arabia, Egypt Army
SYRIA	National Party People's Party Independents	Army Foreign powers	Communists Arab Socialists Ba'th	Army Foreign powers
EGYPT	Wafd Liberal Constitutionalists Sa'dists Independent Wafdist Bloc Watani Ittihad Sha'b	Monarch U.K.	Muslim Brotherhood Young Egypt Communists	Streets Political violence Army

acterized as disunited, fragmented, and factionalized, a result of a constant struggle among various and shifting patron-client groupings for power and resources (Azimi 1989).

Confronting Iran's conservative forces were a number of challenger parties that were developing an ability to recruit significant political support on the basis of extensive organization and/or the ideological content of their platforms. The Iran Party was one important such challenger force. This was a nationalist, secular, liberal party that advocated a neutralist foreign policy and European-style social democracy. "The Iran Party advocated antifeudal reforms and propagandized against both old and new wealthy classes; it proposed state-sponsored industrialization to prevent capitalists from further entrenching their oligarchy" (Ghods 1989, 125). It developed a following among women, students, and the professional middle classes, including bureaucrats, journalists, lawyers, doctors, and teachers.

Most important among the challenger parties, however, was the communist Tudeh (Masses) Party. When founded in 1941, the party called for significant socioeconomic reforms designed to improve the living standards of workers, peasants, and the middle class. Importantly, at the outset Tudeh sought to pursue these reforms through parliamentary and constitutional rather than revolutionary avenues (Azimi 1989, 81; Ghods 1989, 126). Tudeh was Iran's best-organized mass-mobilizing political party, and was particularly strong in urban areas. It linked itself tightly to a growing organized labor movement.[5] In 1943 British officials determined that Tudeh was the only party in Iran that possessed nationwide organization (Abrahamian 1982, 291). It continued to expand its organization in the mid-1940s and by 1946 boasted 50,000 to 100,000 members. Around this time a *New York Times* reporter stated that the party and its allies could win as much as 40 percent of the vote in a fair election (Abrahamian 1982, 300). The Tudeh's ideological platform and organizational efforts attracted the support of workers, students, civil servants, and teachers.

Iran's challenger parties thus were calling for important revisions in the property rights regime, taking their messages to workers, peasants, students, and the middle class. In addition, the Tudeh Party in particular was building a modern, mass-mobilizing party structure across Iran. These trends increasingly alarmed Iran's conservative elites (Azimi 1989, 101), driving them to defect from nascent democratic institutions. A first indicator that conservatives would be unwilling to play by democratic rules came when Iran's fourteenth *majles* (parliament) convened in 1944. Numerous polit-

TABLE 7. Caucus Strengths in Iran's Fourteenth *Majles* (1944)

Tudeh Caucus	*Individual Caucus*	*Independent Caucus*	*Liberal Caucus*	*Democratic Caucus*	*Patriotic Caucus*	*National Union Caucus*
(8)	(16)	(15)	(20)	(11)	(26)	(30)

ical forces contested the elections for the fourteenth *majles*, which yielded a 126-deputy chamber that soon separated into seven caucuses. Table 7 indicates these caucuses' names and numerical strengths.

The Tudeh and Individual caucuses (the latter included the Iran Party's deputies) represented the radical left end of the Iranian political spectrum. The Liberal, Democratic, Patriotic, and National Union caucuses each grouped together conservative deputies interested in preserving Iran's socioeconomic status quo. These hailed from different regions, however, and differed with respect to their external attachments: the Democrats and the Patriots were pro–United Kingdom, the Liberals pro–U.S.S.R., and the National Unionists pro–United States. The pro–United States Independents fell somewhere between the left and right extremes on socioeconomic issues.

When the fourteenth *majles* opened for business, the caucuses lined up six against one on the question of whether the shah or parliament should control the military. Only the National Unionists believed the shah should retain that authority, and they were outnumbered. This was parliament's first order of business, and because the vast majority of deputies agreed that parliament should manage the military, "most expected the deputies to assert themselves over the shah and establish a genuine parliamentary democracy" (Abrahamian 1982, 206). This did not come to pass, however, because social conflict intervened, reconfiguring the pattern of partisan conflict in a manner detrimental to the cause of strengthening democratic institutions. Specifically, serious labor unrest broke out in Isfahan. Events there threatened conservatives and drove the Democratic and Patriotic caucuses into alliance with the royalist National Unionists to form a new majority in parliament (Abrahamian 1982, 206–8). The Democrats and Patriots essentially dropped their objection to the shah's control of the military, demonstrating that closing conservatives' ranks to defend the socioeconomic status quo against the Tudeh and Individual caucuses' radical policy agendas was their first priority.

For the next seven years, left-right battles over property rights dominated the political arena. Conservative forces continued to fear Tudeh's potential power. Following the Isfahan events, for example, a conservative newspaper editorialized that

> the Tudeh party, with its satanical doctrine of class struggles, has incited ignorant workers to violate the sacred right of private property and inflict social anarchy upon the industrial center of the country. The uprising proves that the Tudeh is an enemy of private property, of Iran, and of Islam. If the government does not stamp out the Tudeh, the local revolt will inevitably spread into a general revolution. (quoted in Abrahamian 1982, 207)

Faced with challenger forces whose ideological, mass-mobilizing techniques of political recruitment threatened their hegemony in the long term, conservatives continued to defect from nascent democratic norms. They often turned to the local representatives of foreign powers (primarily the United Kingdom and the U.S.S.R.), who enabled them in their antidemocratic behaviors by supporting regional rebellions against the central government and influencing election outcomes in favor of pet elites. Conservatives also turned to the shah and the army he controlled for support against the left. Elections routinely were rigged in conservatives' favor. The Tudeh Party was suppressed and then outlawed. After suffering a gunshot wound at the hands of an apparent Tudeh sympathizer, the shah was also able to restrict the press, declare martial law, and convene a constituent assembly that strengthened the armed forces and amended the constitution to give the shah increased authority relative to parliament.

Faced with these antidemocratic, extraparliamentary moves, the challenger parties also turned to alternative political arenas. In late 1949 Mohammed Mossadeq created the National Front, a coalition of four parties (the Iran Party being foremost among them) that also drew the support of the (now underground) Tudeh Party. After it was outlawed, the latter "abandoned its initial allegiance to constitutional principles and attempts to achieve reform through legal channels" (Ghods 1989, 184). Possessing only 8 of the more than 130 seats in the sixteenth *majles* (1950–1952), and in the face of conservatives' antidemocratic behavior, the National Front turned to the streets for political ammunition. "Mossadeq constantly resorted to street demonstrations to pressure the opposition and thereby 'bring parliament under his influence'"; for its part, the Tudeh Party "revealed its true strength" in April 1951 by orchestrating strikes and street demonstrations in several Iranian cities (Abrahamian 1982, 266–67).

These tactics paid off by scaring conservative deputies into supporting Mossadeq's plan to nationalize Iran's oil industry and, in May 1951, making him prime minister. During the next two years, Mossadeq mounted an intensifying attack on the interests of the conservative deputies and the shah. His government disbanded the senate, launched a propaganda war against wealthy landowning elites, legislated land and tax reforms, and advanced nationalization proposals. Striking at the shah's prerogatives, Mossadeq cut the palace budget, made himself minister of war, and appointed a parliamentary committee that ruled that the Iranian constitution granted control over the military to the government rather than to the shah.

Mossadeq's attacks on the shah and the establishment politicians would not go unanswered. In August 1953 his government was toppled by a conservative-supported military coup that had been conceived by Britain, supported and financed by the U.S. Central Intelligence Agency, and carried out by disgruntled army officers angered by military cutbacks ordered by Mossadeq. The coup crushed both the National Front and Tudeh and made Mohammad Reza Shah *the* key actor in Iranian politics for the following two and a half decades. The shah used considerable U.S. financial aid and Iran's growing oil receipts to purchase the army's continued loyalty (Limbert 1995, 47), to fund development projects, and, with the help of American and Israeli advisors, to build a new internal security organization (SAVAK) to monitor and intimidate would-be enemies of his regime.

Iraq

Iraq gained independence in 1932 but did not begin to consolidate a stable founding regime until 1968. While Iraq was still a constitutional monarchy, from 1932 to 1945 a series of mostly conservative, pro-British cabinets governed the country. Modes of cabinet formation, however, varied widely. Six parliamentary elections took place during these years, but a 1936 coup fomented by a leftist civilian politician in alliance with disgruntled army officers set what would be an oft-followed precedent wherein either explicit or implicit military pressure drove cabinet composition. In addition, a 1941 coup by the anti-British, Arab nationalist Rashid 'Ali al-Gaylani provoked Britain to reoccupy Iraq. For the remainder of WWII, the cabinets that reigned under U.K. protection purged their Arab nationalist rivals from the army, bureaucracy, and school system. By the mid-1940s, conservative, pro-British elites again came to rule Iraq.

These elites benefited from a system of perks established by Britain during the mandate period and sustained by Britain after independence. As the United Kingdom built the Iraqi state apparatus in the 1920s, it granted tax breaks and property rights in land to Iraqi tribal, landholding, and administrative elites in return for the latter's political support (Haj 1997, 81; Tripp 2000, 69). The evolving state administration became a source of significant patronage resources (land, positions within the administration, and so on) with which conservative elites could establish networks of clients among kin, communal, and regional groups. After independence this political economy was sustained by ongoing British aid—in the form of lease payments for military basing rights, the presence of British advisers, and military aid, training, and assistance. Conservative elites sought to defend Iraq's ties to Britain, to preserve the Iraqi state in its existing borders, and to quash proposals for land reform.

In 1945 the regent Prince 'Abd al-Ilah announced that Iraq would embark on a path of social and political reform. This announcement began a decade-long, halting, but nonetheless real experiment in choosing Iraqi cabinets on the basis of competitive multiparty elections. During this period, four ideological, mass-mobilizing parties emerged to challenge conservative landowning and tribal elites' hold over the Iraqi parliament.[6] The Istiqlal (Independence) Party attracted intellectuals, professionals (especially lawyers), and students. The party opposed Iraq's close political ties with and dependence upon Britain and was a strong advocate of pan-Arab political union. It did not, however, espouse radical policy positions with respect to property rights.

Founded in 1947, the National Democratic Party (NDP) grouped together sections of the industrial middle class, a number of progressive agricultural elites, professionals, leftist intellectuals, students, and workers. By April 1947 the NDP's membership stood at 6,961 members (Batatu 1978, 466). Like Istiqlal, the NDP strongly opposed Iraq's ties to the United Kingdom. However, the NDP was not in favor of pan-Arab union and instead wished for Iraq to continue as a sovereign political entity within existing borders. Also in contrast to Istiqlal, the NDP, by 1950, was calling for substantial socioeconomic reforms, including state support for industrialization as well as a land reform proposal that would have confiscated the holdings of many of Iraq's oligarchic elites and distributed these and state lands to landless and poor peasants (Haj 1997, 88). Importantly, at the outset of this experimental period, the National Democrats were committed to pursuing their policy agenda within the parliamentary arena (Haj 1997; Tripp 2000, 114).

A self-proclaimed Arab socialist party, the Ba'th Party espoused redistributive socioeconomic policies and attracted mainly lower-middle-class teachers, students, and urban youth as members (Haj 1997, 91–92). It opposed Iraq's ties with the United Kingdom as well as the existence of the Iraqi state in its current borders, advocating joining a pan-Arab union instead. Though it was committed to popular mobilization (Farouk-Sluglett and Sluglett 1991, 129), the Ba'th Party arrived on the scene relatively late in this experimental period (in the early 1950s) and did not build a substantial following before the period ended. Still, it was part and parcel of the ideological, mass-mobilizing challenger party phenomenon that threatened conservative interests in Iraq.

The Iraqi Communist Party (ICP) was by far the most substantial ideological mass-mobilizing challenger party (Batatu 1978, 466; Farouk-Sluglett and Sluglett 1991, 129; Zubaida 1991, 200). Founded in the mid-1930s, the ICP worked diligently to develop a cadre of leaders capable of organizing and mobilizing the masses, meeting with significant success in this endeavor (Zubaida 1991, 200; Haj 1997, 95–96). For example, it organized Iraqi labor, coming to control twelve of the sixteen labor unions that were licensed in 1946 (Farouk-Sluglett and Sluglett 1991, 126). It also recruited the support of many of Iraq's professional and middle classes and urban intelligentsia, students, petty traders, and recent rural-to-urban migrants. The party was organized not only in the capital but also in Iraq's small provincial towns. In 1947 it could boast between three thousand and four thousand members and a much larger number of supporters and sympathizers; one state official wrote in 1949 that the ICP commanded the loyalty of almost half of Iraq's urban youth (Batatu 1978, 466). The ICP supported the continuing existence of the state in its current borders but opposed Iraq's ties to Britain and called for radical land reform (Haj 1997, 94).

The key policy positions of the mass-mobilizing ideological parties are summarized in Table 8. All of the challenger parties objected to Iraq's close political ties to and dependence upon Britain. Three out of four advocated land reform and other significant wealth-redistributing measures. Two out of four objected to the country's existing borders and sovereign status. These policy positions clashed with those held by conservative parliamentary elites. Importantly, all three policy rifts threatened conservatives' ability to maintain their elite status in Iraqi politics and society. The Iraqi party system of the 1940s and 1950s was thus seriously polarized.

Iraq's party system was also mobilizationally asymmetrical. Given that challenger parties were developing articulate policy platforms and build-

TABLE 8. Parties and Polarization in Iraq, 1940s and 1950s

	CONSERVATIVES	*CHALLENGERS*			
	Independents Constitutional Union Socialist Nation	*Communists*	*National Democrats*	*Istiqlal*	*Ba'th*
Iraq-UK tie?	Pro	Anti	Anti	Anti	Anti
Border status quo?	Pro	Pro	Pro	Anti	Anti
Land reform/ redistribution?	Anti	Pro	Pro	Anti	Pro

ing complex organizations, conservative elites were ill equipped to defend their interests in a democratic context over the long term.[7] Conservative elites' tenure in parliament depended on networks of patronage rather than on impersonal, generalized mass support. Those conservatives that did engage in party organization could access only the political support that fell within the reach of their respective patron-client networks. For example, the conservative Constitutional Union Party encompassed the clienteles of several top Iraqi elites and tribal sheikhs (Tripp 2000, 127). Also, rivalries engendered by competition for access to state patronage resources constrained conservatives' capacity for unified action (Haj 1997, 98; Tripp 2000, 77–78, 129). Many conservatives failed to join parties at all, as indicated by the fact that the elections of the late 1940s and early 1950s typically returned chambers in which 35 to 40 percent of the seats were filled by independents. Competitive dynamics among conservatives also fueled a split within the Constitutional Union Party, with Salih Jabr breaking away to found the Socialist Nation Party in 1951.[8]

Faced with an opposition that not only challenged their ability to sustain their elite status but also was building superior mobilizational capacity, conservatives were decidedly apprehensive when in 1945 the announcement was made that Iraq was to embark on a path of social and electoral reform. Conservative parliamentarians knew well that the growth of the mass-mobilizing ideological challenger parties—if allowed to proceed—would gravely threaten their political, economic, and social status (Grassmuck 1960, 413; Khadduri 1960, 253; Tripp 2000, 117). Spurred on by serious and ongoing strike activity in the 1940s, status-quo elites worried considerably about communism (Farouk-Sluglett and Sluglett 1991, 138; Eppel 1998a, 190). In Marr's words: "The activities of the newly licensed parties . . . soon confirmed the opponents of reform in their belief that an open political system would only lead to an overthrow of the regime itself" (1985, 100).

Conservatives' response to this threat was to pressure the government to backtrack on reform promises and to use all necessary means to keep the opposition from gaining a strong presence in parliament.[9] Their defection from the operation of competitive democratic norms took a number of forms and escalated as time went by. Early on during the experimental period, conservative parliamentarians felled prime ministers who were inclined to liberalize the political arena, rigged elections, limited press freedoms, and arrested and tried opposition party leaders (executing several communists).

Though opposition parties were denied the opportunity to fairly compete for seats in parliament, many of them continued to participate in the (imperfect) elections that were held during this period. At the same time, however, the challenger parties also became increasingly frustrated with and radicalized by continued conservative stonewalling. As a result, the challenger parties turned to two additional, nonelectoral arenas in search of political voice. The first such arena was the streets. Repeatedly between 1945 and 1958, the opposition parties organized strikes and street demonstrations to make their demands known. Because much of their support came from urban areas—whose populations were growing due to rural-to-urban migration—these parties could organize effective protest demonstrations.

Predictably, conservatives responded to these challenger tactics with heightened repression. Successive Iraqi governments used the police and the army to suppress strikes and demonstrations, killing participants in the process. They ordered further arrests, trials, and incarcerations of opposition party leaders (including additional executions of communist leaders) as well as the disbanding of political parties. They imposed martial law intermittently. In August 1954 conservative forces drove the prorogation of the parliament that had been elected in June of that year. The challenger parties, which had joined together in a National Front during the campaign, had managed to win 11 of 135 seats in that body despite government intimidation of voters and vote falsification. This would mark conservatives' final clampdown on possibilities for political liberalization: they banned political parties, unions, and civil society organizations; they targeted communists with a campaign of repression; and they oversaw new, government-controlled elections to elect a servile parliament.

When it came to defending their interests, however, Iraq's conservative elites were not out of the woods yet. This was because the second non-electoral arena to which the challenger parties turned was the Iraqi army. Increasingly, younger army officers opposed the regime's pro-Western foreign policy stance and were sympathetic to challenger parties' ideologies.[10] At the same time, all of the challenger parties cultivated links with officers and noncommissioned elements of the army (Tripp 2000, 143). In July 1958 a group of army officers—in consultation and cooperation with the challenger parties (Haddad 1971, 89; Khadduri 1969, 30–32; Marr 1985, 158)—led a coup that overthrew the monarchy, established a republic, abolished parliament, put an end to elections, and silenced the conservative end of the Iraqi political spectrum. Between 1958 and 1968 the various elements of the Iraqi left then vied with one another for power,[11] and a stable founding regime was not established until 1968. In that year the Ba'th Party instigated a coup and established a one-party authoritarian regime that remained in power until 2003 by using fear and violence, oil wealth, and a large state presence in the economy to suppress domestic dissent.

Jordan

Jordan became independent in 1946, but the nature of the postindependence founding regime that would take root there did not become clear until the late 1950s. For more than a decade the rules governing who held decision-making power in the kingdom would be fluid. Jordan's first independent constitution (1947) located political authority in the monarchy and created a weak parliament to which cabinets were not responsible. October 1947 elections returned a parliament of sixteen independents and four members of the government-sponsored al-Nahda (Revival) Party. Demonstrating significant continuity with the legislative councils of the mandate period, these parliamentarians came from Jordan's large-landholding, tribal, and merchant elite families, many of whom had served in the mandate-era councils (Abu Jaber 1969, 228). In general these parliamentarians supported the government and the political status quo (Aruri 1972, 93).

In the early 1950s, however, two developments undermined this status quo. First, the Jordanian monarchy weakened suddenly and substantially. King Abdallah was assassinated in July 1951. His schizophrenic son, Talal, became king in September 1951 but, due to his illness, held the throne for only a year before being removed from office in August 1952. Talal's young son, Hussein, subsequently was named to the throne but was too young to assume it immediately. A regency council ruled on Hussein's behalf from August 1952 until May 1953, when he acceded to the throne at age seventeen. Second, after the first (1948) Arab-Israeli war, in 1950 Jordan annexed the territory known today as the West Bank and granted its Palestinian population full citizenship rights. Relative to the "predominantly rural-nomadic society of Transjordan" (Aruri 1972, 89),[12] Jordan's West Bank citizens possessed a larger middle class and were more educated, urbanized, politically organized, and radical.[13] Moreover, these were reluctant citizens. Most Palestinian Jordanians intensely resented Abdallah for having annexed the West Bank rather than seeing to it that an independent Palestinian state was established. Indeed, Abdallah's assassin was an angry Palestinian.

The infusion of some 800,000 Palestinians into the Jordanian body politic[14] had a dramatic impact on political development in the kingdom. First, the size of parliament's lower house was doubled, now allotting twenty seats to East Bank deputies and twenty seats to West Bank deputies.[15] In addition, embracing the West Bank meant opening up the political system to new groups, which in turn led to a major overhaul of the party system. With elections scheduled for that same year (1950), the importation of established West Bank political parties spurred East Bank Jordanians to organize their own parties, creating a party system that between 1950 and 1957 contained seven main actors.

Jordan's nascent party system was tremendously polarized. Parties disagreed about a long list of issues, beginning with the question of whether or not Jordan should continue to exist within its 1950 borders.[16] Parties also clashed over whether Jordan should be a monarchy or a republic; whether, in a monarchical scenario, the king should reign or rule; whether the public sphere should be secular or Islamicized; and whether or not Jordan should pursue a pro-Britain foreign policy. Table 9 summarizes where each of Jordan's seven political parties stood on these divisive issues.

In addition, the conservative parliamentarians that sought to defend the status quo possessed only patron-client ties to their followers (Aruri 1972, 101) while those parties that challenged the status quo had more modern methods of generating political support. Conservatives formed the Arab Constitutionalist and Community parties—though many did not organize into party forms at all and ran instead as independents. These men represented mainly East Bank large-landholding, tribal, and commercial interests. They favored the status quo regarding property rights and Jordan's borders, and they supported the idea of having a strong monarchy

TABLE 9. Parties and Polarization in 1950s Jordan

	CONSERVATIVES		*CHALLENGERS*				
Party Platforms	*Community*	*Arab Constitutionalists*	*Communists*	*Ba'th*	*National Socialists*	*Muslim Brothers*	*Liberation*
1950 border status quo?	Pro	Pro	Anti	Anti	Anti	Pro	Anti
Monarchy?	Pro	Pro	Anti	Anti	Pro	Pro	Anti
Monarchy: reign or rule?	Rule	Rule	—	—	Reign	Rule	—
Secularism or Islam?	Secularism	Secularism	Secularism	Secularism	Secularism	Islam	Islam
Which foreign power?	U.K.	U.K.	Not U.K. U.S.S.R.	Not U.K. Neutralism	Not U.K.	Not U.K. Neutralism	Not U.K. Neutralism
Wealth redistribution?	No	No	Yes	Yes	Mild	No	No

TABLE 10. Jordanian Election Results, 1950–1956

	Conservatives			*Challengers*				
Election	*Community*	*Arab Constitutionalists*	*Independent*	*Communist*	*Ba'th*	*NSP*	*Muslim Brothers*	*Liberation*
1950	2	8	16	2	2	10	—	—
1951	1	9	14	2	3	11	—	—
1954	0	17	15	2	0	1	4	1
1956	1	4	14	3	2	11	4	1

allied to the United Kingdom. The last was particularly essential, for "only the monarchy secured their position; there would be no place for them in a system without a king" (Satloff 1994, 41). The problem was that their opponents were developing comparatively greater mobilizational capacity. Jordan's five challenger parties—the Communist, Ba'th, National Socialist, Muslim Brotherhood, and Liberation parties—all had platforms with specific ideological content and mass followings based on ideological affinity (Abu Jaber 1969, 248), and many possessed significant organizational apparatuses.[17]

Table 10 demonstrates that the first two elections (in 1950 and 1951) following the annexation of the West Bank returned chambers with a substantial and growing number of challenger deputies—a testament to their parties' popularity and mobilizational skill. In light of concurrent monarchical instability, challengers' growing parliamentary strength allowed them to alter the rules of the political game in their favor. In January 1952 a new constitution was promulgated that identified the Jordanian nation rather than the monarch as the source of political authority. The constitution also enhanced the legislature's authority: cabinets became responsible to parliament and parliament gained the right to override a monarchical veto with a two-thirds majority. A two-thirds majority also could fell a cabinet in a no-confidence vote; in 1953 this was amended such that only a simple majority was needed to bring down a cabinet.

The growing strength of the challenger parties manifested outside of the parliamentary arena as well. In October 1953 Israeli troops attacked a West

Bank village, killing more than sixty Jordanians. When Jordanian troops did not respond to the aggression, the challenger parties organized huge street demonstrations. They called on the government to retaliate against Israel, to investigate the army's failure to respond to the aggression, to dismiss the British officers that commanded Jordan's army, and to cut Jordan's ties to Britain. As British subsidies and the British-led Jordanian army represented two key supports of the monarchy, King Hussein was not pleased with these developments. At the same time, conservative parliamentarians grew increasingly anxious about the challenger parties' power. In Abu Jaber's words, "once the process [of democratization] was begun it was too fast for the East Bankers to assimilate, or later, to accept" (1969, 233).

A period of authoritarian reaction ensued, carried out by the king in tandem with conservative parliamentarians. In May 1954 King Hussein fired the prime minister and asked Tawfiq Abu al-Huda, leader of the Arab Constitutional Party, to form a new government. Abu al-Huda packed his cabinet with individuals who were loyal to the monarchy. When the opposition continued to challenge the government, Abu al-Huda persuaded the king to dissolve parliament. He also banned a number of newspapers, including those of the communists, the Ba'th Party, and the Muslim Brothers. New elections took place in October 1954. Through a combination of restrictive laws and electoral fraud, Abu al-Huda made sure that the poll returned a conservative, pro-status-quo parliament containing a dramatically diminished challenger presence. He then formed a new government that continued clamping down on political freedoms.

Antidemocratically shut out of parliament after 1954, the challenger parties turned to three alternative arenas to pursue their political aims. The first was the Jordanian army. At independence the army had consisted of troops drawn mainly from the sons of East Bank tribal families who were loyal to the monarchy. During the 1950s, however, the army grew by a factor of nearly three as it drew into its ranks West Bank and urban East Bank residents likely to be more radical in their personal politics. Challenger penetration of the army was also facilitated in March 1956 when King Hussein, bowing to public opinion, dismissed the British officers who commanded the army. The men who replaced the departing officers were a politically heterogeneous lot but included several who sympathized with the challenger parties (Satloff 1994, 147). The challenger parties capitalized on both developments and worked to develop allies and political support within the army (Cohen 1982, 237–44). Most pivotal for future developments would be Hussein's choice of Ali Abu Nuwar as the army's chief of staff, for Abu Nuwar was known to his contemporaries as a Ba'thist and as a personal friend of Ba'th leader Abdullah al-Rimawi (Vatikiotis 1967, 128; Satloff 1994, 163).

The other two arenas to which the challenger parties appealed were the streets and foreign powers. In December 1955 and January 1956 the challenger parties organized a series of violent demonstrations and riots to protest rumors that Jordan would join the Baghdad Pact, a British-led anti-communist alliance. These disturbances—during which demonstrators railed against British imperialism and the Jordanian monarchy—were supported by Saudi Arabian financial aid and Egyptian radio propaganda designed to prevent Jordan from acceding to the pact (Dann 1989, 30; Haddad 1971, 492–94).

In the face of public opinion so expressed, King Hussein chose not to accede. Still, opposition-led unrest and demonstrations continued through the first half of 1956. Now the demand was that Jordan abrogate the 1948 Anglo-Jordanian Treaty, the source of Jordan's pro-British foreign policy and significant annual subsidy. Threatening though these were to King Hussein's position, he called for new elections. The October 1956 poll was "the freest ever held in the Kingdom" (Agwani 1969, 150) and returned a chamber in which the strength of the conservative parties was much diminished while that of the challenger parties was substantial. The NSP won a plurality and the king asked its leader, Sulayman al-Nabulsi, to form a government. Nabulsi's cabinet included six NSP members, one Ba'th deputy, one communist (as agriculture minister), and three independents. Nabulsi virtually excluded the conservative, pro-monarchy parties and parliamentarians from his cabinet.

The Nabulsi government's initiatives threw into stark relief the degree to which Jordan's party system was polarized. While the king and the conservative parties sought to preserve Jordan's ties to the West, the Nabulsi government abrogated the Anglo-Jordanian Treaty, broke diplomatic relations with France, and strengthened Jordan's ties to China, the Soviet Union, Egypt, and Saudi Arabia. While the king and the conservative parties wished to preserve Jordan's independence, the Nabulsi government publicly began to question the legitimacy of the continuing existence of the state of Jordan (Haddad 1971, 498). As a first step toward integrating Jordan into a larger Arab entity, the Nabulsi government called for economic union with Syria. It also met with an Egyptian representative on the subject of standardizing the curricula of Egyptian and Jordanian schools. These latter actions appear to have convinced the king that allowing competitive politics to operate in the kingdom "would be a mortal risk" (Dann 1989, 45).

This conclusion was reinforced in April 1957 when the Nabulsi government retired director of security Bahjat Tabara, "on whom [the king] relied in domestic matters" (ibid., 52).

King Hussein knew that he could not tolerate much more such activity from the Nabulsi government without endangering his throne. "Domestic conservatives . . . were equally disturbed with the new political trend in the country" (Aruri 1972, 139). The king and conservative parliamentarians again defected from nascent democratic norms. On April 10, 1957, King Hussein fired Nabulsi and worked to form a new cabinet that would be more sympathetic to his interests. Again thwarted in parliament, the challenger parties turned to their allies in the army for help in confronting the king. This strategy culminated in an attempted coup d'état against the monarchy led by units of the army that were sympathetic to the challenger parties. Key army regiments loyal to the king scuttled the coup attempt. Not yet fully subdued, the challenger parties held a congress in Nablus on April 22, 1957. There they issued a "proclamation to the people" calling for a series of measures that would have destroyed the monarchy as well as for a general strike and demonstrations in support of those measures. This turn of events "convinced Hussein that nothing but brute force applied at once . . . could save him and the Hashemite state from disaster" (Dann 1989, 60–61).

King Hussein proceeded to create an authoritarian monarchical regime. In this endeavor the king had the support of pro–status quo parliamentarians and other conservative Jordanian elites. From these, he constructed a new cabinet—featuring the Community Party's Samir Rifa'i as deputy prime minister—that faithfully carried out his will. On April 25 the king declared martial law, banned political parties, and forced more than a dozen radical deputies out of parliament. "Never again would the regime permit truly free elections and the parliaments that have followed since 1959 . . . were to be more conservative, handpicked supporters of the regime" (Abu Jaber 1969, 239). Purged of its radical officers, the army henceforth became an unquestioned pillar of Hussein's regime. Finally, Eisenhower Doctrine–driven U.S. financial aid helped Hussein solidify both the army's support for the monarchy and his hold over the political arena more generally.

Syria

At independence, multiple parties competed for power in a political arena in which the operation of competitive elections and parliament were central to determining who would wield power in Syria (Picard 1980, 148). Syria's party system, however, was polarized, pitting the conservative National and People's parties against the radical Communist, Ba'th, and Arab Socialist parties. The People's and National parties' members came from elite backgrounds, but their domestic policy preferences differed. The People's Party articulated capitalists' economic preferences, including land reform and other welfare-enhancement measures for peasants with a view to enlarging the Syrian market. The National Party represented mainly landowners who were opposed to reforming the rural status quo. At the outset of the interim transitional period, the People's Party cooperated with one of the radical challenger parties out of a shared concern for peasants' welfare. However, as the years went by, the political power of the challenger parties mounted while their policy demands became increasingly extreme. In the face of these developments the People's Party fell into political lockstep with the National Party, and both parties fought to preserve a liberal bourgeois political-economic status quo.[18]

Three important challenger parties sought to overturn this status quo. The policy platform of the Syrian Communist Party (PCS) fluctuated over the years, but during the 1950s—by which time it was "the best-organized political party in the country" (Kaylani 1972, 17)—it strongly championed peasants' rights and interests against those of their landlords (Batatu 1999, 120). Internationally, the PCS developed strong ties to Moscow and to international communism. The Arab Socialist Party advocated the abolition of feudalism, upper limits on landholdings, distribution of land to peasants, and other radical socioeconomic reforms.[19] The Ba'th Party promoted a socialist agenda that included "state ownership of banks and large industry, a labor code, unionization and minimum wages, a welfare state, and, most radical in this society of great estates, land reform" (Hinnebusch 1989, 16). This agenda was "designed to eradicate the economic power, and hence political domination, of the big landowners, business and commercial magnates" (Kaylani 1972, 6).

Clearly, then, the Syrian party system was polarized over the issue of property rights. The challenger parties' calls for nationalization and land reform threatened conservative landowning and industrial actors' ability to maintain their elite status over time. Later, as the case narrative will demonstrate, Syria's parties also were in conflict over what the proper borders of the political community should be: some advocated the status quo, some a merger with Iraq, and some a broader merger with all Arab countries.

Syria's conservative parties entered the transitional period having to confront challenger parties that appeared poised to outpoll them in the not-so-distant future. Conservative elites grouped together into nonideological, narrowly organized patron-client parties. The National and People's parties had "non-existent" platforms or programs; their goals were "to obtain power and the advantages that were linked with power, which were redistributed to the mass of kin relations, clients and allies who had assured their electoral victory" (Picard 1980, 144–45). Kaylani refers to them as "groupings rather than political parties . . . [that] emerged after independence largely shapeless and disorganized" (1972, 9–10). Furthermore, election data from the transitional period (see table 11) demonstrate that a significant portion of Syria's traditional conservative elite did not join parties and instead ran for parliament as independent candidates.[20]

In stark contrast, Syria's challenger parties were developing articulate ideological platforms and building modern organizations with significant grassroots mobilizing capacities. The challenger parties recruited followers on the basis of ideological kinship rather than personal allegiance, imposed strict discipline on their followers, and built complex, hierarchical party organizations (Picard 1980, 147). The Communist Party was "superbly organized and very ably led" (Kaylani 1972, 10) and succeeded in putting down substantial roots among peasants (Batatu 1999, 119). In 1950 Akram al-Hawrani's Arab Socialist Party (ASP) was able to attract as many as forty thousand people from the countryside when it convoked in Aleppo the first peasant congress in Syria's history. In the same year it probably counted no fewer than ten thousand members (Batatu 1999, 128). The Ba'th Party worked throughout the 1940s to build a network of branches and sub-branches in Syria's provinces. At this time the Ba'th's popularity and organizational strength lay primarily among rural Syria's college and secondary-school teacher and student populations (the latter were growing rapidly during this period), as well as with civil servants, doctors, and lawyers from Syria's cities and towns. In 1952 the Arab Socialist and Ba'th parties, their followings quite complementary, merged into a single party (under the Ba'th name) to more effectively counter their conservative opponents (Kaylani 1972, 14).

When independence came to Syria in 1946, conservatives dominated parliament. They could not be complacent about domestic political trends, however, in the face of the challenger parties' mobilizational initiatives. What's more, Akram al-Hawrani, elected to parliament in 1943, was calling for electoral law reform. With help from his Ba'thist allies and other reform-minded deputies, Hawrani succeeded. In 1947 citizens would for

TABLE 11. Syrian Election Results, 1949–1961

Parties/Elections	*1949*	*1954*	*1961*
National Party	13–14	14–25	13–20
People's Party	43–45	27–32	25–32
Tribal Deputies	9	9–18	13
Independents	31–51	46–55	76–83
Communists	—	1	—
Arab Socialists	1	n/a	n/a
Ba'th	4	16–22	15–24
Other	7–8	19	24
Total Seats	114	141–142	170–173

SOURCES: Data for the table were compiled from Kaylani 1972, Picard 1980, Batatu 1982, Seale 1965, Torrey 1969, Devlin 1976, and Khader 1984. For many cells, only ranges can be given because sources reported differing election results. The 1949 election results were in part the product of conservative-directed fraud and manipulation; the 1954 and 1961 elections, by contrast, were legitimately competitive (Picard 1980, 145).

the first time directly elect their representatives in one-stage elections. Conservatives now correctly sensed even more of a threat from the emerging challenger parties. As Syria's first postindependence elections approached, conservative elites apparently concluded that their electoral prospects were decidedly unattractive. Through fraud and intimidation, they manipulated the outcome to obtain the results they wanted (Picard 1980, 145). Fearing that they would not be able to defend their interests in a democratic context, conservatives defected from nascent competitive rules in Syria.

Having been denied a fair opportunity to pursue their policy preferences through legal channels, challenger parties also defected, turning to sympathetic officers in the Syrian army for the political muscle they concluded they would not be allowed to develop in parliament. In March 1949 army colonel Husni al-Za'im took control of the government with the assistance of challenger party leaders—Akram al-Hawrani and Ba'thist officials in particular (Heyworth-Dunne 1951, 24–25; Kaylani 1972, 12; Torrey 1964, 123, 139n6). The Za'im administration instituted a number of reforms that were consistent with Arab Socialist and Ba'th political proclivities. It initiated public works projects, extended suffrage to educated women, and introduced taxes on personal income, inheritances, and commercial and industrial profits. Za'im also formulated a plan to distribute state land to poor farmers. While not radically redistributive, these measures reflected a leftist agenda on the part of the administration.

This was a turn of events that, if allowed to continue, threatened the status of Syria's propertied, conservative classes (Khader 1984, 8). These apparently learned the lesson that friendly army officers were now a crucial political resource in Syria, for, with help from members of the conservative People's Party (Picard 1980, 154; Torrey 1964, 146), army colonel Sami al-Hinnawi launched a coup that ended Za'im's rule in August 1949. Hinnawi rescinded some of the taxes that Za'im had inaugurated and held elections for a new constituent assembly. Conservative forces tampered with these elections to ensure their preferred outcomes (Picard 1980, 145), and the People's Party won a plurality of seats in the assembly.

In this new assembly, the question of whether or not Syria should pursue political union with Iraq (and possibly Jordan) soon surfaced as a polarizing issue. The conservative National and People's parties supported the measure, while the Arab Socialist and Ba'th challenger parties opposed it. When it looked as though the proposal would pass, the Arab Socialist Party's Akram al-Hawrani again looked to the army for political ammunition. He found support there because many army officers feared what would become of their prerogatives and careers should the Syrian army merge with those of other Arab states (Seale 1965, 85; Devlin 1976, 56). Hawrani plotted with army colonel Adib Shishakli, who took control of Syria in December 1949 in that year's third coup d'état (Torrey 1964, 162; Kaylani 1972, 12–13).

Shishakli allowed the sitting constituent assembly to complete its work and form a new cabinet. But conservatives and independents dominated this and subsequent cabinets and sought to restrict the army's ability to interfere in politics. This was unacceptable to Shishakli and in November 1951 he dissolved parliament and banned the conservative parties. Though he shut down the main challenger parties (the Ba'th and the Arab Socialists) five months later, Shishakli's policy initiatives in many ways mirrored their preferences. During the next two years his administration built schools, hospitals, and infrastructure; provided seeds, equipment, and state land to peasants; made credit available to peasants and small industrialists; raised tax rates on wealthy Syrians; and required merchants to keep books so that they could be properly taxed.

In the early 1950s the logic of the vicious cycle—wherein parties turned to leaders of army factions rather than the electoral arena to advance their causes—intensified. In late 1952 Shishakli arrested several challenger party members and dismissed two dozen army officers for plotting against his regime. These parties were angry at Shishakli for having banned them and were urging certain army officers to confront Shishakli and help return Syria to a civilian regime. Conservatives too, especially the People's Party, were seeking the help of sympathetic army officers with the goal of unseating Shishakli.

In 1954 a conservative coup returned Syria to civilian rule. The People's and National parties, together with conservative-minded independents, held a parliamentary majority. The National and People's parties dominated early cabinets during this period, but their rivalry and infighting opened up political space for increasing leftist influence (Torrey 1964, 276; Kaylani 1972, 16; Tibawi 1969, 398–99; Devlin 1976, 73). The Ba'th Party capitalized on this opportunity. Its cabinet strength increased over the years, culminating in 1958 when the party led Syria into political union with Egypt. Egypt was by far the senior partner in this union, and many strands of Syrian public opinion soon became disillusioned with the undertaking. Nationalizations and land reform laws that were implemented by the union antagonized conservatives in particular. In September 1961, yet another coup was launched by "a wing of the army in alliance with conservative politicians," ending the union with Egypt (Tibawi 1969, 407). Elections subsequently returned a conservative parliament dominated by the People's and Nationalist parties. The governments that followed repealed the nationalization laws, weakened the land reform decrees, and encouraged private enterprise.

Syrian politics would make one more leftward turn before the interim transitional period came to an end. In March 1962 the army arrested the government's conservative leadership and installed a new, more progressive prime minister. His cabinet revitalized agrarian reforms and pursued nationalizations again. Cementing this change, in March 1963 Syria's final military coup took place. This time, the political party that partnered with the army was the Ba'th. The Ba'th had been working for more than a decade to increase its influence within the army's ranks (Ma'oz 1972, 400–401). By the early 1960s the Ba'th had succeeded to such an extent that it could seize and retain power, free from the threat of subsequent countercoups. From 1963 to the present day, Syria has been governed by the Ba'th in alliance with the Syrian army.

Egypt

At independence, Egypt's nascent party system contained two broad types of parties. A large number of conservative parties emerged whose interests and activities revolved around defending the political-economic status quo. In general this meant pursuing only diplomatic channels to rid Egypt of remaining British influence while supporting the socioeconomic status quo and a secular public sphere. With the partial exception of the Wafd, these parties were not ideological, did not articulate specific policy visions for Egypt, and did not have organized mass followings. Instead, for the most part these were little more than elite groupings whose political support at election time rested on patron-client ties. They sought positions in parliament both for patronage reasons and to defend their privileged position in society. Alongside these conservative parties grew three important mass-mobilizing, ideological parties that advocated taking more extreme steps to end British influence and that challenged Egypt's secularism and socioeconomic status quo. The parties in each of these categories are listed in table 12.

The Wafd was the most important party of the period. Its characteristics are not fully consistent with its classification as a conservative patron-client party, yet neither do they qualify the Wafd for "challenger party" status. As chapter 2 established, the Wafd built a mass following for itself, a challenger party trait. Yet the Wafd did not seek a continuously mobilized mass following; instead, it worked to keep "popular political activity episodic and circumscribed" (Botman 1991, 56). And in rural areas, the Wafd reeled in the vote via "conservative" means—by tapping the party's patron-client links to rural landlords and the peasants whose political behavior they influenced (ibid.). Similarly, consistent with the challenger party "profile," the Wafd was an ideological party—but only to the extent that the main plank in its political platform was a (massively popular) call for Egyptian independence. By the 1930s and 1940s, advocating for the end of remaining U.K. privileges in Egypt did not differentiate the Wafd from the other parties and forces in the political arena. All shared this same sentiment. At the same time, beyond its anti-British rhetoric, the Wafd never articulated a specific social and economic policy vision for Egypt (Botman 1991, 58; Terry 1982, 160).

Indeed, policy-wise, the Wafd was a conservative party that defended the political and economic status quo. Its founders were a group of landowning aristocrats and well-off urban professionals committed to

TABLE 12. Egypt's Political Parties, 1936–1952

Conservative Patron-Client Parties	*Mass-Mobilizing, Ideological Challenger Parties*
Wafd	Muslim Brotherhood
Liberal Constitutionalists	Young Egypt/Socialist Party
Sa'dists	Egyptian Communist Party
Watani	
Ittihad	
Sha'b	

Egypt's "existing capitalist structures which they anticipated dominating" (Terry 1982, 208). Though trade unions regularly supported the Wafd, when in power the party assented to the suppression of strikes and consistently rejected workers' demands for socioeconomic reform. It never advocated land reforms or economic nationalization; instead, it defended "the . . . socioeconomic positions that were held by the majority of the Egyptian elite" (Botman 1991, 56). Indeed, as the 1940s unfolded, the Wafd leadership "began to speak more obviously in the accents of vested interests" (Mitchell 1993, 38). The Wafd's conservatism explains its preference for episodic and circumscribed mobilization. It sought sufficient mass support to compete successfully in elections, but preferred subsequent *de*mobilization so as to avoid having to contend with a populace that, once activated, might demand "more far-reaching social and economic changes which most of the Wafd was not willing to consider" (Terry 1982, 207). This analysis places the Wafd in the conservative category due to its socioeconomic policy instincts as well as the fact that, over the course of the time period considered here, the party changed in important ways, coming more and more to resemble this category's profile.

Several other parties joined the Wafd in the conservative patron-client category. An early split within the Wafd led to the creation of the Liberal Constitutionalist Party (LCP) in 1922. Relative to the Wafd, LCP members—mostly prominent landowners—were more moderate and gradualist in their attitude toward negotiations with Britain over Egypt's political status. The king created and funded the conservative, pro-palace, Ittihad Party in 1925 to defend the monarchy's interests against Wafd and LCP attacks. In 1930 Ismail Sidqi created the Sha'b, a conservative, relatively pro-monarchy party populated primarily by wealthy landowners. The (politically quite minor)

Watani Party had Islamist leanings and took a hard line regarding negotiations with Britain over the content of Anglo-Egyptian relations. All of these "core" conservative parties lacked clearly articulated platforms and organized their political support along patron-client rather than ideological, mass-mobilizing lines.[21]

From the 1920s through the early 1950s the Wafd was electorally by far the majority party. However, it was prevented from governing Egypt for all but a very few years. The British and/or the Egyptian king routinely blocked the Wafd from ruling by forbidding or dismissing governments with which they took issue. Britain's ability to do so stemmed from the military forces it still maintained in and near Egypt, while Egypt's 1923 constitution gave the king far more than a constitutional monarch's powers, including the right to dismiss parliament. The "core" conservative parties also played a part in denying the Wafd the power it had earned at the polls. Aware of their marked electoral inferiority relative to the Wafd yet wishing to access power, the LCP, Ittihad, and Sha'b regularly enabled Britain's and the king's antidemocratic instincts by either backing or serving in undemocratically constructed cabinets. Threatened by the Wafd's mass following and superior electoral prospects, the core conservative parties—along with the United Kingdom and the king—were the first to defect from nascent democratic norms.

These defections affected the Wafd in two ways. First, being unfairly blocked from power eventually corrupted the Wafd (Gordon 1989, 1992). Perhaps concluding that its opponents could not be bested, the Wafd joined them. In the 1940s and early 1950s the Wafd appeased and even protected the king's and Britain's interests in return for being allowed to govern. Catering to antidemocratic actors rather than the electorate, the Wafd joined the "core" conservative parties in defecting from the rules of democratic competition. Also, as the other conservative parties routinely did, the Wafd took full advantage of the opportunities for patronage and nepotism that cabinet control offered (Gordon 1989, 197–98; Terry 1982, 254). Second, the trying political waters the Wafd was forced to navigate divided the party (Gordon 1989, 1992), with the Sa'dists splitting away in the late 1930s, and the Independent Wafdist Bloc doing so in 1942. These developments fragmented and weakened the Wafd as a political force.

As it became corrupt and fragmented, and because it never articulated an attractive social and economic policy vision, the Wafd lost its mass following—particularly in urban areas—in the 1940s and 1950s. During and after World War II, rising unemployment and inflation hurt especially the poor but also the middle class. Extremely unequal landholding patterns and trends in the agricultural sector squeezed peasants. The Wafd's refusal to consider land or other progressive economic reforms alienated much of its mass support (Terry 1982, 262), rendering the Wafd more akin to the "core" conservative parties. The Wafd lost its mass following to three genuinely mass-mobilizing, ideological challenger parties that, over time, earned the political allegiance of urban youth, workers, and the middle class as well as substantial numbers of rural Egyptians.

The most important challenger party was the Muslim Brotherhood. Established in 1928 by Hassan al-Banna, the Muslim Brothers sought to make Islam the organizing principle in Egypt's society, economy, and politics. It was extremely hostile to the British presence in Egypt and did not believe that the conservative parties were doing enough to end it. Gaining the support of civil servants, students, urban labor, urban middle classes, and rural Egyptians, the Muslim Brothers' organization grew from a scant four branches in 1929, to three hundred in 1938, to two thousand in 1949. Mitchell estimates the Brotherhood's late 1940s membership at between 300,000 and 600,000 and suggests that the party could boast another half million "sympathizers" (1993, 328). By the end of WWII "the Muslim Brothers . . . had seriously eaten into the traditional Wafdist strongholds" (ibid., 309).

Young Egypt was the second-most important challenger party.[22] It also was strongly opposed to the United Kingdom's continued presence in Egypt. In its early years, Young Egypt promoted patriotism and national pride, social and economic development, and a conservative, martial, personal ethic that disapproved of alcohol and various forms of what it considered immorality. After 1938 the party focused increasingly on class conflict. By 1940 the party's platform called for free medical care and social insurance for all citizens (Vatikiotis 1978, 75). In 1949 the party renamed itself the Socialist Party of Egypt and its program called for radical land reform, agricultural collectivization, nationalization of industry and public utilities, a social security scheme, and income and inheritance taxes (ibid., 77). Though Young Egypt had been in decline for most of the 1940s, when it reemerged, renamed and more radical, in 1949, it built momentum. In 1950 it succeeded in electing a member to parliament who went on to propose land reform legislation. By 1951 the party operated sixty-five local branches, and its two journals—which regularly condemned the conservative parties—circulated to 100,000 to 200,000 readers per week.

The third challenger party was the Communist Party. Communist organization underwent two iterations during this period in Egyptian political history. In the early 1920s a communist movement got under way and began to build trade union support but remained weak due to internal factionalism, its failure to mobilize peasants, and its aloofness from the nationalist struggle (Botman 1987, 80). Communism returned to the Egyptian scene during the early 1940s when several communist organizations were founded—this time "highly nationalist, and critical of Egypt's traditional political culture" (ibid., 84). The extent of the communists' popularity was demonstrated in 1947 when they organized a strike of some twenty-seven thousand workers in Cairo (Agwani 1969, 45). By 1952, "communist strength in Egypt was estimated at 5,000 card-carrying members" (ibid., 48).

As these three challenger parties emerged and grew in the 1930s, 1940s, and 1950s, Egypt's conservative parties took note and were alarmed. Not only did the challenger parties advocate radical policy preferences that would have undermined conservatives' elite status, but the former also were well organized and building mass followings. The challengers thus represented a serious political threat to the conservative parties, whose political support depended on patron-client links only. The conservative parties' reactions to the challengers not surprisingly tended to be repressive. In another form of defection from democratic rules, the conservatives repeatedly blocked the challengers' ability to function freely and to run for parliament.

Egypt's early conservative governments, for instance, were quick to block communist organizing. In the early 1920s communist leaders were arrested, their allied trade unions dismantled, and the party finally shut down in 1925. In the 1930s Young Egypt had stated its intentions to work within the constitutional system to achieve its goals (Jankowski 1975, 37). It sought to contest the 1938 election, yet could not, because none of its members were old enough to run. The government rejected Young Egypt's repeated demands that the minimum age for deputies be lowered from thirty to twenty-five. In 1941, the government suppressed the party for three years. In that same year the Muslim Brothers decided to participate in national elections. The party entered the 1942 election campaign, but then withdrew under pressure from the Wafd to do so (Mitchell 1993, 309).[23] In 1945 the Brotherhood again contested parliamentary elections, running candidates in a number of electoral districts. However, the government manipulated the results of these elections—"believed to have been among the more obviously dishonest held in Egypt"—such that the Brothers were defeated in ostensibly safe constituencies (ibid., 33). In 1948 the Brotherhood was dissolved and suppressed.

Barred from functioning freely and participating in elections, the challenger parties increasingly adopted public stances that were disloyal to and critical of Egypt's nascent democratic institutions. Unable to compete in the 1938 elections, Young Egypt began to denounce the electoral process as unrepresentative. The organization also became more supportive of authoritarian rule (Jankowski 1975, 60, 37). For their part, Muslim Brotherhood leaders criticized the political system and overall social order in Egypt. At the same time, all three challenger parties turned to alternative arenas in the pursuit of power. They took to the streets, leading strikes, marches, protests, and demonstrations that often turned violent. They engaged also in explicit acts of political violence, including assassination campaigns and bomb attacks on U.K. targets. The Muslim Brothers developed paramilitary formations as well as significant contacts with disenchanted officers in the Egyptian army. By the early 1950s, public order had broken down altogether. This situation both motivated and facilitated a July 1952 coup by army officers that led to the establishment of a stable authoritarian regime in Egypt.

Conclusion

In postindependence Iran, Iraq, Jordan, Syria, and Egypt, competitive elections for seats in powerful parliaments to a large extent determined who would wield policy-making power. Political parties contested these elections and sought inclusion in cabinets. Yet polarization and mobilizational asymmetry characterized all five nascent party systems. Conservative elites committed to maintaining the political-economic status quo faced off against challenger forces intent on significantly altering the status quo through radical shifts in property rights, borders, foreign allegiances, and/or regime fundamentals. Conservatives failed to organize into party form at all or formed nonideological parties whose political support rested on a limited base of patron-client ties. Challenger forces, meanwhile, were building modern party structures with articulate, strident ideological platforms. In so doing, challengers were laying the groundwork for a capacity to substantially outpoll conservatives. Threatened thus by the challenger parties, conservatives defected from nascent democratic rules by rigging elections, suppressing challenger parties, and supporting monarchs and foreign powers in antidemocratic actions. Faced with such defections, challenger parties also defected from democratic rules and turned to alternative arenas such as the streets and the army in the pursuit of power. These dynamics hollowed out democratic arenas, paving the way for the establishment of authoritarian regimes.

Conservatives were always the first to defect. They did so based on expectations regarding *long-term* rather than immediate election outcomes. In Iran, Iraq, Syria, and Egypt, challenger parties did not achieve substantial parliamentary presences during interim transitional periods. They typically won between a handful and a couple of dozen seats—far fewer than would constitute a parliamentary majority anywhere. Yet suffrage norms were changing in ways that constrained conservatives' ability to control elections and maximized the masses' impact on election outcomes. While conservatives stood at the helms of parties that relied on face-to-face, patron-client ties for constituents and that did not offer attractive ideological programs to the masses, they watched as the challenger parties did the opposite. The latter were building more modern, cell- or branch-based party structures and recruiting individuals indirectly on the basis of forceful ideological platforms calling for significant changes in the status quo designed to shift resources away from conservative elites toward the masses. For these reasons conservatives could rationally reach the conclusion that, over time, challenger party organizations would outdistance their own ability to generate votes in free and fair elections.

Sociological and technological trends would have reinforced the calculus that challenger parties would become the more powerful mobilizers in democratic elections in the long run. Conservatives' patron-client parties were in large part built on traditional hierarchical relations that held in predominantly agricultural societies. For example, prominent landowners' clienteles included those who worked their lands, who existed in debt relationships to them, and so on; these were the actors whose political behavior landowners could influence. But the Middle East was modernizing during the interim transitional periods under consideration here, and a key element of that process was rural-to-urban migration. Peasants were leaving the land in large numbers and moving to cities in search of better economic opportunities (Owen and Pamuk 1998, 98–99; Khader 1984, 2; Eppel 1999, 419; Stork 1982, 29; Avery, Hambly, and Melville 1991, 231). The population of Baghdad, for instance, doubled between 1922 and 1947 (Farouk-Sluglett and Sluglett 1991, 126). Across the region, this dynamic shrank conservatives' clienteles while generating a significant new stratum to which challenger parties appealed (Haj 1997, 83, 96; Eppel 1998a, 195; Avery, Hambly, and Melville 1991, 251, 259). Meanwhile, radios came into widespread use during this period, and challenger parties used them to disseminate their ideological platforms broadly (Plascov 1981, 113; Marr 2004, 62), a development that also threatened to weaken conservative parties in the long run.

Two types of evidence indicate that conservatives were well aware of these trends and were fearful about their ability to maintain their elite status over the long term. First, many resisted demands that electoral rules be changed in ways that would harm their own parties' performance. Egyptian conservatives refused Young Egypt's request that the minimum age of parliamentary deputies be lowered. In Iraq, conservative elites resisted reformers' calls for the country to move from two-stage elections to direct elections. They lost this battle in 1952 when the temporary military administration of army general Nur al-din Mahmud, installed after widespread riots triggered the cabinet's resignation, decreed a new electoral law providing for direct elections in order to appease an agitated populace. Second, as the case studies noted, conservative-directed vote rigging was ubiquitous during interim transitional periods. While resisting electoral change entails inertia rather than effort, vote rigging required the expenditure of resources and effort to effect desired outcomes. In other words, vote rigging was a costly behavior, indicating that conservatives engaged in it because the costs of not doing so were unacceptable in their minds. Conservatives clearly believed that much more support for challenger parties existed than the election results of the period actually reflect.

So while in every case but Jordan conservatives were holding the line for the time being in terms of parliamentary control, there was every reason for them to believe that to do so legitimately, under free and fair democratic competition, would be impossible in the long run. As a result, conservatives defected from nascent democratic norms, putting numerous obstacles in the way of challenger parties' translating their organizational and ideological strengths into proportionate parliamentary presences. Opposition parties were harassed and suppressed, and elections were almost always tampered with. These defections triggered reciprocal defections by challenger parties as the latter grew increasingly frustrated that they could not translate their growing mass support fairly into parliamentary power.

In making a set of party-centered causal claims, this study does not mean to suggest that other actors were irrelevant to founding regime outcomes in Iran, Iraq, Jordan, Syria, and Egypt. Clearly, the preferences and behavior especially of monarchs and militaries pushed these countries toward authoritarian rule. However, the room for maneuver accorded to these actors, as well as their ability to accumulate political power, depended in significant respects on *party* elites' choices and behavior. For example, in Syria, Iraq, and Jordan, armies were not unitary actors but rather were politically factionalized—in large part the result of rival parties' efforts to lobby their officers' support. Similarly, in Iran and Jordan, kings were young and vulnerable at the start of the transitional periods during which democratic institutions might have been strengthened. In both cases, one or more parties chose to ally with these kings and their authoritarian ambitions; these decisions bolstered the monarchs' positions. Though the Egyptian king began the period of contested regime rules in a relatively stronger constitutional and political position, parties' choices reinforced his authority as well. Parties' decisions and behavior thus shaped the parameters within which monarchs and militaries acted.

6

Depolarization, Increased Mobilizational Symmetry, and the Consolidation of Competitive Politics in Turkey

Chapter 6 analyzes the four iterations of two-party confrontation that constituted the drama that unfolded as the Turkish political community struggled during its interim transitional period (1920–1950) to agree upon a new set of rules of the political game. In part extending the arguments of chapter 3, it demonstrates that center-periphery conflict manifested itself in all four such confrontations (see table 13). Though the center nearly always maintained the upper hand, it faced repeated challenges from the periphery. The peripheral "Second Group" challenged the central "First Group" in the Ankara-based parliament that oversaw the Turkish War of Independence between 1920 and 1923. In 1923 Kemal turned the First Group into the Republican People's Party (RPP), which faced challenges in 1924 and again in 1930 from would-be opposition parties that had strong support in the periphery. When the opposition Democrat Party was established in the late 1940s, it represented the newest iteration in a long history of peripheral organizing against central elites.

The analysis will show, however, that while these fights still turned on the center-periphery cleavage, they did so now in a new way. For more than a century prior to 1918, center and periphery had done battle—with both protagonists remaining relatively cohesive. After 1918, as the Turkish Republic was born and the shape of its founding regime was contested, rifts within the center burst forth. In each of the four subsequent instances of two-party confrontation, a subset of disgruntled central elites aligned with peripheral forces in order to challenge dominant central elites over the emerging rules of the game. In doing so, these dissenting central elites availed themselves of the impressive mobilizational capacity that peripheral elites possessed thanks to the dense networks and social relationships that were a legacy of nineteenth-century Ottoman political development. The challenges that these opponents posed to the ruling RPP were thus quite significant. The ruling RPP suppressed the first three challengers it faced between 1920 and 1950. However, it acquiesced to free and fair electoral competition with the fourth (the Democrat Party), thereby inaugurating a competitive founding regime in Turkey.

Chapter 6 argues that two key trends in the interim transitional period help explain these outcomes. First, political debate became progressively less polarized. In Turkey, regime fundamentals were the primary polarizing issues in the political arena. The men who held power throughout the interim transitional period, repeatedly squaring off against challenger parties, were a new and insecure elite. Military men, civil servants, intel-

TABLE 13. Anatomy of Two-Party Conflict in Turkey

Protagonists	*Center (central government)*	*Periphery (local notables)*
Parties	CUP, 1908–1918 First Group, 1921–1923 Republican People's Party, 1923–	HİF, 1911–1912 Second Group, 1922–1923 PRP, 1924–1925 FRP, 1930 Democrat Party, 1946–
Social sectors involved	Civil servants Military officers Intellectuals	Wealthy landowners Commercial sector Clerics and religious jurists
Preferences	Higher taxes Concentration of power in centralized state Secularization of politics Augmented role for state in economy and society	Lower taxes Checks and balances in a decentralized or federal state Against secularization of politics Minimal role for state in economy and society
Networks facilitating collective action	Army Central bureaucracy Professional schools	Administrative council system Proto-parliamentary assemblies and parliaments

lectuals, and teachers, they were the products of the westernizing reform efforts undertaken by the Ottoman Empire in the nineteenth century: the creation of a modern army, the expansion and strengthening of the state, and the development of a new collection of secular professional schools designed to staff these institutions. By the early 1920s this new elite accumulated sufficient power to snuff out the Ottoman Empire, the sultanate, and the Islamic legal and educational institutions that buttressed them. In their stead they constructed a secular, republican, westernizing Turkish state that reflected their political preferences and secured their status as political elites.

These "new" status-quo elites (the First Group and then the RPP) suppressed their first three challengers (the Second Group, the Progressive Republican Party, and the Free Republican Party) because the latter confronted them on policy issues—republicanism and secularism in particular—on which they were unable to compromise. For an opposition party to threaten republicanism and/or secularism was to target the political structures that conferred elite political and social status on those who held power, threatening them with relegation to the backwaters of a political community returned to some sort of monarchical and/or Islamist footing. Status-quo elites were unwilling to countenance this, and repeatedly repressed challenger parties perceived as threatening in this regard.

Over time, opposition elites gradually became reconciled to the acceptable parameters of debate. By the time the Democrat Party (DP) emerged in 1946, politics had depolarized considerably. This challenger party was credibly committed to republicanism and secularism; it argued with status-quo leaders over issues less threatening to the latter's elite status, such as how (de)centralized government should be and the proper extent of state economic intervention. Depolarization facilitated Turkey's transition to competitive politics, because reassuring ruling RPP elites that they would be able to continue to compete to maintain their elite status increased the chances that the RPP would agree to fair electoral competition with the DP.

Turkey's party system was also characterized by increasing mobilizational symmetry as the years passed. At the start of the interim transitional period, the RPP was quite handicapped relative to its opponents where its ability to attract mass electoral support was concerned. Thus the RPP suppressed its first three opponents also for the reason that it did not believe it had the mobilizational capacity to defend its interests in a competitive context. By the 1940s, however, the picture had changed. Beginning in the 1930s, the RPP worked hard to augment its organizational breadth and depth and grassroots appeal. More confident now that it could hold its own in free and fair elections, the RPP allowed such elections to go forward in 1950.

The Relevance of Bipartism for Polarization Levels

Before proceeding with these arguments, it is important to link this discussion with that provided in chapter 3 by arguing that Turkey's two-party system helped facilitate the depolarization dynamic that altered the political arena in important ways between 1920 and 1950. Many scholars have noted correlations between party number and polarization levels in party systems; some assert a causal link between the two. Duverger argued that two-party systems would tend toward moderate politics and that larger numbers of parties would increase polarization in party systems (1954, 387–88). Downs provided the formal underpinnings for Duverger's intuition as to why two-party systems should produce centripetal dynamics (1957). Sartori (1976) suggested that systems with three to four parties can conduct moderate politics but that polarization and centrifugal politics arise when the number of parties reaches five or six—particularly if antisystem parties are represented among them. Mainwaring and Scully show that the number of parties correlates with polarization levels in Latin American party systems, and they imply that the former may help bring about the latter (1995, 29–31).

There is, however, good reason to question the intuition that party systems with just two or three parties will necessarily manifest centripetal rather than centrifugal tendencies. Sani and Sartori, for instance, show that in advanced Western democracies, party system fragmentation (that is, the number of relevant parties) does not correlate with polarization (1983). The Turkish case also is instructive. Here we will observe a two-party system that in the 1920s was quite polarized—so much so that Atatürk had many of his political enemies executed in the later part of the decade. Yet by the late 1940s the same two-party system had become substantially less polarized. The Turkish case supports others who have cautioned that at any given moment, two-party competition may well exhibit centrifugal rather than centripetal dynamics (Linz 1978; Mainwaring and Scully 1995). It also demonstrates that while the number of parties stays constant, polarization levels can vary.

The cases considered in this study suggest that a different dynamic may explain the correlations that sometimes occur between the number of parties and polarization levels. Rather than the number of parties influencing these levels in some mechanical way, the relationship may hold because, in polarized systems, a large number of parties may hinder prospects for depolarization. The logic behind this claim begins with the assumption that elite choices and behavior constitute intervening variables between potentially polarizing contextual factors (socioeconomic, ideological, international, and so forth) and actual levels of polarization. Prospects for depolarization therefore should depend on elite actions, and the number of party players may affect party leaders' willingness and/or ability to participate in a depolarizing dynamic.

Consider the contrast between the Turkish and Iraqi cases. Between 1920 and 1950 four opposition parties confronted Turkey's ruling RPP in sequence. The RPP suppressed the first three oppositions, each time sending clear signals as to the parameters within which it would tolerate partisan competition. The opposition understood that it would not be given the chance to compete until it conformed to these strictures. The Democrat Party did so when it emerged in 1946, and the RPP agreed to hold free and fair elections in 1950. The case suggests that the smaller the number of players in a polarized party system, the smaller the number of party leaders who must make appropriate decisions in order for depolarization to take place. In the Turkish case a single latent opposition seethed under RPP hegemony. Only one leadership had to adjust its strategy, given RPP signals, to give competitive party politics a lease on life. When the conservatives who dominated the Iraqi government in the mid-1940s saw that four of five newly licensed parties threatened their interests in profound ways, they too suppressed their opposition. For depolarization to have occurred in the Iraqi case, *four* party leaderships, each beholden to specific constituencies and in competition with one another for popular support, would have had to adjust their behavior. Clearly, this was a much taller order, for if one challenger party had moderated for the sake of depolarization—while its peers did not—it would have risked the appearance of "selling out" in the face of conservative pressure, driving its constituents to switch allegiances to the other, still-strident challenger parties.

In sum, in party systems with large numbers of players, depolarization should be difficult. This factor may help explain the correlations that exist between large numbers of parties and polarized politics in some sets of cases. By contrast, the fewer the number of players in a given party system, the smaller the number of actors that must moderate their stances for depolarization to occur. Let us turn now to the evolution of two-party competition in Turkey.

Two-Party Confrontation in the Wartime Parliament, 1920–1923

Chapter 3 left off with the Turks mobilizing to fight an independence war against their would-be occupiers after World War I. With the fate of the political community hanging in the balance, elites of the center and periphery closed ranks. In March 1920 Mustafa Kemal convened a new Turkish parliament in Ankara to direct the fight against occupying powers. Members of the last Ottoman parliament in İstanbul who could evade the occupying powers and make their way to Ankara joined the new body. In addition, each nonoccupied county was to send five elected representatives to the assembly. Local administrative council members and leaders of the Defense of Rights societies were the secondary electors in these elections (Sezgin and Şaylan 1983, 2044). Given these procedures, the new parliament not surprisingly was an amalgam of central military, bureaucratic, and intellectual elites and of peripheral notable elites (Özbudun 1976, 43; Rustow 1959, 528–29). Among the parliamentarians were civil servants, military officers, lawyers, engineers, doctors, newsmen, clerics, farmers, merchants, tribal chiefs, and dervish order leaders (Kabasakal 1991, 92–93).

Conflicting perspectives on the future of the political community went hand in hand with this diversity in parliamentarians' backgrounds. "Some saw the war as an effort to liberate the sultan-caliph from the hands of the enemy so that his sovereignty might be restored" (Turan 1994, 112). Peripheral elites tended to group in this camp. "Others felt that the sultan's government was a collaborator with the enemy and as such should be gotten rid of" (ibid.). Kemalist-led central elites espoused this view. Conflict over the fundamentals of how Turks would and should be governed made for a heterogeneous, intractable parliament (Zürcher 1994, 166; Rustow 1959, 547) that posed substantial governing challenges for Kemal. To manage the new assembly, in May 1921 Kemal organized his partisans into a parliamentary group known as the First Group. In early 1922 the Second Group organized itself to oppose the First Group. These two groups were "to be the basis of the fundamental bipartite framework that has dominated the political scene throughout the Turkish Republic" (Yerasimos 1987, 70).

In important respects this rivalry embodied the classic, late-Ottoman center-periphery conflict described in chapter 3. Second Group members were politically and socially more conservative than First Group members (Frey 1965, 308). Zürcher writes that "the *Second Group* . . . represented a clearly different section of society than the . . . *First Group* . . . mullahs, jurists and commercial groups, and had been based on local interests more than the *First Group*" (1984, 160). Indeed, the data suggest that many Second Group members were local notables. A higher proportion (73 percent) of Second Group members represented the province they were born in than was the case in the First Group (61 percent) (Demirel 1995, 141).[1] Second Group members also were only half as likely as First Group members to be speakers of French or English (ibid., 147). Moreover, the Second Group "strongly supported education through religious schools" and "passed a statute prohibiting the consumption of alcohol" (Mardin 1973, 181). Consistent with the peripheral "profile," then, Second Group members were local leaders, less exposed to the languages and ways of the West, and hostile to secularization.

Probing further into the First and Second Groups' memberships reveals, however, that this round of bipartite political competition did not pivot strictly along traditional center-periphery lines. Zürcher notes that the Second Group included many former CUP officials (1994, 163)—men of the center, that is. Indeed, the proportion of civil and military officials was 48.5 percent in the First Group and 49.2 percent in the Second Group (Demirel 1995, 149–50). Considered together with available qualitative evidence, these data suggest that the Second Group was an alliance between newly disgruntled central elites and peripheral elites whose hostility toward the center was long-standing. The latter had long objected to secular, westernized central elites' efforts to expand the state's power over society and to the economic and cultural consequences of those initiatives. They resented the Western template for reforms advocated by the center and wanted to avoid a rupture with Ottoman governing institutions (Finefrock 1979, 5; Dodd 1991, 31). Centrist Second Group members were more sanguine about such reforms but began to oppose Kemal because they feared he would exclude them from the exercise of power.

Specifically, during political-military crises associated with the independence war, Kemal obtained an increasing amount of authority relative to parliament (Finefrock 1979, 4). As more and more power concentrated in his hands, many became anxious that Kemal would establish a dictatorship, and this anxiety triggered the coalescence of the Second Group (Demirel 1995, 379). Many former CUP officials who joined the Second Group felt that their contributions to the independence war were going unrewarded in the distribution of power that was emerging in the new parliament. These men resented Kemal's ascendancy (Zürcher 1994, 163).[2] Others, including military rivals of Kemal, joined the Second Group out of opposition to the prospect of a dictatorship under Kemal. These disaffected central elites allied themselves with peripheral leaders in the Second Group,[3] which sponsored a number of initiatives designed to limit Kemal's authority. What united these otherwise unlikely allies was a shared desire—albeit for different reasons—to preserve the new parliament's sovereignty, thus preventing a concentration of power in Kemal's hands (Demirel 1995, 613).

Kemal did not relish the challenge posed by the Second Group. The following recollection of İsmet İnönü, a military officer and Kemal's close associate, is telling.

> During the War of Independence, more than once Atatürk told me that he had arrived at the conclusion that the Assembly had become a stumbling block vis-à-vis our efforts to save the country. On one of those occasions Atatürk sent me a telegraph saying, "From this point onwards it will not be possible for us to work with the Assembly. What is your opinion on how the military and the country would react to our doing away with the Assembly?" (quoted in Heper 1998, 176)

Yet until the war was won, Kemal had no choice but to tolerate the opposition. He needed the resources that the Second Group's provincial elite members and their local networks of influence were providing: men, materiel, and financing for the war effort. Granting them a voice in parliament was the quid pro quo that assured their continued cooperation.[4]

At the same time, contending with an opposition that held fundamentally different views regarding the future shape of the political community convinced Kemal that he would have to alter parliament's composition in order to implement his reform agenda successfully. Turkish politics was polarized; the gap in political preferences between center and periphery was too wide. Notable elites in the provinces had a proven track record of opposing central elites' reform efforts. Worse, they possessed significant organizational capacity in the form of their dense local networks. Kemal knew that his secularizing, westernizing reforms would be doomed in a democratic parliament in which the periphery was represented, and thus he shut the periphery out of the assembly.

The war winding down, in December 1922 Kemal announced he would turn the First Group into a political party, the People's Party. He then carefully managed parliamentary elections in 1923 so as to produce an assembly filled with individuals who were sympathetic to his leadership and political vision. His People's Party vetted and selected all candidates, gutting the elections of any dimension of real choice for citizens. Not a single Second Group member was reelected to parliament. Moreover, those members of the First Group who hailed from peripheral backgrounds[5] were much less likely to be reelected than First Group members whose origins were military and civilian officialdom (Demirel 1995). For example, of the thirty First Group members who were military officials, twenty-three sat in the second assembly while only seven failed to be reelected. By contrast, of the twenty First Group clerics, six survived while fourteen were excluded. In addition, reelected First Group members were likely to have attended military academies and other higher educational institutions in İstanbul, while those not reelected tended to have either a religious or only a secondary level education.

The Republican People's Party and the Progressive Republican Party, 1924–1925

The 1923 elections thus returned control over the Turkish state to the political center, now dominated by Kemal. The newly elected parliament grappled with momentous issues right away. Under Kemal and his core RPP allies' leadership,[6] Ankara replaced İstanbul as the capital of the Turkish political community in October 1923. Later that month, the government extinguished the centuries-old Ottoman Empire, declaring Turkey a republic. In March 1924 it abolished the caliphate and secularized the country's educational system. In March and April 1924, the assembly debated and adopted a new constitution. Thus began the Turkish political and cultural revolution for which Kemal is famous.

Though Kemal had thoroughly manipulated the 1923 elections, the new assembly still contained many deputies who would not unconditionally follow his will. As fundamental changes were made to the form and foundations of the political community, many members of the assembly grew increasingly uncomfortable with the undemocratic tactics Kemal sometimes employed to legislate reform. They were also uncomfortable with the degree to which reforms were augmenting his personal political power. In November 1924, twenty-nine such members of parliament formed the opposition Progressive Republican Party (PRP). Made up largely of former CUP officials, the PRP parliamentary leadership "took its strength from intellectuals, bureaucrats and the military" (Zürcher 1984, 160–61). These were individuals who "believed in the Unionist notion of collective or collegiate leadership" and objected to "the reins of power being gathered in the hands of an individual [Kemal] who brooked no rivals" (Ahmad 1991, 70). As had been the case with the Second Group, an important dimension of the PRP phenomenon was rifts at the political center caused by Kemal's rise to power, with dissenting central actors cleaving off into organized opposition against that trend.

But the PRP was not solely a party of disaffected central elites. The political stances taken by the PRP, as reflected in its program and rhetoric, indicate that the party was an alliance between marginalized central actors and peripheral forces. The PRP's program included many principles that were consistent with long-standing peripheral political preferences. These included reducing state tasks to a minimum, the rule of law and nonarbitrary government, democratization and the placing of checks on executive power, administrative decentralization, free trade and economic liberalism, and respect for religious beliefs and convictions.

Trends in PRP organizing also suggest that the party entailed an alliance between angry central actors and local notables in the provinces. PRP organizing proceeded rapidly (Sezgin and Şaylan 1983, 2048; Yeşil 1992, 244; Usta 1994, 28). By the end of December 1924 the PRP was completely organized in the province of Sivas. The party was extensively organized in the province of Trabzon by the end of February 1925 (Usta 1994). Though the party was in existence for only seven months, PRP branches were established in İstanbul,[7] Ankara, Urfa, İzmir, Samsun, Eskişehir, Siverek, Erzurum, Ordu, Karahisarı Sahip, Amasya, Sinop, and Maraş. In addition, PRP activists applied to local authorities for permission to open party branches in Mardin, İzmit, Erzincan, Adana, Mersin, and Kastamonu. Elites in numerous other towns contacted top PRP leaders requesting copies of the party's manifesto and program for the purpose of opening branches in their locales (Yeşil 1992, 254).

The evidence suggests that these auspicious organizational beginnings occurred because central PRP leaders tapped the dense, provincewide local networks of peripheral notable elites who had long opposed unchecked central governmental power and objected to Kemal's policies. Members of the Second Group—many of whom were local notable elites from the provinces—were key local supporters and organizers of the PRP in the provinces (Tunaya 1952, 612; Sezgin and Şaylan 1983, 2048; Kabasakal 1991, 115; Karpat 1991, 49; Yeşil 1992, 247; Usta 1994, 29). The Urfa PRP branch's leadership included numerous local notables, artisans, and tradesmen

(Yeşil 1992, 249). Moreover, Usta's research on the PRP in Trabzon province shows that Defense of Rights leaders (recall that many of these were local notables) who quit the organization when Kemal turned it into a branch of the People's Party were instrumental in PRP organizing (1994, 28–29). Moreover, his data demonstrate that notables and merchants made up a large proportion of party leadership (ibid., 29). Within just two months, PRP branch offices were created in the provincial capital, in all county seats, and in many district seats (ibid., 30–31).

Thus while the PRP's founders hailed from the RPP, the First Group, and/or the CUP, the PRP's local organizers and supporters were men of the periphery—local notable elites who in the past had filled out the ranks of the Second Group and the HIF. As had been the case with the Second Group, different motivations drove the two components of the PRP alliance. Marginalized central elites were less antagonistic to centralized state power and reforms than were the peripheral notables in the alliance, who opposed central elites' political and cultural reforms and wished to maximize their own local authority. But for marginalized central actors frustrated by Kemal's rising personal hegemony, making common cause with the periphery emerged as an obvious political strategy. In Özbudun's words, "had th[is] opposition part[y] been in existence for a sufficient length of time, [it] would conceivably have capitalized on the discontent in the periphery. The temptation to do so would be too great for almost any opposition party to resist" (1976, 42). Not only did PRP founders understand that deep discontent existed in the periphery; they also knew that the periphery could be organized quickly and effectively in support of the party if they tapped into provincial notables' networks.

Kemal's government banned the PRP in June 1925, in part because the parties' positions were polarized. Kemal sought to use the powers of the central government to push through revolutionary westernizing and secularizing reforms. Nonnegotiable issues were that the community be a secular republic and that the constitution provide for significant concentration of powers in the assembly that he controlled. The PRP challenged these values. Early on, PRP leaders discussed making İstanbul the Turkish capital and creating a second, Senate-like parliamentary chamber (Zürcher 1991, 55). The former would have erased the symbolism of Kemal's decision to move the capital to Ankara, away from the historic seat of the Ottoman Empire; the latter would have weakened his control over parliament. The PRP program called for minimization of state tasks, administrative decentralization, and respect for religious sentiments and beliefs. Furthermore, the PRP called on Kemal to be a neutral, "above-party" president. All of these demands either were direct rebuffs to Kemal's political vision or would have constrained his ability to implement his vision.

Though the PRP made efforts to reassure Kemal that it was allegiant to the republic and that it would not accept religious "reactionaries" into its organization (Yeşil 1992, 247–48, 260–61), Kemal doubted several PRP leaders' commitment to the Republic (Zürcher 1991, 156). What's more, scholars have concluded—and the ruling party reasonably can be assumed to have feared—that the mere existence of an opposition party would trigger other expressions of political hostility against the Kemalist regime. Rustow writes that the PRP "quickly became a rallying point for opponents to [Kemal's] ambitious reform programme including monarchists, separatists and Islamic conservatives" (1991, 14). Dodd concurs: "The danger was that any appeal to traditional forces in society by an opposition political party, like the Progressive Republican Party, would almost certainly have led to the overthrow of the revolution" (1991, 32). For Kemal and his political allies, then, the costs of tolerating the PRP were unacceptably high because in a competitive electoral environment, they believed they would not have been able to reproduce their elite status.

The aftermath of the PRP interlude further demonstrates the political distance that Kemal sensed separated the two parties. Subsequent to learning of a conspiracy against his life, Kemal used the 1925 Law on the Maintenance of Order and its associated system of Independence Tribunals to try and to execute many of his political enemies. More than 7,500 people were arrested and 660 executed under the umbrage of this law (Zürcher 1994, 181), including six former PRP deputies. That dissidents plotted the assassination of the president, and that the president would take such extreme measures to shift the balance of political power sufficiently in his favor to allow him to pursue his political vision, testify to the degree of polarization that characterized the confrontation between the ruling RPP and the opposition PRP.

Polarization, however, did not constitute the sole barrier to the emergence of competitive politics at this juncture in Turkish history. Kemal and his RPP refused to countenance the rise of the PRP also due to asymmetry in these parties' respective vote-getting abilities. Since both parties articulated specific (and diametrically opposed) programmatic platforms, asymmetry hinged on organizational issues. While both parties worked to build modern organizations characterized by systems of branches that blanketed the country, the parties that opposed the ruling RPP began the interim transitional period with a noticeable head start.

The PRP represented an alliance between disgruntled central elites and the elites of the periphery who had long opposed the idea of unchecked central governmental power. Thanks to the institutional innovations that had evolved beginning in the mid-nineteenth century to manage center-periphery conflict (that is, the provincial administrative council system and parliament), peripheral elites were linked together in dense networks that crisscrossed all of Turkey's provinces and that penetrated downward through the county, district, and subdistrict administrative levels. These networks constituted a boon to opposition-party builders. Indeed, PRP organizing proceeded rapidly in the short period of time that unfolded before the RPP shut it down. Also, because peasants historically had sided with their local notable leaders against the center and because peasants were beholden to their local elites through various patron-client linkages (landlord-tenant, creditor-borrower, marketer-food producer, and so on), the PRP would likely have generated significant electoral support from the masses in Turkey's countryside.

By contrast, in 1924 the RPP did not possess a nationwide organization capable of mobilizing effectively at the grassroots level. Chapter 3 demonstrated that at the opening of the nineteenth century, the center's authority in the periphery was extremely thin and mediated by powerful local notables. Indeed, the drama of nineteenth-century Turkish politics revolved around the center being forced to grant increased political rights and privileges to peripheral actors in return for the latter's support for center-initiated reform efforts. When center-periphery conflict first manifested in party form as the CUP faced off against its rapidly organizing HIF opposition in the period from 1910 to 1912, the CUP's organizational reach and sociopolitical influence in the Anatolian periphery were spotty. CUP elites hailed largely from the army and the bureaucracies and professional schools of the capital; any party created by such an elite would have to be built in top-down fashion. Not surprisingly, the CUP's branch network extended neither to all major cities nor below the county level. While CUP leaders coordinated Turks' resistance to occupation during the war of independence, they relied on peripheral elites' provincial networks to mobilize the men and materiel necessary to achieve victory.

Beginning in 1923, the Republican People's Party embodied the "center." Like its predecessor, the CUP, the RPP at that time lacked a well-elaborated apparatus as well as mass grassroots support. The RPP commenced a nationwide organizational effort in the summer of 1924. While the RPP successfully developed branches in cities and towns, it did not penetrate to the village level of Turkish society. Moreover, Kabasakal characterizes the branches that it did establish as "skeletons"—consisting primarily of administrators, lacking numerous members, and devoid of mass popular support or even interest (1991). The RPP "was not successful in stimulating peasant participation" (Payaslıoğlu 1964, 428). The party's influence in the southeastern Kurdish provinces—an extremely disaffected peripheral area that had been seeking independence—was particularly tenuous (McDowall 1996, 189–95).

The Republican People's Party and the Free Republican Party, 1930

The Independence Tribunals had a chilling effect on expressed political opposition in the late 1920s, allowing Kemal to push through many of his secularizing, westernizing reforms. In 1929 his regime allowed the Law on the Maintenance of Order to lapse. Substantial political discontent still existed, however, and in August 1930 the Free Republican Party (FRP) formed to confront the power monopoly wielded by the RPP. Kemal actually encouraged this development, hoping that it would serve as a controlled channel for the expression of the dissent he knew existed, preventing that dissent from exploding in forms that would threaten the republican regime and the reforms that symbolized it (Çavdar 1983, 2053). Kemal also wanted to shake the RPP out of the self-satisfied, lethargic, and sometimes corrupt state that its power monopoly had fostered (Karpat 1991, 51; Zürcher 1994, 186–87).

Kemal clearly intended for the new opposition party to function within strict parameters. He required FRP leader Ali Fethi Okyar to guarantee that the party would not challenge the regime's republican and secular foundations (Çavdar 1983, 2054). Kemal and Okyar bargained over where on the political spectrum the party would be located and how many assembly deputies it would have (Kabasakal 1991, 119). While Okyar hoped the FRP would have an assembly strength of 120 deputies, Kemal countered that 40 to 50 would suffice.[8] Kemal personally selected many of the assembly members who would go over to the FRP, and these tended to be his close friends and/or highly trusted deputies.

Like the Second Group and PRP before it, the FRP represented a political amalgam: its leaders were elites of the center, while its views and support base rendered it a peripheral challenge to the center. The fifteen deputies who made up the FRP's parliamentary group were "hardly distinguishable from the RPP in terms of the social background characteristics of its deputies" (Özbudun 1976, 41–42). They tended to come from military and official occupational backgrounds, to have been born either abroad or in western Turkey, and to be highly formally educated (Frey 1965, 342). In other words, the leaders of the FRP were central elites. Yet, though Okyar was a close and trusted friend of Kemal, his sympathies had been known to lie with conservative leaders (Weiker 1973, 74). Kemal had made Okyar prime minister in 1924 to temporarily assuage his conservative opponents at the time of the PRP's creation. Moreover, the FRP drew support from those local notable groups in the periphery that long had opposed the centralizing, interventionist political center: merchants, landowners, and members of the free professions (Çavdar 1983, 2055; Yetkin 1987, 115).

Peripheral support was assured by the FRP's statute (SCF 1930a) and program (SCF 1930b), which articulated an agenda consonant with peripheral interests. These documents called for political control over the executive branch and argued that citizens' own initiatives and visions should drive local administration. The FRP advocated limits on the boundaries beyond which the state should not intervene in society, and it supported a number of civil liberties, among them religious freedom. FRP documents criticized RPP economic policies as overly extractive, interventionist, and arbitrary. The party pledged to end tax collection irregularities and ensure that taxes did not exceed people's ability to pay. It also opposed state intervention in the economy that crowded out private entrepreneurship.[9] Instead, the FRP pledged to nurture private economic and financial enterprises through a variety of policy mechanisms. Furthermore, the party promised to eradicate usury and facilitate the delivery of low-interest credit to villagers and farmers. All of these themes resonated with core peripheral constituencies and their long-held complaints about the central government as corrupt, arbitrary, overly expansive, and hostile to Islamic religious practices.

Within just a few months, the FRP organized itself in a comprehensive way in thirty-seven of Turkey's sixty-three provinces, and networks of peripheral notable elites were pivotal to this achievement. The party's provincial chairman in Kars was a native and former mayor. The FRP chair in Adana was a local journalist who had been an active organizer of the Adana and Kayseri regions' Defense of Rights societies during the independence war. Likewise, Samsun province's FRP chief, Şefik Avni, was a respected local politician who had served as that province's area commander during the independence war. While Okyar and top FRP leaders selected these chairmen, the party's organizational success stemmed in large part from less centralized, more grassroots efforts. Avni used his provincial contacts to designate party organizers in Samsun's towns and villages, as well as in the neighboring regions of Amasya and Merzifon, within a span of just two months (Weiker 1973, 120–21). "Fethi [Okyar] was unable to control the many Free Party branches which sprang up overnight—often literally so" (ibid., 141).

Municipal elections were approaching in October, and peripheral actors were keen to make their presence felt by confronting RPP candidates with FRP opponents (Weiker 1973, 122). The masses flocked to the FRP "like an avalanche" (Çavdar 1983, 2055). Applications for party membership deluged FRP branch offices. Large, enthusiastic crowds greeted FRP leaders as they traveled around the provinces. In October 1930, the FRP—still only two months old—won 30 of 512 seats in municipal elections. As the elections allegedly were conducted in a fraudulent manner in most provinces, this small number of FRP seats won has been judged an opposition success (Kabasakal 1991, 122).

The elections would be among the last of the FRP's endeavors, however. The opposition's strong electoral showing and massive popularity stunned Kemal and the RPP regime (Heper 1998, 178). The latter were caught unaware of the depth and extent of citizens' unhappiness with the status quo. Within a month, the RPP suppressed the FRP, in part because it feared that the opposition party would threaten Kemal's reforms. Although Okyar had reassured Kemal that the FRP would uphold secularism and republicanism, and although FRP documents echoed these commitments, events convinced ruling party elites that Okyar was not adequately monitoring who was joining the party and acting in its name in the provinces. The RPP believed that antiregime elements—both on the left (communists) and the right (conservative, religious reactionaries)—were infiltrating the FRP and that their presence endangered the republic (Tunaya 1952, 628; Frey 1965, 341). "In the view of observers at many levels of Turkish society and at many points on the Turkish political spectrum, the Free Party by the time of its demise had become counter-revolutionary" (Weiker 1973, 148). Polarization thus prevented competitive electoral politics from taking hold in Turkey in 1930.

Importantly, however, the Turkish party system of 1930 was less polarized than that of 1924. The PRP had acknowledged the principle of republicanism but had not mentioned secularism in its program. Ultimately, party leaders' commitment to both principles was suspect in the eyes of the RPP. The party was shut down and several of its leaders were hanged two years later. RPP signals about the acceptable scope of contestation did not go unheeded. Six years later, FRP leaders were careful to proclaim their loyalty to both republicanism and secularism.[10] Their sincerity was not questioned, but their inability to guarantee partywide commitment to these principles led to the FRP's downfall. Several Turkish scholars have characterized the FRP (in a denigrating way) as not being as authentic, aggressive, or oppositional as was the PRP.[11] The analysis presented here suggests that FRP leaders, rather than demonstrating timidity or ineptitude, were acting instead in a pragmatic manner, hoping to usher in a transition to competitive electoral politics by agreeing to keep contestation within RPP-dictated parameters.

If Turkey's party system was too polarized to support the emergence of competitive politics in 1930, it was also too mobilizationally asymmetrical. In the years following the PRP's suppression, the RPP worked to further elaborate its organizational apparatus across Turkey; in 1930 it was still engaged in this endeavor, though not in the turbulent and rebellious Kurdish southeast (Kabasakal 1991). At the same time, the radical westernizing and secularizing reforms implemented by Kemal and the RPP perplexed and alienated many of the rural masses, reducing the RPP's potential for successful grassroots mobilization. By contrast, the FRP looked to be enjoying enormous, rapid success in opening branches and in attracting mass enthusiasm and support. Given the circumstances, the RPP concluded that it could not have held its own against the FRP in a competitive context. It thus shut the latter down in an effort to defend the core political principles that guaranteed its members' elite status in society.

The Aftermath of the Free Republican Party Episode

The 1930s would be a pivotal decade with respect to the emergence of competitive politics in Turkey. Having briefly countenanced and then quickly repressed two opposition parties that had been both ideologically and mobilizationally threatening, the RPP initiated a number of efforts designed to shore up its most dearly held political values and interests. It proceeded on two tracks. First, the RPP worked to depolarize the political arena through attempts at manufacturing intra-Turkish consensus with respect to national history and identity, political culture, and language. Second, the ruling party worked to make the political arena more mobilizationally symmetrical by augmenting the party's organizational apparatus and levels of potential mass support.

Decisions taken by the RPP regime during the 1930s underscored its surprise and distress at the signs that antiregime elements—especially religious and conservative ones—still existed and sought voice through rival parties. From the RPP's perspective, the FRP episode had exposed a gulf in worldviews between the party and the people. The RPP regime subsequently launched a number of related initiatives that were designed to bridge this gap. In Kemal's words, spoken in November 1930,

> We are compelled to work more actively each day, as if there were many other political parties to be faced, to spread our ideas into every group of the people, and into the remotest villages. (quoted in Weiker 1973, 157)

These "idea-spreading" initiatives aimed at promoting a new, widely held national identity consonant with the RPP's political values. That they were undertaken at all bolsters the claim that polarization prompted the closing of the FRP. The initiatives also served as signals as to the parameters within which the regime would tolerate contestation.

Perhaps the bluntest initiatives were new and systematic efforts to indoctrinate citizens with the regime's values. In 1934 the "History of the Turkish Revolution"—that is, the Kemalist revolution as interpreted by Kemalist elites—became a compulsory school subject. In 1937 the six principles that came to symbolize Kemalism (republicanism, secularism, nationalism, populism, statism, and revolutionism) were inserted into the constitution. Of this move prominent RPP leader Recep Peker said:

> This . . . will uplift all our citizens in their future existence with a spirit of wholeness and togetherness, and will be a firmer step toward national unity . . . citizens . . . will become a greater and more powerful, unshakable aggregate believing together in a common set of basic principles appropriate to the structure of the nation . . . Just as it is now the case that no-one inside this nation may work against the Republic which is guaranteed in our Constitution, in the future, any activity of internationalism which is the opposite of populism, of liberalism which is the opposite of étatism, clericalism which is the opposite of secularism, or reaction which is the opposite of revolutionism, all these will be banned. (Weiker 1973, 237)

In addition to laying down these explicit political-ideological markers, the regime engaged in broader efforts to shape Turks' self-perception and worldview. One such effort involved historical myth-making. In 1931 the regime created the Society for the Study of Turkish History and charged it with researching and propagating a new theory that Turks' historical roots ran much deeper than the Ottoman and Islamic eras. Instead, it asserted that ethnic Turks founded many of the ancient world's great civilizations, including the Sumerian and the Hittite. "The theory aimed to give Turks a sense of pride in their past and in their national identity . . . [i]t was one of the means whereby the Kemalist leadership tried to construct a new national identity and strong national cohesion" (Zürcher 1994, 199). This theory, too, became a compulsory course in schools.

A second broader effort was language reform. For centuries a linguistic gulf had divided literate Ottoman-Turkish elites from the common people. Relative to the latter, largely illiterate group, the former spoke and wrote a Turkish that was heavily inflected with Arabic and Persian words and grammatical constructs. Language reform initiatives in the 1930s aimed to "purify" Turkish by purging it of its Arabic and Persian influences. Weiker argues that the regime's goal was to "eliminate the great differences between spoken and written Turkish which retarded national unity" (1973, 232). Also, in much the same vein as the aforementioned historical myth-making, in 1935 the regime supported the propagation of the Sun-Language Theory, which held that all world languages had developed from a single primeval tongue that closely resembled Turkish and, therefore, that all languages had developed *through* Turkish.

In addition to spearheading these efforts to depolarize Turkish politics, the RPP also set out in the 1930s to "level the mobilizational playing field" between itself and its latent opposition. It took a first step in this direction when it suppressed a network of social institutions called the Turkish Hearths. The Hearths had promoted positivism and secularism among the population, ideals that did not run counter to RPP thinking. But the Hearths advocated pan-Turkish nationalism rather than a nationalism that corresponded to existing borders. Moreover, the Hearths were run by elites who were independent of the RPP; indeed, many of their leaders and branches reportedly had been tied to the FRP (Yetkin 1987, 117–18; Kabasakal 1991, 152–53; Üstel 1997, 338–39). The RPP perceived the Hearths as both an ideological and mobilizational threat. Announcing their closing, Kemal remarked that "there are some periods in the history of nations when all moral and material forces must be gathered together and made to work in the same direction to reach definite goals" (quoted in Weiker 1973, 171).

The RPP regime did not stop here, however. After the FRP episode, Kemal and his top lieutenants took a hard look at their party and concluded that it was in need of reforms that would bring the party closer to the people

(Kabasakal 1991). İsmet İnönü, a close confidant of Kemal's, admitted that the party "had lost touch with the people" (Kinross 1965, 518). The party reforms pursued by the RPP in the 1930s included overhauling and extending the party's organization and holding new, local-level elections for party branch administrators. Also, by the late 1930s, the RPP regime had finally managed to pacify the rebellious Kurdish-inhabited southeastern portion of the country (Kirişçi and Winrow 1997, 105). This allowed it to begin establishing a solid party presence there. Indeed, in 1946 the RPP announced it had finally succeeded in establishing branches in every Turkish district (Prather 1978, 88n7).

Perhaps the most significant RPP effort initiated in the 1930s, however, was the building of "People's Houses" (in larger towns and cities) and "People's Rooms" (in smaller towns and villages) across Turkey. These were community centers run by the RPP, which funneled the assets of the recently suppressed Turkish Hearths into the initiative. Their establishment seems in part to have been designed to further depolarize the Turkish political arena. According to Peker, the Houses' function would be to "bring Turks together in cultural activities, and heighten national unity" (quoted in Weiker 1973, 173). "The political goal of the Houses was to persuade as many people as possible in the countryside that Turkish nationalism was their new religion and Republicanism their modern political identity" (Karpat n.d., 69). The Houses sought to effect this persuasion through lectures and propaganda films.

However, the RPP built People's Houses and People's Rooms also for the purpose of reducing the mobilizational asymmetry that had characterized its confrontations with challenger parties. For RPP leaders, the community centers could help achieve this goal in two ways. First, they represented extensions of the party's organizational apparatus. Second, they were designed to improve the image of the RPP in the people's eyes and, in so doing, to attract increased mass support to the RPP. The People's Houses and Rooms sought to carry out this latter task by sponsoring a variety of activities. They offered reading, writing, and vocational skills classes to local communities. They also opened libraries, ran sports and cultural programs, offered social-work services, and attempted to find work for unemployed citizens. Indicative of the importance the RPP placed on increasing its connections to the masses, the RPP committed significant resources to the People's House initiative during the 1930s and 1940s: by 1945 it had built 438 People's Houses and 2,688 People's Rooms (Tunaya 1952, 597).

The Republican People's Party and the Democrat Party, 1946–1950

The manner in which the RPP regime navigated World War II touched off the third iteration of opposition party organizing in the Turkish Republic. In 1940, the RPP gave itself the authority to intervene in the economy as needed (including by confiscating citizens' property) to cope with war-induced disequilibria. In 1942 it passed a law designed to tax those who had profited from the war through speculation and black-market activities. This law was implemented in a harsh and arbitrary manner that shook citizens' confidence in government. In 1945, the government passed a land reform bill that provided for the distribution to peasants not only of state lands but also, under some circumstances, of portions of wealthy landowners' holdings. These laws elicited significant opposition among those who saw them as further instances of authoritarian central elites overstepping the acceptable boundaries of state intervention in the economy and society. RPP deputies with ties to landed interests had fought the land reform bill vehemently but in vain. The day after its passage, four RPP deputies (two of whom hailed from landowning families) proposed pluralizing internal party procedures. When their initiative came to naught, they founded the Democrat Party (DP) and began pushing for the establishment of competitive electoral politics in Turkey.

First established in January 1946, the DP grew extremely rapidly. As table 14 demonstrates, within six months the party had created branch offices in nearly two-thirds of Turkey's 63 provincial capitals and in nearly half of its 472 district seats. "In most provinces, district branches were created in all but the smallest and most remote towns shortly after the establishment of the provincial organization" (Prather 1978, 88). By the end of 1946 the opposition party had extended its presence to 55 provinces, and in 1947 established branches in most of the remaining provinces. "Within four years . . . [the Democrats] extended their organization to cities and towns in most provinces, founding many times the number of local branches that the RPP had founded in the preceding decades" (Rustow 1960, 409).

The DP was able to establish a grassroots organizational presence so rapidly because—like the Second Group, the PRP, and the FRP before it—it represented an alliance between disaffected central elites and peripheral elements. The party's two large-landowning founders notwithstanding, top DP leaders did not differ dramatically in social background or political or economic outlook from RPP elites (Mardin 1973, 185; Özbudun 1976, 50–52; Prather 1978, 148). Top government and cabinet posts under DP adminis-

TABLE 14. Pace of Democrat Party Organizing in Turkey, 1946

Date	DP Branches in Provincial Capitals	DP Branches in District Seats
March 1946	16	36
April 1946	26	75
June 1946	37	168
July 1946	41	200

SOURCES: March, April, and July data from Albayrak 1992, 184; June numbers from Prather 1978, 87.

trations disproportionately were held by central elites—that is, men with high levels of formal education who came from "official" occupational backgrounds in the bureaucracy, the military, and the school system (Frey 1965). These central DP elites had a party to build, however, and significant challenges accompanied this task. The DP's "four founders were able to lead very few other parliamentarians out of the ranks of the RPP, nor could they capture large blocks of the RPP organization" (Prather 1978, 42). As a strategy for growing the party, therefore, the DP chose to capitalize on longstanding peripheral resentment of the central government.

This strategy would succeed because many of those who lived in the countryside were politically predisposed against the ruling party. During the RPP's tenure in power, new resentments had compounded the periphery's historical antagonism toward the center. The agricultural sector had been squeezed to finance the rebuilding of the country after WWI and the independence war, which had damaged its infrastructure considerably (Mardin 1973, 183). The RPP regime had taxed and policed the countryside intensely, suppressed expressions of popular faith, and done little to improve rural living standards (Zürcher 1994, 215–16). On material, financial, and cultural grounds, then, many residents of the periphery resented the center. If it could be mobilized, the periphery harbored the votes the DP would need to topple RPP rule.

The DP mobilized the periphery in two ways. Ideologically, it packed its platform with stances designed to appeal to peripheral elements. The DP "seemed to put more emphasis on the satisfaction of local demands" (Frey 1965, 173) and advocated granting increased authority to local government. The DP backed landowners' interests by opposing land reform legislation. The party appealed to private sector merchants and industrialists by criticizing excessive state intervention in the economy. Finally, the DP promised peasants increased attention and services, as well as greater official toleration of and support for the private pursuit of religious faith.

The DP also mobilized the periphery organizationally, using politically sympathetic provincial elites and their local networks to elaborate the party's electoral base. Certain landowning and merchant elites in every province had supported the ruling RPP. Indeed, they were crucial partners of the ruling party's mainly bureaucratic, intellectual, and military cadres because they kept order in the countryside (Frey 1965, 219; Mardin 1973, 182; Rustow 1991, 16). However, when the RPP began to pass laws targeting property rights in the early 1940s, a large number of these provincial notables were alienated from the regime (Payaslıoğlu 1964, 423; Özbudun 1976, 46; Zürcher 1994, 216). These notables left the RPP and went over to the opposition, which was proposing to defend landed interests and private capital against state encroachment. Notables leaving the RPP coalition joined other prominent local families who had been drawn to the DP for reasons of policy preference and due to rivalries with (once) pro-RPP notables (Rustow 1991, 16).

These notables' provincial networks were crucial ingredients of the DP's eventual organizational and electoral success. Notables' links to voters in the countryside were in part economic. Villagers often depended on prominent landowners for crop marketing services (Karpat 1959, 112–13) as well as credit and social assistance (Mardin 1973, 183). They often turned to merchants for credit, medical assistance, and dispute resolution services (Prather 1978, 275–77). Notables were also linked politically to rural voters. To some extent their political influence derived from their economic and social roles in the lives of smaller producers and peasants. In addition, as chapter 3 demonstrated, local notables had long been intermediaries between the central state and its subjects—at first quite directly, and, later, through the operation of the local administrative council system. This relationship continued through the first half of the twentieth century. Karpat characterizes the wealthier landowners as "a semi-urbanized group who deal with the populations of both towns and villages, and exert political influence in both areas, as was seen in the political struggle after 1946" (1959, 113). Lewis tells us that peasants voted for the DP "under the guidance of their own rural leadership" (1968, 316).

Notables' links to local voters have been identified generally as resources prized by Turkish political parties seeking to build their local organizations (Payaslıoğlu 1964, 423). The DP was no exception.

> The Democrats wisely sought to reach followers in sizeable aggregates. Most of their potential supporters were to be found in readily identifiable groups—in small villages or extended families which could be arranged into larger units through the offices of lineage leaders, merchants, local notables, or others with ties into these groups. (Prather 1978, 302–3)

One way the DP built support, then, was by recruiting merchants and local notables to head up district and provincial party offices; when it did so, it gained the political support of the villagers those elites wielded influence over. Between 61 and 78 percent of the DP's provincial committee members came from economic backgrounds (that is, they were merchants and farmers), while 17 to 30 percent were professionals, and just 2 to 4 percent were in officialdom (Prather 1978, 158). In other words, provincial elites from traditional local notable backgrounds—that is, whose wealth derived from landowning, commerce, and industry—were the backbone of the DP's local organization.

The DP also built support by identifying locally influential and connected notable elites as candidates for parliament (Frey 1965, 173; Prather 1978, 76). Relative to RPP governments, when the DP took over in 1950, deputies under DP rule were less educated, less familiar with foreign languages, less often drawn from "official" occupations (the civil service, the military, and teaching/educational administration), more often drawn from the "professions" (law, medicine, and so on) and "economic" occupations (that is, commerce and agriculture), less disproportionately drawn from İstanbul, tending to hail from the "more locally oriented areas of Anatolia," and more often born in the province they represented (Frey 1965, 187). Of the transition from RPP- to DP-controlled parliaments, Frey concludes that "the deputies have changed from being primarily a national elite group, oriented toward the tutelary development of the country, to being primarily an assemblage of local politicians, oriented toward more immediate local and political advantages" (ibid., 196). Thus the DP amassed considerable political support by acquiring the votes of peripheral parliamentary candidates' rural clienteles.

Why did the RPP agree to compete in elections with its new and powerful rival? A key reason the RPP tolerated the DP was the fact that, by the late 1940s, Turkey's party system was significantly less polarized than it had been during the 1930 FRP opposition experiment. For the first time the RPP faced an opponent it trusted not to undermine the institutions it cherished. The RPP was not suspicious of the DP's top leaders and their policy preferences. DP leaders "were all Kemalists of long standing who espoused the same basic philosophy as their opponents with only a difference in emphasis" (Ahmad 1993, 103). The fact that DP founder Celâl Bayar was "trusted as someone who subscribed to the fundamental tenet of secularism, undoubtedly eased the acceptance of the existence of an opposition party by the Kemalist bureaucracy" (Zürcher 1994, 221). Though DP leaders opposed the extent of the state's intervention in the economy, "by 1946 it was no longer possible to make any convincing arguments that the anti-*étatists* were also politically 'reactionary'" (Weiker 1973, 274)—that is, individuals who would work to erode Turkey's secular and republican foundations.

DP leaders took pains to reassure the RPP about their intentions and positions. They knew that "it was necessary to convince at least the moderates in the People's Party that the new organization was led by people who were basically Kemalist and that a measure of toleration and freedom could be accorded to it" (Prather 1978, 151). According to Toker, Bayar secured Turkish president and RPP leader İsmet İnönü's approval of the DP's first program prior to publicizing it. That event included the following exchange.

> *İnönü:* Does it contain an article saying "we respect religious beliefs" the way the Progressive Republicans' did?
> *Bayar:* No sir. It states that secularism does not mean irreligion.
> *İnönü:* Never mind. Will you oppose the Village Institutes or the primary school campaign?
> *Bayar:* No.
> *İnönü:* Are there differences in foreign policy?
> *Bayar:* No.
> *İnönü:* In that case, okay. (quoted in Toker 1970, 112–13; translation mine)[12]

The DP's program explicitly accepted the RPP's six core political principles. In the run-up to the 1950 elections the DP "gave assurances that [a] change of government would not affect any specific social class or the regime and its principles" (Karpat 1959, 239–40). Moreover, as it organized, it was careful to screen out of its local activist pool any individuals who might have struck the RPP as politically reactionary (Prather 1978, 50).

Unlike the PRP and the FRP, the DP did not challenge the institutions that protected RPP elites' status as such: republicanism and secularism. Its core interests thus protected, the RPP could more easily accede to demands that it compete on a fair electoral playing field with the DP. The fact that the RPP stepped down from power when the DP won a parliamentary majority in the 1950 elections also demonstrates the extent of party system depolarization. The ruling party would have been much less likely to accept its defeat gracefully if it had felt that defeat meant its permanent banishment from the political elite. But a democratic, secular republic would guarantee it political voice as a parliamentary opposition as well as the ability to return to power in subsequent elections.

A second key reason for the RPP's willingness to compete with the DP was the fact that, by the late 1940s, Turkey's party system was significantly more mobilizationally symmetrical than it had been during the FRP and PRP interludes. Though between 1930 and 1946 the RPP had expended considerable effort to level the mobilizational "playing field" between itself and its latent opposition (by extending the party's organizational apparatus, establishing the People's Houses and Rooms, and so on), the record suggests that the ruling party still felt mobilizationally outclassed in the mid-1940s. For while the RPP agreed to compete with the DP in free and fair elections in 1950, it rigged Turkey's 1946 election (Prather 1978, 88). This was the first election in which the DP challenged the ruling party. It was also Turkey's first *direct* (single-stage) election, and originally it had been scheduled to take place in 1947. In the face of the DP's emergence and rapid growth, however, the RPP moved the election up so that the DP would not have time to organize completely and compete in all electoral districts. The ruling party evidently was not yet confident that it could hold its own in a fair poll.

Indeed, between 1946 and 1950 the RPP continued to work to achieve mobilizational parity with its opponent. Historically, the party's central committee had monopolized the process through which RPP parliamentary candidates were selected. In an attempt to enhance its candidates' popularity and potential for attracting mass support, the party now gave its local branches a larger say in designating candidates for parliament. In some cases, this led to the appointment of more locally born individuals as RPP candidates.[13] The RPP also deepened its organization across the Turkish countryside. Between 1946 and 1950 the RPP "opened more local branches than it had in the previous quarter-century" (Rustow 1966, 123). A passage from the report of the 1947 congress of the RPP's central Ankara district is similarly revealing.

> In 1946 the opposition succeeded in mobilizing and winning over citizens of every kind of opinion by utilizing all of their skills, including lies, slander, and

> misinformation. Today we are moving into a transitional phase wherein their success will be undone . . . Doubtless the RPP is indebted to these attacks for the fact that, in the last year and a half, its organizational strength has grown much greater than that which it had achieved prior. (CHP 1948, 13; translation mine)

Finally, the RPP also aggressively expanded the People's House network. In four years it added 40 Houses and 1,634 Rooms to the grid it had begun back in the 1930s (Tunaya 1952, 596–97).

In sum, in the two decades that intervened between the RPP-FRP confrontation and the RPP-DP confrontation, the ruling party made concrete progress in shrinking the yawning chasm that had existed between itself and its opponents where mobilizational capacity was concerned. By 1950 party leaders had good reason to feel more confident about the party's ability to do well in free elections, even against a well-organized opponent. Many in the party indeed believed that the RPP would win in 1950. The emergence of increased mobilizational symmetry in Turkey's two-party system, therefore, helps explain why the ruling party yielded to fair, competitive elections in 1950.

Conclusion

Center-periphery conflict continued to be a powerful force structuring two-party confrontation as an ongoing trend in the Turkish political community. Now, however, that conflict intersected with new, intracenter rifts, and the result added an important new dimension to two-party competition in Turkey. As Kemal and his party rose to power and proceeded with reforms, their power monopoly was repeatedly challenged. On four successive occasions, disaffected central elites founded opposition parties (the Second Group, the PRP, the FRP, and the DP). In each instance central elites teamed up with their peripheral counterparts to achieve joint goals. Central elites appealed to peripheral notable leaders on an ideological level, emphasizing one or more policy themes that had traditionally characterized the periphery's demands of the center. Peripheral elites in turn provided their central partners with organizational capacity and mass support.

Competitive electoral politics became consolidated in the Turkish case due to two developments in the party system. First, with each successive instance of opposition organizing, the party protagonists became progressively less polarized. Kemal suspected that PRP leaders were allegiant neither to the republic nor to its secular public sphere. When the RPP became convinced that individuals opposed to these principles were infiltrating the FRP's ranks, the latter was shut down as well. In both instances, opposition parties threatened core institutions that guaranteed RPP members' status as elites over the long term. The DP, by contrast, did not threaten these institutions. It argued with the RPP over the extent to which government should be centralized, the state should intervene in the economy, and economic policy should target the agricultural sector. Still, in part because these policy debates did not endanger the core infrastructure of RPP elites' status, the RPP acceded to fair electoral competition with the DP and then turned power over to it when the former lost the 1950 election.

Second, Turkey's two-party system was becoming more mobilizationally symmetrical. The ruling RPP began the interim transitional period substantially handicapped relative to its opponents where organization and mass support were concerned. Whereas peripheral elite actors could draw on dense networks of association as well as close ties to the masses in order to build popular opposition parties, the Turkish center historically had lacked a firm presence in the countryside. The ruling RPP was cognizant of this weakness and repressed the PRP and FRP when these parties looked to be enjoying enormous success in their mobilizational efforts. Especially during the 1930s and 1940s, the RPP worked to remedy this handicap by consolidating its control over Turkey's southeast, by dramatically fleshing out its organizational apparatus in Turkey's provinces, counties, districts, and subdistricts, and by building thousands of People's Houses and People's Rooms. With the 1950 elections looming, the RPP had reason to believe that it would be able to hold its own against the DP in mobilizing voter support. This facilitated the RPP's decision to allow a free and fair election to go forward.

Those who are familiar with this case will note, aptly, that the depolarization and increased mobilizational symmetry that characterized Turkey's party system at the end of the interim transitional period were not the only factors rendering the 1950 poll free and fair. International factors strongly affected this outcome as well. In the late 1940s Turkey was fielding expansionist threats from the Soviet Union and wished to align itself with the West in the emerging Cold War scenario. Many therefore argue that RPP leaders presided over political pluralization in the belief that doing so would help Turkey acquire the moral and material support of the Western alliance.

Indeed, the details and chronology of Turkish democratization suggest that the international environment played a pivotal role in driving political pluralization in 1950. Yet international context cannot stand alone as a complete account of the founding of a competitive regime in Turkey at that time. Depolarization and increased mobilizational symmetry in the party system dramatically reduced the threat to the RPP posed by the advent of free and fair electoral competition. This made it easier for RPP elites to choose to showcase Turkey to the West as a like-principled, plural polity by tolerating the DP. In addition, international context fails to explain fully the RPP's willingness to step down from power when it lost the 1950 election. That argument implies that the RPP would have yielded to its opposition regardless of the latter's ideological stripes. Yet the RPP had spent two decades in power implementing Atatürk's westernizing, secularizing political agenda—a legacy it cared fiercely about defending. Had the DP not been led by elites with credible secular credentials who assured the RPP that Kemal's reforms would be preserved in the event of a DP victory, the transition very well might not have gone forward when the DP won the 1950 election. Basic policy compatibility between the parties arguably was at least as pivotal to the transfer of power as international circumstances were.

Readers also will observe that the Turkish case diverges from the multiparty cases considered in chapter 5 in a key respect other than the fact that its party system at the end of the interim transitional period was characterized by mobilizational symmetry and a lack of policy polarization. In the five cases of multiparty systems giving way to authoritarian rule, when faced with antidemocratic defections on the part of conservative status-quo parties, challenger parties also defected from democratic rules, turning to alternative arenas in the pursuit of power. This set in motion vicious cycles that hollowed out democratic forms and beckoned the eventual establishment of authoritarian rule. The same did not occur in Turkey. When Kemal and his allies repressed the Second Group, the PRP, and the FRP, the political elites and social forces that were the motors behind these challenger parties did not turn to the army, the streets, and so on for political ammunition. Instead, they laid low.

They did so for a number of reasons, not the least of which were the draconian measures taken by the RPP to silence its opposition—especially in the aftermath of the PRP interlude. In addition, comparable alternative arenas to those used by challenger parties in the breakdown cases were not available in Turkey. First, there was no monarch to turn to; Kemal had eradicated the sultanate when he abolished the Ottoman Empire. Second, Kemal and the RPP kept close watch over the army, seeking to deny opponents the ability to politicize it against their reformist regime. The army also was one of the pillars of the political "center" in Turkey; as such, it was naturally associated with rather than critical of Kemalist reforms (Karpat 1970, 1659) and would have loomed as an unreceptive target for peripheral lobbying efforts. Third, Turkey in the 1920s and 1930s was not as modernized as were the other five cases, wherein the vicious cycles that destroyed nascent democratic bargains began in the 1940s and 1950s. Still a predominantly rural country, Turkey possessed neither a large student population nor large urban underclasses; in other words, the "street" was not yet a political arena available for use to challenger parties.

This difference from the other cases is crucial because it bought the Turkish political community important time during which nascent democratic institutions could be salvaged. Only the RPP party was sullying democratic norms. Had challenger parties done so as well, competitive politics likely would not have triumphed in Turkey. Yet this difference was not determinative as to the shape of Turkey's founding regime. That challenger parties did not defect from democratic norms did not ensure that competitive politics would be the endpoint of the trajectory of Turkish politics during the interim transitional period. Instead, key changes in the characteristics of Turkey's party system—the fact that it became significantly less polarized and the fact that it became significantly more mobilizationally symmetrical—facilitated the establishment of a competitive founding regime there. These were the pivotal explanatory variables that accounted for authoritarian founding regimes in the multiparty breakdown cases, rendering the juxtaposition of the breakdowns to the Turkish case a revealing analytical exercise.

CONCLUSION

The Arguments in Middle East and Comparative Perspective

*This study has sought to improve our understanding of the reasons why most contempo*rary Middle East states evolved authoritarian regimes in the postimperial period and why Turkey is a notable exception to this rule. It has emphasized the pivotal role played by party actors in the regime-formation processes that unfolded in ten countries in the region as political elites navigated critical historical junctures when old rules had crumbled and new rules were open to be shaped. The analysis combines attention to party system characteristics with an understanding of democratic regimes as political-institutional bargains that are viable only if no relevant actor wishes to defect. The book asserts that regime outcomes in the region can be understood most systematically not as the ineluctable result of cultural attributes, levels of modernization, or class configurations, but instead as the relatively more contingent product of the features of indigenous party system characteristics at a specific point in time.

In Tunisia, South Yemen, and Algeria, because single preponderant parties dominated postindependence politics, there was no bargaining over the rules of the game. No other actors possessed sufficient stature to force nationalist parties to the bargaining table. The latter simply did as they pleased, and the result was immediate authoritarian rule. In Iran, Iraq, Jordan, Syria, and Egypt, authoritarian regimes also took root, but only after interim transitional periods had unfolded. While all five countries had an opportunity to build upon fledgling competitive institutions, polarization and mobilizational asymmetry in their party systems drove parties to defect from democratic arrangements, clearing the way for the establishment of dictatorship. During Turkey's interim transitional period, the party system became decreasingly polarized and increasingly mobilizationally symmetrical over time. The ruling RPP defected from pluralizing experiments in 1924 and 1930 because its opponents' platforms and/or support base threatened its ability to maintain its elite status. By the late 1940s, however, the opposition had moderated its platform and the ruling RPP had much improved its grassroots organizational presence. These developments in large part facilitated the inauguration of competitive politics in Turkey beginning in 1950.

Ultimately, the claims advanced here are probabilistic rather than deterministic. The study argues on empirical and theoretical grounds that party system polarization and mobilizational asymmetry each will independently lower the probability that a given nascent democratic bargain will survive, because these dynamics will shape the calculations of those actors whose acquiescence is crucial if democracy is to be viable. As these are not the only variables that bear on possibilities for democracy, not all countries with fledgling competitive institutions and troubled party systems will fail to settle on competitive politics. At the same time, polarization and mobilizational asymmetry are central variables that, holding constant all other pertinent factors (such as the external environment, wealth levels in society, and political culture), should render the survival of nascent democratic bargains problematic.

In addition to demonstrating the relevance of party system characteristics for founding regime outcomes in the Middle East, the book also explored the determinants of several key party system characteristics themselves. This analysis produced evidence for the causal relevance of explanatory factors that are quite familiar to comparativists who ponder party number questions. That is, electoral rules and the extent and type of societal cleavages formed part of the explanation for the shape of party systems in the six multiparty cases considered here (Iran, Iraq, Jordan, Syria, Egypt, and Turkey). However, the study also brought to light the crucial role that outside actors played in structuring regional party systems. The impact of imperial powers' policies on the sociopolitical standing of traditional elites, and imperialists' responses to traditional elites' demands for independence, had much to do with the number of parties that occupied national political stages at independence. Finally, the book highlighted the importance of preexisting social capital for party-building enterprises. This dynamic appeared most prominently in the Turkish case, which evolved a two-party system not only due to majoritarianism and center-periphery conflict, but also due to crucial elite networks that allowed the periphery to develop a unified rather than a fragmented response to the overbearing center.

Turkish Exceptionalism Revisited

Turkey is exceptional in the Middle East because it was the only state in the region to emerge in the postimperial era having developed competitive political institutions—institutions that have survived to the present day. This is the observation that drives the premise of this study. The Introduction acknowledged, however, that the extent of Turkish exceptionalism was not limited to the nature of its founding regime. Prior to the critical independence juncture, Turkey differed from much of the Middle East in other ways as well. It was never colonized. It had constituted the core rather than a peripheral region of the Ottoman Empire. It would have scored higher on a "stateness" scale than many of its neighbors. Many of the ways in which Turkey diverged from its neighbors before the interim transitional periods this study focuses on *do* bear on the fact that a competitive founding regime emerged there. To date, however, no one has linked these traits in a systematic, causal fashion to the emergence of competitive politics. This study facilitates, and now turns to, this important task.

Characteristics that made Turkey unique in the region prior to the start of founding regime formation processes—in particular, the fact that Turkey escaped Western imperial domination—shaped the features of Turkey's postindependence party system in important respects. Those, in turn, nurtured the emergence of a competitive electoral regime. Let us first consider the ways in which Turkey's uniqueness was relevant to the "number of parties" variable. Single preponderant parties developed in those countries wherein imperial powers' policies weakened indigenous traditional elites, imperial powers were intransigent in the face of traditional elites' demands for independence, and, hence, second-generation elites inclined to mass mobilize took over the mantle of nationalist movements. Those preponderant parties were then able to immediately install authoritarian rule at independence. The fact that Turkey escaped imperial domination seems to have precluded the emergence there of a single preponderant party, thus closing off this route to dictatorship.

The other regional route to dictatorship originated in polarized, mobilizationally asymmetrical party systems containing four or more parties.

The fact that Turkey had just two parties facilitated depolarization and, thus, political pluralization. Chapter 3 argued that Turkey's two-party structure was, in part, the product of the manner in which center-periphery conflict unfolded—with the center *sustaining* its attempts at gaining increased control over the periphery over a significant period of time. This center-periphery conflict led to the building of the provincial administrative council system, creating elite networks in the countryside that facilitated collective action among peripheral elites who sought to challenge the center. These institutions—and the social capital they produced—took decades to establish. The fact that the Turkish political community escaped imperial domination meant that there was time for these processes to come to fruition, free from external interference. In this respect, the lack of a colonial past helped Turkey shape a two-party system, which in turn was conducive to political pluralization.

The lack of a colonial past also worked to shield Turkey from important sources of polarization that were present in the multiparty breakdown cases. While the Ottomans certainly had their share of conflicts with the West, the fact that neither France nor Britain ever took over direct control of the Turkish political community's fate made for a comparatively smooth relationship between Turks and the West. By contrast, direct Western domination in Iraq, Jordan, Egypt, and Syria made for a much rockier relationship with the West—indeed, one that polarized those communities. In these countries, overlapping generational and socioeconomic cleavages developed wherein older traditional indigenous elites who were co-opted by and who cooperated with the imperial powers became objects of scorn to younger, less well-off, radicalizing sectors of the population. The latter were increasingly resentful of the Western presence and formed the core of the challenger parties, while the former formed the core of the conservative status-quo parties. By virtue of the fact that Turkey escaped direct colonial control, it was spared this important potential source of party system polarization.

The lack of a colonial past also insulated Turkey's party system from the kinds and levels of polarization that were present in the multiparty breakdown cases because it meant that Turkey's interim transitional period commenced in a different, less polarizing time period with respect to world-historical developments. Turkey became an independent state in 1923. Decolonization processes in the multiparty breakdown cases, however, did not take place until the 1930s (in Iraq and Egypt) and 1940s (in Jordan and Syria). At around the same time, two major international conflicts began brewing that would polarize party systems in the latter four multiparty cases.

First, in the British-controlled Palestine Mandate, communal tensions between Jews immigrating from Europe and the resident Palestinian Arab population turned increasingly violent in the 1930s and 1940s. The drama and tragedy of Palestine accentuated the cleavage between conservative, pro-West parties and radical, anti-West parties in the multiparty breakdown cases. Britain played a key role in facilitating Jewish immigration into Palestine. Radical, anti-West elements in neighboring Middle East countries equated British actions with continued Western imperialism and intrusion in the region. For many of the challenger parties in the multiparty breakdown cases, then, Palestine was a cause célèbre. On the other hand, conservative status-quo party elites—by virtue of their self-interested ties to Western powers—tended to take a more moderate line on Palestine. The Palestine conflict thus exacerbated party system polarization, especially in Iraq, Jordan, and Egypt. The conflict did not, however, have the same impact in Turkey, which commenced its interim transitional period in 1923, well before violence erupted in Palestine.[1]

The second major international conflict that polarized party systems in the multiparty breakdown cases was the Cold War, which took shape in the late 1940s. For these political communities that already were divided along a pro- versus anti-West cleavage—in part due to colonial legacies and in part due to the Palestine conflict—the Cold War not surprisingly deepened divides. Conservative status-quo party elites tended to seek to align with the West while challenger parties looked to the Soviet Union for inspiration and for financial backing. Furthermore, Cold War ideological competition between capitalism and rival, radically redistributive political-economic models inspired the clash of the very disparate economic policy agendas that were proposed by conservative status-quo parties on the one hand, and by their socialist and communist party challengers on the other. Turkey was insulated from this potential source of polarization as well. Beginning its interim transitional period in the early 1920s, Turkey's party system was well along the road to depolarization by the time the Cold War shook the rest of the Middle East.

In several important respects, then, the fact that Turkey escaped the fate of nearly all its Middle East neighbors by avoiding formal subjugation to a Western European power helped make possible the development of a postindependence party system that would be auspicious for the eventual establishment of a competitive founding regime there. It would be a mistake, however, to overstate the explanatory import of this aspect of Turkish "exceptionalism" for founding regime outcomes. After all, Iran also never fell under formal, direct foreign control. As occurred in the late-nineteenth-century Ottoman Empire, the dynamics of domestic politics in early-twentieth-century Iran led to the creation of a national parliament, which in turn encouraged multiparty politics. Yet Iran's party system developed very differently from Turkey's—for at least two reasons unrelated to lack of a formal imperial interlude.

As noted at the end of chapter 3, center-periphery conflict played out quite differently in Iran than it did in Turkey. Unable to make substantial inroads in terms of establishing an authoritative presence in the periphery, the center threw up its hands and resorted to divide-and-rule tactics. Nothing even remotely like the set of tiered, territory-wide administrative council institutions developed by the Ottomans took root in Iran that might have rendered its outlying areas more politically cohesive. Additionally, Iran's population was considerably more fragmented and heterogeneous than Turkey's, including along ethnic, linguistic, and tribal lines. Iran's differences in these respects encouraged a proliferation of political groupings rather than a two-party system. This comparison suggests that key aspects of state-society relations in the Turkish political community (that is, the relative balance of power between center and periphery, and the relative homogeneity of Turkish society) were as important for shaping its postindependence party system—if not more so—than was the fact that it escaped imperial domination.

A final question that must be dealt with here concerns the role that culture and ideas might have played in the regime-formation processes explored in this study. Those who emphasize Turkey's exceptionalism prior to the playing out of these processes aptly note that, physically as well as philosophically, Turkey stood closer to early democratic experiments in Western Europe than did its regional neighbors. Indeed, many in the Turkish elite began to study European languages and visit European capitals during the nineteenth century. Ideas about the virtues of parliamentary democracy without a doubt were circulating among late Ottoman and early republican Turkish elites in ways that were not replicated in the wider Middle East. In addition, Mustafa Kemal Atatürk both admired the West and was determined to remake Turkey primarily along Western lines. Many will wonder, therefore, whether this fact is sufficient to explain Turkey's regional exceptionalism where founding regime type is concerned.

Without negating the causal importance of cultural and ideational factors, the evidence marshaled in this study strongly suggests that Turkey's penchant for the West is insufficient to explain the emergence of competitive politics there. Indeed, it is difficult to see how this facilitated progress toward political pluralization in the 1920s, 1930s, and 1940s except through the most general and diffuse of mechanisms. Certainly, many of the elites who ushered the Turkish political community into the nineteenth and twentieth centuries admired the West, looked to the West for political models to follow, and were open to the ideas and values of Western political discourse. Moreover, these facts surely contributed in 1950 to the successful completion of the historic, peaceful transfer of power from the long-ruling Republican People's Party to its Democrat Party challenger. Both sides could take pride in the moment, and the losers could derive some solace from the fact that their acceptance of defeat indeed put Turkey more on a political par with Western Europe than it had ever been before.

But the evidence presented in chapter 6 demonstrates that these cultural proclivities did not ensure that Turkey would develop competitive politics. After all, who was defecting from competitive electoral norms during Turkey's interim transitional period? Ruling Republican People's Party elites were the culprits here, and these were the very elites who had studied in the West, admired so much about the West, and sought to model Turkey after the West. Peripheral elites generally were less cosmopolitan and less knowledgeable of Western languages than RPP elites were. Were culture to be causally critical to the puzzle pondered here, one would expect that RPP elites would have been the better democrats during the years in which Turks were settling on a postindependence founding regime. This was not the case, however. The RPP repeatedly defected from would-be competitive electoral bargains because polarization and mobilizational asymmetry in the party system threatened its core interests and values. In other words, the party system characteristics highlighted in this study remain central to a satisfactory explanation of the emergence of competitive politics in Turkey.

Reflections on Contemporary U.S. Policy in the Region

Though the focus of this study is historical, its findings suggest important lessons and cautions for U.S. policymakers. Since September 11, 2001, U.S. policy toward the Middle East has shifted both rhetorically and in practice from one that tolerated dictatorships to one that explicitly promotes democratization, both directly (as in Iraq and Afghanistan) and indirectly (as with diplomatic pressures put on the Palestinian Authority and Egypt in recent years). The Bush administration's conviction that dictatorship breeds terrorism has driven this shift, and substantial American financial and human resources have been committed to the effort. While the administration's public pronouncements insist that the goal of a democratic Middle East is achievable via its interventions, the arguments of this book suggest at least two crucial grounds for concern that this confidence may be misplaced.

First, the scope of the challenge is immense. This book conceives of democracy as a bargain that can survive only if all important political actors agree to play by its rules. One key determinant of whether or not actors will do so is the extent to which party systems are polarized—that is, whether they include parties whose policy platforms threaten the ability of other party leaders to maintain their elite status. Defined this way, polarization is a serious problem in the region. The problem is perhaps most visible in Iraq, where a largely Sunni insurgency is reacting in part to that community's concern that democratic rules will institutionalize Shi'ite political hegemony—a privilege Sunnis had enjoyed during the Ba'thist era. The problem arises in a second respect to the extent that secular Iraqis fear that Shi'ite hegemony will ultimately yield a regime that is Islamist in complexion. Conflict of this type is endemic in the region, for nearly everywhere the most vocal, organized political forces opposing entrenched authoritarian regimes are Islamist in nature. These realities suggest that immense obstacles will have to be overcome if the United States is to achieve its stated policy of democratizing the region.

Second, it is quite possible that the United States' goals are unrealistic given an important tension in U.S. policy that is not widely recognized in the public discourse on this issue. On the one hand, U.S. policymakers are clearly cognizant of the dangers of polarization for democracy's prospects. The administration has promoted inclusive interim governance arrangements designed to reassure rival Iraqi elites that their interests and futures will not be destroyed by democracy. For instance, the constraint that a final Iraqi constitution cannot be ratified if it fails to obtain majority support in three or more provinces is meant to signal Sunnis—who are a majority in three provinces—that their interests and preferences will have to be taken into account by Iraq's emerging democratic processes. The hope is that this and other gestures will procure Sunnis' allegiance to nascent democratic norms.

On the other hand, the United States itself is a polarizing force in the Middle East. This problem is particularly evident in two arenas: Iraq and the Arab-Israeli conflict. Western imperial domination over Iraq, Jordan,

Egypt, and Syria worked to polarize those communities such that nascent democratic norms unraveled during interim transitional periods. This dynamic pitted elites who chose to cooperate with the imperial powers against elites who were incensed at the Western intrusion. Similar processes are at work today in Iraq because the U.S. invasion and occupation have forced its citizens to choose sides. While a great many have chosen—for whatever reason—to work with or for U.S. officials to further the project of building a new, democratic Iraq, these individuals have incurred the wrath of those Iraqis who advocate a policy of non-engagement with the United States. Assassinations of cabinet officials and repeated attacks on Iraqis enlisting in the army and security forces are the most extreme manifestations of this divide. The tension embedded in U.S. policy, therefore, is that it is seeking in Iraq to build institutions that cannot survive unless politics depolarizes at the same time that, arguably, its very presence on the ground is raising polarization levels.

This problem is made all the more acute by the legacy of a half-century of previous U.S. policy decisions toward the region that have earned it the resentment of many Middle Easterners. Its support of regional dictatorships that dealt harshly with domestic dissidents has generated substantial anti-U.S. sentiment. So too did the U.S.-led sanctions imposed on Iraq during the decade following the first Gulf War. Perhaps most inflammatory, however, has been the United States' stance vis-à-vis the Arab-Israeli conflict. This conflict, which already in the 1930s and 1940s was a source of domestic political polarization in Middle Eastern states, has continued to fester as a political irritant for decades—decades that have only intensified emotions given that they have seen multiple wars and the four-decade-long Israeli occupation of the West Bank and Gaza Strip. The United States has long been perceived by Arab states as sharply biased toward the Israeli position. This has polarized domestic politics, especially in states such as Egypt and Jordan, whose regimes have chosen to moderate their stance toward Israel out of a desire to curry U.S. favor. Such decisions distance regimes and the elites associated with them from general public opinion. Perceptions of U.S. bias also fan the flames of anti-American sentiment in the region, a fact that renders the U.S. presence in Iraq all the more polarizing.

It is not at all clear, therefore, that U.S. policy can succeed in the region. The sheer magnitude of the challenge, together with the fact that the U.S. carries important baggage with it as it attempts to intervene in regional political dynamics and promote democratization, suggest that public concerns over current strategy and resource commitments to the region are well founded. They also tell a cautionary tale should this or any future administration entertain the possibility of further democratizing interventions in the region.

Contextualizing Theories of Middle East Authoritarianism

Where the founding of dictatorship is concerned, this study is instructive because it puts certain arguments about Middle East authoritarianism into important context. Many have asserted, for instance, that regimes in the region are authoritarian because states have successfully availed themselves of significant oil and foreign aid revenues. These revenues allow regimes to "purchase" domestic political peace while releasing them from having to tax their citizens, thereby cutting off the "no taxation without representation" mechanism that allegedly triggers demands for accountable rule (Luciani 1987).

While not unproblematic, this rentier hypothesis is in many respects intuitively plausible.[2] In light of the regime-formation processes described in this study, however, it stands at best as an incomplete explanation for Middle East authoritarianism. After all, the political impact of state coffer-filling rents should depend on the prior distribution of political power across societal groups. For example, in the preponderant single party cases, rentier theory helps explain how ruling parties maintained their hegemony once they came to control postcolonial states. The Algerian state, for example, has profited handsomely from the exploitation of its considerable natural gas and oil reserves; those profits have bolstered FLN rule. Yet the theory can tell us little about how and why the FLN rose to a hegemonic position in the first place—something this study has sought to explain.

Similarly, in the multiparty breakdown cases, rentier theory tells us little about why incipient democratic institutions foundered and how authoritarian rule emerged. It does, however, illuminate how those who held power at the close of interim transitional periods maintained their authoritarian rule. For example, the Iranian oil industry was not yet nationalized in 1953 when the Shah's authoritarian rule commenced. Oil revenues accruing to the state were modest during the interim transitional period (1941–1953) as Iran's polarized, mobilizationally asymmetrical party system set that nation on a course for authoritarian rule. After 1953, the Shah used U.S. financial assistance and increasing oil revenues to support his regime. If the party system had been less polarized and more mobilizationally symmetrical, and if parties had been able to cooperate to curb the Shah's power and consolidate parliamentary rule (as it seemed they might in 1944), the increasing oil revenues that accrued in later years might have helped consolidate fledgling democratic institutions by increasing the size of the political "pie."

The larger point is that the rentier income variable, which is alleged to explain Middle East authoritarianism, does not become causally relevant until the founding regime-formation processes this study has focused on have come to an end. At that point, rentier income helps explain how founding regimes maintained themselves, but it cannot tell us why these regimes were competitive or authoritarian in the first place. The same liabilities characterize the argument that the towering of strong, powerful, interventionist states over weak civil societies facilitates authoritarian rule in the region. Sivan dates the origins of this state-society imbalance to the mid-nineteenth century and implies that it worsened in the twentieth century (1997). It is true that authoritarian regime "founders" deployed resources (rents included) in ways that strengthened their states and weakened their societies. But this perspective cannot illuminate the reasons why and the processes through which contemporary authoritarian regimes were founded in the first place, giving those in power political carte blanche to (further) weaken society relative to the state.

In the end, assertions linking rentier income and/or dysfunctional state-society relations to Middle East authoritarianism are arguments about the maintenance rather than the creation of authoritarian regimes. As such, they are important and relevant, especially for questions concerning prospects for future transitions in the region. But because they black-box the agents and processes through which such authoritarian regimes were established in the first place, these accounts and arguments are incomplete. They obscure important variations in the paths countries traveled to authoritarian rule; and they conceal important explanatory variables underlying those paths, variables this study has highlighted.

The Argument in Comparative Theoretical Perspective: Parties, Class, and Agency

At the same time that this study sheds light on the emergence of competitive politics in Turkey and on the establishment of authoritarian regimes in much of the rest of the Middle East, its research design and findings suggest some important lessons with respect to the broader comparative enterprise of theorizing regime formation processes. In terms of the analytical approaches that dominate work in this field, the Introduction noted that political culture and modernization theory both are correlational constructs; neither can specify the relevant actors whose decisions and behavior actually produce regime configurations. Yet the ten cases analyzed here show regime configurations to be the product of struggles among concrete, purposive political actors over what the "rules of the game" will be at given critical junctures. Political culture and modernization theory therefore do not appear to be the most useful primary methods with which to approach comparative regime formation and regime type questions.

The third approach, class structure, does not share this liability that agents are not specified and explicitly theorized. Scholars who work in this tradition identify social classes as the pivotal agents that shape political systems. Perhaps it is due in part to the fact that they speak convincingly to agency issues that Barrington Moore's and Rueschemeyer, Stephens, and Stephens' books are enduring, important works in comparative politics. Indeed, the class approach is the most potent rival to that taken in this study, which focuses instead on political parties as the pivotal agents shaping outcomes, and which investigates party-building processes and party system characteristics to explain regime type. Yet for world-historical time periods in which political parties exist, party system characteristics are a crucial complement to class structure considerations when analyzing regime formation processes.

This claim may be substantiated in part by noting important parallels between this study's insights and those revealed by the debate about whether class structure or party system characteristics better explain regime outcomes in interwar Europe. Here scholars ask why most of about a dozen newly democratic European regimes survived this turbulent time, while a handful broke down into authoritarian rule. This puzzle mirrors the portion of this study that asks why, of the six countries that began postindependence interim transitional periods with parliaments, elections, and plural party systems, only Turkey established a competitive regime. The situation of Europe's young democracies in the period following WWI resembled that of the multiparty cases considered in this study. In interwar Europe, democratic institutions were relatively new, the international community provided little support for democracy, communism and fascism were powerful currents, and socioeconomic conditions were not sufficiently positive to guarantee democratic durability (Ertman 1998, 476–77). Ertman's judgment is that "Western Europe's first-wave democracies were highly susceptible to breakdown." As chapter 5 demonstrated, much the same can be said for the Middle East's fledgling parliamentary systems.

Rueschemeyer, Stephens, and Stephens (RSS) (1992) believe that class is the analytic key to sorting out which democracies survived and which ones broke down. They assume that landlords will be democracy's enemies, that workers will be its friends, and that the bourgeoisie will be ambivalent. They want to argue that, because workers have the most to gain from full-suffrage democracy, working classes were by and large responsible for democratic breakthroughs. Democratic breakdown occurred in those few countries wherein state/landlord/bourgeois alliances prevented the working class from doing its democratizing work. But RSS must admit that a wide array of class configurations brought democracy into being. Where workers were in the forefront of democratizing movements, they needed allies from elsewhere in society. In other cases, other social classes such as the urban middle class or the small peasantry took the lead in pushing for democracy, "with the working class playing only a supportive role" (RSS 1992, 141). Thus, very little in the way of generalizable theoretical lessons results from using class as the main analytic tool of explanation. Indeed, RSS employ a stable of additional variables (including civil society, state structure, and transnational structures of power) in tandem with class logic to explain variation in their cases.

At the same time, RSS provide quite a bit of evidence for the causal importance of party system characteristics for interwar European regime outcomes. They note the crucial role of parties as "mediators" between class interests and political outcomes.[3] In addition, their case discussions feature support for the claim that levels of polarization in party systems shaped regime outcomes. RSS recognize this theme and caution readers that polarization is *not* a decisive variable, pointing out that Sweden and Norway democratized despite high levels of polarization (142).[4] Yet RSS make another strong statement about the importance of party system characteristics—this time hinting at the importance of mobilizational asymmetry and the concerns of conservative parties—when they write that

> once democracy was installed, the party system became crucial for protecting the interests of the dominant classes and thus keeping them from pursuing authoritarian alternatives. Democracy could be consolidated only where there were two or more strong competing political parties at least one of which effectively protected dominant class interests. (1992, 9)

Similarly, Ertman argues that democracy survived in those interwar European countries where the status-quo parties felt secure in their ability to muster enough electoral support to maintain a parliamentary presence sufficient for defending their interests. By contrast, democratic rule broke down in Germany, Italy, Portugal, and Spain because parties representing conservative elements were nonexistent, weak, or fragmented. When strong leftist parties emerged (and politics became polarized) in these countries, conservatives doubted their ability to protect their interests in a competitive electoral arena and threw their support behind initiatives to install authoritarian regimes capable of quelling the threat from the left. Ertman further argues that conservative parties' weakness in these cases stemmed from organizational handicaps. Conservative parties either were linked only marginally to voluntary associations or were built on patron-client ties, while left parties were strongly linked to voluntary associations (for example, unions and youth groups), giving the latter an important organizational and electoral advantage.

In other words, both RSS and Ertman find that party system characteristics were crucial to the regime trajectories of newly democratic interwar European countries. Their works suggest that high levels of polarization in party systems threaten the survival of nascent competitive politics, as does this study. In addition, both emphasize the centrality of conservative, status-quo parties' perceived ability to defend their interests in elections and parliaments to the viability of new democratic arrangements. In much the same vein, this study finds that nascent competitive politics could not be strengthened and consolidated in countries where party systems were characterized by mobilizational asymmetry, that is, where status-quo parties felt that challenger parties would outpoll them because of their superior ability to amass electoral support through both ideological and organizational means. In the Middle East as well as in interwar Europe, then, party system characteristics seem to furnish a more robust and parsimonious account of regime trajectories than do class-based analyses. The balance of this chapter offers some concluding theoretical reflections as to why this might be the case.

One of the most compelling claims of comparative politics work in the class analysis tradition is the Marxist conviction that, when it comes to politics and political behavior, people are motivated in large part by material interest. It would seem to be even more valid to assert that people's political activities will be directed primarily by economic interest during critical historical junctures when a community is reformulating the rules of the political game. To the extent that such rules strongly influence the distribution of societal resources over the long term, material concerns are likely to be at the forefront of actors' calculations and behavior in a regime-founding context.

Indeed, much of the empirical material presented in this study supports the assertion that material interest drives politics to a significant extent. In the multiparty breakdown cases, a key dimension of the confrontation between conservative parties and their challenger party opponents was a clash of diametrically opposed economic policy agendas. The former favored the preservation of a status quo that served their material interests well, while the latter advocated radical revisions of the political-economic order that would have redistributed resources away from traditional elites and toward the masses. Similarly, center-periphery conflict in the Turkish political community turned in large part on divergent political-economic visions. Central elites sought to augment the state's control over the national economy to funnel resources toward reform initiatives that they favored, while peripheral elites fought to limit the state's economic role, advocating instead a more laissez-faire approach that furthered their economic interests. In the single preponderant party cases, it was the class backgrounds and interests of second-generation elites that predisposed them toward both mass mobilization and the creation of authoritarian one-party systems after independence.

The stuff of politics is in large part a struggle over material wealth and the parameters within which citizens can access it. Yet it does not follow that class actors should be the only agents that are privileged in investigations of regime formation processes. As the Introduction pointed out, classes are often divided. The multiparty breakdown cases discussed in chapter 5 illustrate the possibility of divided classes. In Iraq, Jordan, Syria, and especially Egypt, conservative status-quo elites acted not "as one" but rather through two or more political parties, as well as through independent parliamentarians. Egypt's and Syria's conservatives competed more than they cooperated with one another, ultimately undermining conservatives' political interests. The assumption that one or another class in society will act in concert for a given political objective due to shared material circumstances thus is problematic. The fact that classes can be divided and vulnerable to internecine struggles undermines efforts to theorize regime formation on the basis of assumptions about classes' preferences and anticipated political behavior.

A second, related reason that class actors should not necessarily be privileged agents in regime formation research is that it is wrong to assume that the objective existence of a given social class will necessarily result in collective action in the political realm by that class. Katznelson criticizes many works of class analysis because they "conflate class structures, world views, and organizational activities as if the first *necessarily* entails the others" (1986, 7). He counters that "people sharing motivational constructs . . . may or may not act collectively to transform disposition to behavior" (19). The Iranian multiparty breakdown story serves as a striking case in point. There, conservative elites failed to organize into party form at all. This had important political consequences, for it drove them to defect from democratic rules when confronted by popular, well-organized challenger parties. The fact that classes cannot be counted on to organize politically for the pursuit of common goals also makes efforts to theorize regime formation exclusively from a class perspective problematic.

A third problem with anchoring regime formation theorizing too tightly to class variables is hinted at by scholars working in the class analysis tradition itself. Both RSS and Luebbert, for example, acknowledge the causal relevance of parties either as "mediators" between class interests and political outcomes or as classes' "representatives." Yet neither RSS nor Luebbert uncovers a systematic cross-national relationship between class structure and party system structure, nor is either study concerned with identifying one. What's more, a number of comparativists have noted that, empirically, similar class structures have translated into varying party system structures (Luebbert 1991; Burton et al., 1991). This study has demonstrated that several nonclass variables affect party system structures. These include electoral rules, social cleavages other than class (region, ethnicity, language, ideology, and so on), choices made by outsiders (such as the actions taken by imperial powers), and the extent and nature of a society's stock of social capital that is available for party-building initiatives.

The absence of consistent linkages between class structures and party system structures presents a problem for class-centered analyses of regime formation processes. This is so because if parties are classes' representatives or agents, and if similar class structures can and do yield *varying* party system structures, then an important intervening step in regime-building processes is left untheorized if party system characteristics are not taken seriously. This is particularly the case in settings wherein parliaments and elections structure at least a portion of the emerging rules of the political game, because these institutions will frame parties' incentives, opportunities, and constraints in ways that may have little to do with class structure or class concerns. Because parties are the vehicles through which political interests must pursue power and influence in parliaments, party system characteristics strongly influence political elites' calculations as to how they can best defend their interests and pursue their preferences. This study has demonstrated that if key actors conclude that a given party system configuration threatens their core values and interests, they are likely to defect from democratic norms and throw their weight behind antidemocratic actors, institutions, and initiatives. Competitive politics emerges only when no key actor reaches such a conclusion.

Analytically, these observations highlight the importance of taking political parties, party system characteristics, and the determinants of these very seriously when asking and answering questions about macrohistorical phenomena such as regime formation. The insights of class analysts are crucial, and RSS, Luebbert, and others have been extremely sensitive to the fact that other variables in addition to class are key elements of satisfactory answers to the questions they address. Likewise, a narrow focus only on political parties, to the neglect of parties' class bases and material inclinations, would make for sterile and superficial theorizing. But because classes often are divided, because classes do not necessarily act collectively in pursuit of shared interests, and because class structures do not translate in a one-to-one fashion into party system structures, complementing attention to class factors with a rigorous analysis of party-related variables is likely to be necessary if systematic, generalizable findings regarding regime trajectories and regime type are to be generated. At the same time, focusing on parties and party system characteristics sensitizes scholars to the ways in which social classes are or are not acting collectively, and are or are not divided—allowing us to ask key questions about the historical, institutional, and sociological factors underlying class behavior.

NOTES

Introduction

1. These interventions occurred in 1960, 1971, 1980, and, arguably, in 1997, when pressure from the military forced the coalition government headed by Necmettin Erbakan (of the now-outlawed Islamist Welfare Party) to step down.

2. Here I follow Schmitter and Karl who, in an influential essay, explicitly refined conventional comparative politics definitions of "democracy" to specify that "popularly elected officials must be able to exercise their constitutional powers without being subjected to overriding . . . opposition from unelected officials" (1991, 81).

3. Political liberalization refers to actions such as the enlargement of individuals' and groups' freedoms of speech and movement and freedom from arbitrary state actions. Following Ibrahim (1995, 43–52), liberalizing and democratizing progress was made during the Third Wave and beyond in Algeria, Jordan, Yemen, Tunisia, Egypt, Morocco, Lebanon, Kuwait, and Saudi Arabia—although, in many cases, retreats and reversals subsequently transpired.

4. These include democratic elections in the Palestinian Authority and Iraq, the holding of municipal-level elections in Saudi Arabia, and the announcement by Egyptian President Hosni Mubarak that more than one candidate will be able to contest future presidential elections there.

5. See the analyses contained in Posusney and Angrist 2005.

6. See Brynen, Korany, and Noble (1995, 6–10) for a concise but comprehensive overview of this literature—and its critics.

7. A strong and un-nuanced statement of this point of view appears in Kedourie 1992. Huntington offers a relatively more balanced assessment (1991, 307).

8. Here Inkeles and Smith (1974) exemplify the paradigm, arguing based on

survey data that subjects across the globe were undergoing personal psychosocial transformations—from "traditional" to "modern" men—as they partook of the expanding educational systems, mass media circuits, and factory-based labor markets that emerged in industrializing societies.

9. See Diamond 1992 for a survey of these works.

10. A second prominent argument holds that, in the face of Soviet demands for political and territorial concessions, the Republican People's Party acceded to political pluralization out of a belief that doing so would help Turkey acquire the economic and military support of the emerging Western Cold War alliance (see Yılmaz 1996). Chapter 6 will show that this is only a partial explanation of Turkey's competitive regime outcome, one that leaves important elements unaccounted for.

11. Clearly, such an approach can be employed only in places and times in which parties exist.

12. He himself states that mass material interests are the motor force of his argument (1991, 6).

13. The set of cases treated in this book therefore excludes Libya, North Yemen, and the Gulf States (Saudi Arabia, Kuwait, Bahrain, Qatar, the United Arab Emirates, and Oman) because political parties either did not exist at all or played extremely marginal roles in regime-formation processes after independence. Though Lebanon's postindependence political stage technically did include political parties, it is excluded because, due to electoral law design, political parties were not the primary actors in the parliamentary system that was established there at independence in 1943. From that time until the start of civil war in 1975, the maximum share of parliamentary seats won by parties was only one-third; the vast majority of members of parliament were independents (Harik 1975; Baaklini, Denoeux, Springborg 1999).

14. Analytically, the tenth case (Morocco) falls somewhere in between the first and second categories and will be treated in chapters 1 and 4.

15. For the eight countries that had been controlled by Britain or France, transitional periods began at independence. Turkey's transitional period began in 1923. The Ottoman Empire experienced its terminal collapse in that year when rival Turkish political-military leaders defeated the armies that had invaded following WWI, declared Turkey a republic, and began fighting over the republic's future political structure. For Iran, 1941 began an analytically equivalent transitional period. In that year a new, weak king assumed the throne, inaugurating an era lasting more than a decade during which political parties struggled with one another and with the shah to shape Iran's post–WWII regime.

16. The logic here is consonant with and informed by Dahl's (1971) classic formulation that polyarchy is difficult to establish when governments would endure

high costs if they tolerated their oppositions, as well as by Alexander's (2002) more recent claim that democracies become consolidated when the right believes that the left is fundamentally and predictably a moderate political force.

17. Ertman (1998) makes similar observations regarding certain interwar European party systems; his work strongly influenced the development of the argument of this book.

18. Many specialists on the study of Turkey characterize politics during this time as single-party rule (Karpat 1959, vii; Zürcher 1994, chapters 10 and 11; and Özbudun 1976, 45) because the first two opposition parties to challenge the RPP enjoyed legal existence only for very brief periods of time. Yet chapter 6 will show that these opposition parties demonstrated considerable organizational ability and garnered widespread popular support. These realities meant that RPP rule was vulnerable to challenge in ways that single-party regimes in Tunisia, South Yemen, and Algeria never were, helping to ensure that Turkey's political trajectory was pluralistic. Conceiving of Turkey's as a nascent two-party system thus has an important analytical payoff.

19. See Mahoney and Rueschemeyer 2003 for a discussion of the achievements of this approach, the analytical tools it employs, and the methodological issues its practitioners confront.

20. I am referring to the Ottoman Empire. Though its territory shrank significantly in the early twentieth century, and though Ankara replaced İstanbul as the Turkish capital in the 1920s, the residents of Eastern Thrace and the Anatolian peninsula—the territories that constitute modern Turkey—have long been members of the same political community.

21. This occurred in Libya, Lebanon, Syria, Iraq, Jordan, and Palestine/Israel.

22. I thank Paul Salem and Lisa Anderson for flagging this research design concern.

23. I thank Vickie Langohr for this observation.

1 *The Emergence of the Preponderant Single-Party Systems*

1. See Yashar (1997), chapter 7, for a discussion of the relevance of controlling the countryside for political outcomes.

2. Approximately 239,000 French settlers resided in Tunisia in 1946, or 1 for every 14 Tunisians; 984,031 French lived in Algeria in 1954, or 1 for every 9 Algerians (Kahler 1984, 317).

3. French intransigence is explained in part by the fact that Tunisia and Algeria were settler colonies. The presence of large numbers of settlers created an important interest group in French politics that opposed decolonization (Fry 1997, 140;

Kahler 1984, chapter 5). South Yemen represented an important strategic outpost from which the British were very reluctant to depart.

4. For the core of this argument regarding the transfer of control over nationalist movements to second-generation elites, I am indebted to Moore 1970.

5. These were pieces of land used as endowments: they could not be sold or divided up, and a designated individual (in the case of private *habous* land) or institution (in the case of public *habous* land) received the profits from their cultivation.

6. Other French administrative policies further weakened tribal identity and undermined the stature and influence of traditional tribal chiefs (Anderson 1986, 150, 154).

7. Archives du Ministère des Affaires Etrangères (AMAE), Bobine 638/Volume 297/Folio 9. All translations are the author's.

8. Protests were used to bring the French to the negotiating table and had to be carefully controlled so that they could be halted when they had achieved the intended political objective. When negotiations broke down, the party would then again activate popular pressure (Moore 1965, 45).

9. Protectorate documents for the years 1945–1955 contain references to hundreds if not thousands of acts of civil disobedience orchestrated by the ND across the entire country. A more complete inventory of protest methods includes gatherings, marches, and demonstrations; boycotts; strikes by workers and students; work stoppages by merchant and commercial enterprises; and public meetings. See the Archives Nationales de Tunisie (ANT), Série Histoire du Mouvement National.

10. These institutions were kept officially and legally separate from the ND in an attempt to protect them from the repression routinely suffered by the ND.

11. According to protectorate authorities, in 1954 UTAC had 240 branches nationally, and UGAT had 237 (AMAE 639/298/47).

12. The party also built a youth organization, the Neo-Destour Youth, which by independence numbered 100,000. This apparatus was used to "keep public order at party rallies and provide young militants for the party" (Moore 1965, 37).

13. As with UTAC, UGAT, and UGET, the ND and the UGTT purposely retained separate institutional identities so that the repression that befell the ND did not harm the union. Beginning in 1950 the UGTT's membership in the International Confederation of Free Trade Unions gave it an extra source of political insulation and protection.

14. French protectorate documents contain numerous additional reports of speeches in which ND leaders exhort their party faithful and Tunisians generally to remain united (behind the ND) lest the French successfully divide the population and, in so doing, retain the protectorate. See ANT Carton 50/Dossier 45/Folio 72 and 50/8/72; and AMAE 638/297/93 and 639/298/5. Indeed, actions that were found

to facilitate dissension within the party were grounds for a member's exclusion from the party (see *Règlement du Parti Libéral Constitutionnel Tunisien 1934* in AMAE 638/297/53a-b).

15. For examples of such critiques, see *Le Neo-Destour* (n.a., n.d.), 21–28, and AMAE 652/318/7.

16. A third, much younger party was Mekki ben Azouz's conservative, pro-French Parti National Tunisien, created in 1950. For French judgments as to this party's political insignificance, see AMAE 652/318/58 and 652/318/13.

17. For French conclusions as to the PCT's weakness, see AMAE 652/319/252, 652/319/12-16, 652/319/55-58, and 652/319/147.

18. PCT weakness derived from the fact that Tunisians had no real voice in party decision making (Kraiem 1997, 353) and that its ideology focused on internationalist, pro-Soviet principles rather than Tunisian nationalism (Interview E).

2 *The Emergence of the Multiparty Systems*

1. For more on this constitutional revolution in Iran, see Abrahamian 1979.

2. In part the lack of intransigence corresponded to British obligations as a mandatory power. In addition, Britain sought to avoid an intensive, expensive oversight role. Instead, its goal was to cut costs by training a competent indigenous administration and army that in time would be capable of governing independently—yet remain sympathetic to British influence and interests (Bannerman 1995, 222).

3. Tibawi notes that France was obligated under the terms of its mandate to prepare Syria for self-governance (1969, 338). Khoury observes that France, exhausted from WWI, felt it had few resources to commit to Syria. Its trade and investment relationships with its North African holdings (especially Tunisia and Algeria) were much stronger (1987, 46–50). As chapter 1 demonstrated, its commitment to retaining those holdings was stronger as well.

4. Evidence that this dynamic played out during the mandate period may be found in Khoury 1987: 301, 329–30, 361, 471.

5. For more details on this period, see Torrey 1964 and Ma'oz 1972.

6. For more on these dynamics, see al-Sayyid-Marsot 1977 and Vatikiotis 1991.

7. For example, the 1906 law saw each province electing either six or twelve deputies; the capital city, Tehran, elected sixty deputies to parliament. The 1909 law saw districts sending between one and nineteen representatives to parliament (see laws in Browne 1910).

8. Electoral laws discussed in this section can be found in Davis 1947 and 1953. The exceptions are Iran's 1906 and 1909 statutes, which can be found in Browne 1910.

9. Egypt possessed a comparatively homogeneous population, and it conducted elections according to majoritarian principles with single-member districts. Two factors help explain the large number of parties present in Egypt's political arena. The Egyptian population was divided along economic and ideological lines. In addition, as chapter 5 will detail, parliamentary politics became perverted such that even small parties with tiny parliamentary blocs could access significant cabinet power and its associated privileges. Incentives thus existed for rival elites to build additional parties. This explanation is consistent with Cox's argument (1997) that electoral structures such as rules for the selection of presidents and prime ministers will affect how district-level outcomes aggregate into national party systems.

10. Batatu tells us, for example, that the Arab Socialist Party appealed to peasants of various religious stripes (1999, 128). Heydemann stresses that Syrians overcame religious and regional differences when they had common material interests at stake (1999, 42).

3 *The Emergence of Bipartism in Turkey*

1. Turks did fight a war of independence following WWI in which they repelled the occupying armies of several invading countries. This war, however, was not analytically equivalent to the independence battles fought by Tunisian, South Yemeni, and Algerian nationalists. The Turkish struggle pitted one sovereign power (the Ottoman Empire) against several others. The empire possessed an army, and Turkish leaders used those army units that retained their autonomy following the Ottomans' defeat in WWI to repel foreign aggression. Building a political party thus was not a necessary strategy for Turkish leaders during the independence war.

2. While Cox (1997, 56) notes that majoritarian rules normally operate in systems wherein citizens vote for individual candidates rather than lists (indeed, he cites only four contemporary exceptions to this pattern), in Turkey citizens voted for lists.

3. Public goods are goods that portions of the populace cannot be prevented from consuming and whose supply is not diminished when some consume.

4. See Olson 1965 and Putnam 1993.

5. From its origins in the late thirteenth century, the Ottoman Empire expanded to become the last great empire to dominate much of the lands that ring the Mediterranean Sea. At its peak, Ottoman sultans controlled North Africa (with the exception of Morocco), parts of the Arabian Peninsula, the Levant, Anatolia, and the Balkan region. This study, however, focuses on the events and trends that shaped politics in those imperial lands that lay inside the borders of contemporary Turkey. This includes two regions: "Anatolia," the peninsula east of the

Bosphorus Straits that constitutes the bulk of Turkish territory, and "Rumelia," the much smaller piece of territory west of the straits and east of the borders of Greece and Bulgaria.

6. For an influential discussion of the politics of this notable class, see Hourani 1966.

7. As set out in the 1839 *Hatt-ı Şerif of Gülhane* reform edict (an English translation can be found in Hurewitz 1956, 113–16), the sultan identified local notables' greed and lawlessness as partially responsible for the empire's decline. He proclaimed the central government's intent to better protect its subjects' lives, dignity, and property through fair, direct taxation; just conscription practices; and other legal reforms. This edict ushered in what is known as the *Tanzimat* (Reform) era (1839–1876). The center hoped that, in addition to improving the efficiency of the tax collection system, these reforms would improve subjects' loyalty to the multiethnic empire, which in the nineteenth century was increasingly threatened by secessionist movements.

8. See Shaw 1969, 63–64, for details on the mechanics of these elections. With the creation of these elective notable positions, the principle of representation was established for the first time in the Ottoman periphery (Davison 1966, 98).

9. These were then rejected, amended, or implemented according to the preferences of the center.

10. Shaw later notes that between eighty and a hundred notables acted as electors in each district (1969, 66–67).

11. An English rendition of the constitution may be found in Kili 1971, 150–59.

12. The constitution was also promulgated in part as a way to diminish pressures from foreign powers who were intervening in Ottoman politics, ostensibly on behalf of the empire's non-Muslim minority communities (Davison 1966, 107).

13. Writing about Mithat Paşa, an architect of the constitution, Karpat concludes that "Mithat Paşa viewed the Constitution and the Parliament of 1876, not only as devices to limit the sultan's authority, but also as methods of establishing a system of balances and cooperation between the major social groups—the propertied groups and the bureaucracy, represented politically by the local and central governments respectively . . . The search for a viable balance between central and local power was a pressing problem born not of political idealism but of recognition of middle-class power" (1972, 267–68).

14. Not coincidentally, this is exactly the kind of countervailing power the provincial administrative councils wielded over centrally appointed provincial officials by the end of the *Tanzimat* reform period.

15. On the military dimension of this phenomenon, see Rustow 1964, 360. Another important networking mechanism was membership in religious orders

and Masonic lodges in and around İstanbul, a trait shared by many top CUP officials (Tunaya 1988, 22; Kabasakal 1991, 27).

16. For details on these and other political parties of the period, see Tunaya 1988.

17. These numbers are taken from a document published in Tunaya 1988 (299).

18. Güneş's research supports this conclusion. He shows that the organizers of HİF branches in the Eskişehir area were from the Zeytunzade family, one of the most important notable families of the province. Between 1878 and 1908, the family had taken the administration of the *kaza* in which they lived into their own hands. "They had arrived at a position of significant political strength," and used their business ties and connections to recruit party members (1992, 470, translation mine).

19. Tanör (1992) documents a total of twenty-eight such congresses. More generally, he offers an in-depth treatment of the Defense of Rights societies, their organization, political philosophy, activities, congresses, and impact on Turkish political development.

20. There are at least two possible explanations for this pattern of center-periphery (im)balance of power. First, only a very small portion of Egypt's territory is habitable: a thin strip of land on each bank of the Nile. The river in turn allows the center—leaders in Cairo—to project power over the periphery easily relative to the challenges central elites in İstanbul faced in governing Anatolia. Second, the position of Egypt's tax-farming notable elites had been weakened by the French occupation, easing Muhammad Ali's task when he sought to alter the fiscal status quo (Hourani 1966, 55).

4 *Preponderant Single Parties and Immediate Authoritarian Rule*

1. One indicator of the kinds of "fruits of victory" available to successful nationalist parties comes from Tunisia, where in the years following independence, the Tunisian army doubled, the police force tripled, and the national guard more than quintupled in size, their ranks filled out by party activists (Tlili 1988, 15–17).

2. Zawiya membership was estimated to stand at 300,000 in 1952 (Moore 1965, 12n5).

3. See AMAE 638/297/90-93 for accounts of their conflicts in that year.

4. A French Foreign Ministry telegram dated October 27, 1955, stated that "it appears increasingly likely that [Ben Youssef] has important sums at his disposal" (AMAE 639/298/194a).

5. French authorities noted the UGTT's growing political restiveness as early as 1954 (AMAE 639/299/99).

6. Indeed, their loyalty was now reinforced by the flow of state patronage that Bourguiba directed.

7. Other sources suggest that such behavior was typical of the ND. According to protectorate authorities' reporting, in 1955 the ND carried out an intimidation campaign against the old Destour Party, disrupting its meetings and sometimes committing violence against its leaders (AMAE 639/298/165-167).

8. Abdallah (1963b, 594) tells us that the country was divided into eighteen "rather extensive" electoral districts to ensure that local personalities were not tempted to oppose the ND.

9. These were the Law of Ill-Gotten Gains (August 13, 1957) and the Law of National Indignity (November 19, 1957). Moore describes the legal proceedings that ensued as harsh and arbitrary (1965, 88–90). Though Bourguiba habitually pardoned the condemned within one to two years, these policies sent a stern signal to this stratum of society.

10. Bourguiba eliminated the Zitouna schools two years later in the context of a massive education reform that provided for a unified, predominantly secular school system in Tunisia. All that would remain of the Zitouna was a faculty of theology, which was integrated into the University of Tunis (Moore 1965, 54).

11. See République Tunisienne, n.d., for the text of the constitution itself.

12. The assembly was newly elected every five years through majoritarian rules that privileged the ND. From 1962 to 1981, no other political parties could oppose the ND in elections.

13. The NLF broke with Nasser as independence neared.

14. For example, Kostiner writes that, "In Dathinah, . . . it was the children of wealthy *Fallahs* [peasants] who studied in Aden where they took up the ideas of revolutionary Arab nationalism. On their return, they spread their new ideas among the local Dhamki, al-Mansuri and al-Husayn tribal groups" (1984, 97–98).

15. Given that an interim transitional period elapsed between independence and the start of Morocco's founding regime, it is important to explain why the case is treated in this chapter rather than in chapter 5. First, Morocco shares with the Tunisian, South Yemeni, and Algerian cases the fact that its European colonizer was at least *partially* intransigent in the face of calls for independence. Second, postindependence Moroccan politics did not possess a key element shared in common by the cases discussed in chapter 5. Specifically, multiparty elections and parliaments did not figure in immediate postindependence politics, a time when the king struck crucial blows in his contest with Istiqlal. Morocco therefore had significantly less potential for evolving a competitive founding regime than did Iraq, Iran, Jordan, Syria, and Egypt.

5 *Polarization, Mobilizational Asymmetry, and Delayed Authoritarian Rule*

1. Sharabi's (1960) distinction between bloc parties and doctrinal parties, and Zubaida's discussion of "the distinction between the 'politics of the notables' and the politics of ideologically-based political parties" (1991, 199) informed my thinking about the salient differences between conservative and challenger parties, as well as their causal importance for regime outcomes in the region.

2. I thank Marsha Pripstein Posusney for raising this as an important contextual factor.

3. During this era, only Syria allowed women—with a certificate of primary education—to vote.

4. Abrahamian (1982) provides helpful descriptions of parliamentary politics during this period, including details on the various caucuses or "fraksiuns" that operated during the successive parliamentary sessions.

5. One demonstration of Tudeh's strength occurred in July 1946 when the party organized an oil workers' strike in southern Iran: tens of thousands of workers participated.

6. For more on these "challenger" parties, see Grassmuck 1960, Haj 1997, Farouk-Sluglett and Sluglett 1991, Tripp 2000, and Zubaida 1991.

7. For more on the conservative parties, see Batatu 1978, Grassmuck 1960, Khadduri 1960, and Tripp 2000.

8. This party was "socialist" in name only. Jabr "was only one of many who in that decade wrapped themselves with the cloak of socialism in the hope of borrowing a little of its popularity" (Batatu 1978, 466).

9. The narrative in the next three paragraphs is culled from Marr 1985, Tripp 2000, and Haj 1997.

10. For more on the politics of the Iraqi army at this time, see Haj 1997 and Farouk-Sluglett and Sluglett 1991.

11. The narrative does not detail developments between 1958 and 1968 because the 1958 revolution, in abolishing parliament and elections, decisively ended Iraq's flirtation with competitive norms and ensured that democracy would not result from the experiment. Political dynamics during the next decade, while determining what *kind* of dictatorship emerged, were fundamentally different from the phenomena that are the foci of this chapter.

12. Hereafter, "Transjordan" will be used in the text to refer to the East Bank (of the Jordan River).

13. Agwani notes that trade unions, professional associations, and political parties existed in the West Bank (1969, 72).

14. Transjordan's (East Bank) population was around 400,000 prior to the 1950 annexation.

15. Dann points out that because the West Bank constituted two-thirds of Jordan's population, the twenty-twenty allotment overrepresented East Bank Jordanians (1989, 6).

16. For example, the communists objected to Jordan's annexation of the West Bank and the Ba'th thought Jordan should merge with neighboring Arab states.

17. For more detailed discussions of these parties, see Agwani 1969 and Aruri 1972.

18. For more details on this shift over time in the People's Party's alliances, see Heydemann 1999.

19. Illustrative of politics' polarization in Syria was the fact that the Arab Socialist Party's institutional predecessor in 1943 adopted as its slogan "Fetch the Basket and the Shovel for the Burying of the Agha and the Bey" (quoted in Batatu 1999, 124). "Agha" and "Bey" are terms denoting prominent landowning notables in Arab society.

20. It should be noted that, by 1954, many of parliament's independents (as many as thirty) were sympathetic to challenger rather than conservative parties; this trend continued into the 1961 election (Devlin 1976).

21. For general evidence to this effect, see Botman 1991, 58, 65, and Terry 1982, 227, 294. For party-specific evidence see Botman 1991, 67, and Terry 1982, 156, on the Liberal Constitutionalists; Botman 1991, 67, on Ittihad; Botman 1991, 68, on the Sha'b; and Terry 1982, 156, on the Watani Party.

22. See Jankowski 1975 for a detailed portrait of this party.

23. In return, the Wafd promised the Brotherhood "freedom for the movement to resume full-scale operations" and "government action against the sale of alcoholic drinks and against prostitution" (Mitchell 1993, 26–27).

6 *Depolarization, Increased Mobilizational Symmetry, and the Consolidation of Competitive Politics in Turkey*

1. Frey's numbers are very similar: 71 percent versus 59 percent (1965, 310).

2. Kemal had been a member of the CUP, but he was not part of the inner circle of leadership that was involved in creating the *Karakol*, *Teşkilat-ı Mahsusa*, and Defense of Rights societies. As Kemal gained control of the nationalist movement, he criticized the CUP and worked to undermine what was left of its organization, creating many political enemies for himself. For more on these dynamics, see Zürcher 1984.

3. This conclusion is consistent with Mardin's characterization of the Second

Group as "mainly the party of notables led by alienated members of the official class" (1973, 181).

4. Consistent with this claim, Demirel observes that the creation of an elective national assembly—the Ankara parliament—was the only way Mustafa Kemal could overcome the opposition of the various Defense of Rights societies to centralization of the nationalist movement under his control (1995, 69).

5. Approximately 22 percent of First Group members were local notables (Demirel 1995, 140). Demirel and Frey (1965, 308) both provide data implying that one reason for the otherwise unlikely affiliation was that local notables representing provinces that were under foreign occupation may have had a stronger sense of the military exigencies Turkey was facing and sided with the First Group to give Kemal the authority he needed to win the independence war.

6. The People's Party changed its name to the Republican People's Party in 1924.

7. Demand for an opposition party was particularly high in İstanbul, whose denizens resented the fact that Kemal had made Ankara Turkey's capital. The PRP had thirteen branches in the city and, in an interview in early 1925, PRP leader Kara Vasıf Bey estimated PRP membership there at around ten thousand (Yeşil 1992, 255).

8. In the end, the FRP's assembly strength never exceeded fifteen.

9. The FRP acknowledged that a role existed for the state in economic arenas wherein private initiative failed to advance the republic's development goals; however, it inserted this statement into the document only at Kemal's insistence (Barlas 1993, 161).

10. Tunaya contrasts the FRP to the PRP in this way: the goal of the latter, in his mind, was to *destroy* the Republican People's Party while the goal of the former was only to *control* the Republican People's Party (1952, 624; emphasis added).

11. See, for example, Tunçay 1983, 2021, and Tunaya 1952, 624.

12. Many would cite İnönü himself as an important explanatory factor for the RPP's newly tolerant attitude toward its political opponents in the late 1940s. Heper (1998) depicts İnönü as committed to the norm of democratic multiparty competition, and his stewardship unquestionably facilitated Turkey's transition. As the exchange between him and Bayar suggests, however, his democratic commitments were not unconditional. Heper tells us that, for İnönü, the state that Atatürk had created "had primacy over democracy" (132), that İnönü was always concerned with safeguarding the Kemalist regime, but that by the mid-1940s, he had concluded that "the country had made great progress in democracy and, consequently, the Republican reforms were no longer under a threat" (144). İnönü was not a democrat come-what-may: the survival of the Kemalist regime mattered first and foremost, and multiparty competition could be tolerated only as long as the regime was not threatened. Depolarization thus enabled İnönü to act on his democratic instincts.

13. See Prather's discussion of events in Artvin province in 1946, where, for the first time in the history of the republic, some of the RPP's candidates for that province were local men (1978, 76 and n81).

Conclusion

1. It should be noted as well that, in terms of ethnicity, Turks are not Arab, the emerging Arab-Israeli conflict was less potentially polarizing by virtue of the fact that Turks, while Muslim, do not have the same sense of fellow feeling with Palestinians that Arab Middle Easterners do.
2. See Waterbury 1997 and Okruhlik 1999 for evaluations.
3. Luebbert (1991) joins RSS in conceiving parties as classes' "representatives."
4. Luebbert makes the identical point (1991, 309).

BIBLIOGRAPHY

Abdallah, Ridha. 1963a. "Structures et évolution du Néo-Destour." *Revue Juridique et Politique d'Outre-Mer* 17, no. 3 (Juillet-Septembre): 385–428.

———. 1963b. "Le Néo-Destour depuis l'indépendance." *Revue Juridique et Politique d'Outre-Mer* 17, no. 4 (Octobre-Décembre): 573–657.

Abidi, Aqil Hyder Hasan. 1965. *Jordan: A Political Study, 1948–1957.* New York: Asia Publishing House.

Abrahamian, Ervand. 1979. "The Causes of the Constitutional Revolution in Iran." *International Journal of Middle East Studies* 10, no. 3 (August): 381–414.

———. 1982. *Iran Between Two Revolutions.* Princeton, N.J.: Princeton University Press.

Abu Jaber, Kamel S. 1969. "The Legislature of the Hashemite Kingdom of Jordan: A Study in Political Development." *Muslim World* 59, nos. 3–4 (July-October): 220–50.

Agwani, M. S. 1969. *Communism in the Arab East.* Bombay: Asia Publishing House.

Ahmad, Feroz. 1969. *The Young Turks: The Committee of Union and Progress in Turkish Politics, 1908–1914.* Oxford: Clarendon Press.

———. 1991. "The Progressive Republican Party, 1924–1925." In *Political Parties and Democracy in Turkey*, ed. Metin Heper and Jacob M. Landau, 65–82. London: I. B. Tauris.

———. 1993. *The Making of Modern Turkey.* London: Routledge.

Akşin, Sina. 1971. "İttihat ve Terakki Üzerine." *Ankara Üniversitesi Siyasal Bilgiler Fakültesi Dergisi* 26, no. 1 (March): 153–182.

Albayrak, Mustafa. 1992. *Türk Siyasi Tarihinde Demokrat Parti* (1946–1960). Ph.D. dissertation, Hacettepe University, Ankara, Turkey.

Aldrich, John H. 1995. *Why Parties? The Origin and Transformation of Political Parties in America*. Chicago: University of Chicago Press.

Alexander, Gerard. 2002. *The Sources of Democratic Consolidation*. Ithaca, N.Y.: Cornell University Press.

Almond, Gabriel A., and Sidney Verba. 1963. *The Civic Culture: Political Attitudes and Democracy in Five Nations*. Princeton, N.J.: Princeton University Press.

Anderson, Lisa. 1986. *The State and Social Transformation in Tunisia and Libya, 1830–1980*. Princeton, N.J.: Princeton University Press.

———. 1995. "Democracy in the Arab World: A Critique of the Political Culture Approach." In *Political Liberalization and Democratization in the Arab World*. Vol. 1, *Theoretical Perspectives*, ed. Rex Brynen, Bahgat Korany, and Paul Noble, 77–92. Boulder: Lynne Rienner.

Anghie, Antony. 2002. "Colonialism and the Birth of International Institutions: Sovereignty, Economy, and the Mandate System of the League of Nations." *New York University Journal of International Law and Politics* 34, no. 3 (Spring): 513–633.

Archives du Ministère des Affaires Etrangères, Quai d'Orsay, Paris (AMAE). Série: Tunisie 1944–1955. Bobines 638, 639, 652, Correspondance Politique et Commerciale. Consulted at the Institut Supérieur d'Histoire du Mouvement National, Tunis, Tunisia.

Archives Nationales de Tunisie (ANT). Série: Histoire du Mouvement National. Carton 50, Informations générales, situation politique, activités Nationalistes .

Arjomand, Said Amir. 1988. *The Turban for the Crown: The Islamic Revolution in Iran*. New York: Oxford University Press.

Aruri, Naseer H. 1972. *Jordan: A Study in Political Development (1921–1965)*. The Hague: Martinus Nijhoff.

Avery, Peter, Gavin Hambly, and Charles Melville, eds. 1991. *The Cambridge History of Iran*. Vol. 7. Cambridge: Cambridge University Press.

Azimi, Fakhreddin. 1989. *Iran: The Crisis of Democracy*. New York: St. Martin's Press.

Baaklini, Abdo, Guilain Denoeux, and Robert Springborg. 1999. *Legislative Politics in the Arab World: The Resurgence of Democratic Institutions*. Boulder: Lynne Rienner.

Balfour-Paul, Glen. 1991. *The End of Empire in the Middle East: Britain's Relinquishment of Power in Her Last Three Arab Dependencies*. New York: Cambridge University Press.

Bannerman, M. Graeme. 1995. "Hashimite Kingdom of Jordan." In *The Government and Politics of the Middle East and North Africa*, ed. Bernard Reich and David E. Long, 220–39. 3rd ed. Boulder: Westview.

Bar, Shmuel. 1995. "The Jordanian Elite—Old and New." In *The Hashemites in the Modern Arab World: Essays in Honour of the Late Professor Uriel Dann*, ed. Asher Susser and Aryeh Shmuelevitz, 221–28. London: Frank Cass.

Barlas, Dilek. 1993. *Turkey: Etatism and Foreign Relations in the 1930's*. Ph.D. dissertation, University of Chicago, Department of History.

Batatu, Hanna. 1978. *The Old Social Classes and the Revolutionary Movements of Iraq*. Princeton, N.J.: Princeton University Press.

———. 1982. "Syria's Muslim Brethren." *Merip Reports* 12, no. 9:12–20.

———. 1999. *Syria's Peasantry, the Descendants of Its Lesser Rural Notables, and Their Politics*. Princeton, N.J.: Princeton University Press.

Bausani, Alessandro. 1971. *The Persians: From the Earliest Days to the Twentieth Century*. Trans. J. B. Donne. London: Elek Books.

Baynard, Sally Ann. 1995. "Arab Republic of Egypt." In *The Government and Politics of the Middle East and North Africa*, ed. David E. Long and Bernard Reich, 303–25. 3rd ed. Boulder: Westview.

Bellin, Eva. 2000. "Contingent Democrats: Industrialists, Labor, and Democratization in Late-Developing Countries." *World Politics* 52 (January): 175–205.

———. 2002. *Stalled Democracy: Capital, Labor, and the Paradox of State-Sponsored Development*. Ithaca, N.Y.: Cornell University Press.

Bennoune, Mahfoud. 1988. *The Making of Contemporary Algeria, 1830–1987: Colonial Upheavals and Post-Independence Development*. New York: Cambridge University Press.

Berman, Sheri. 1997. "Civil Society and the Collapse of the Weimar Republic." *World Politics* 49, no. 3 (April): 401–29.

Bidwell, Robin. 1983. *The Two Yemens*. Boulder: Westview.

Botman, Selma. 1987. "The Egyptian Communist Movement in Historical Perspective." *Journal of South Asian and Middle Eastern Studies* 10, no. 3:78–94.

———. 1991. *Egypt from Independence to Revolution, 1919–1952*. Syracuse: Syracuse University Press.

Brown, Leon Carl. 1964. "Stages in the Process of Change." In *Tunisia: The Politics of Modernization*, ed. Charles A. Micaud, Leon Carl Brown, and Clement Henry Moore, 3–68. New York: Praeger.

Browne, Edward G. 1910. *The Persian Revolution of 1905–1909*. Cambridge: Cambridge University Press.

Bruhn, Kathleen. 1997. *Taking on Goliath: The Emergence of a New Left Party and the Struggle for Democracy in Mexico*. University Park: Pennsylvania State University Press.

Brynen, Rex, Bahgat Korany, and Paul Noble. 1995. "Introduction: Theoretical Perspectives on Arab Liberalization and Democratization." In *Political Liber-*

alization and Democratization in the Arab World. Vol. 1, *Theoretical Perspectives*, ed. Rex Brynen, Bahgat Korany, and Paul Noble, 3–28. Boulder: Lynne Rienner.

Bujra, A. S. 1970. "Urban Elites and Colonialism: The Nationalist Elites of Aden and South Arabia." *Middle Eastern Studies* 6, no. 2 (May): 189–211.

Burton, Michael, Richard Gunther, and John Higley. 1991. "Introduction: Elite Transformations and Democratic Regimes." In *Elites and Democratic Consolidation in Latin America and Southern Europe*, ed. John Higley and Richard Gunther, 1–37. Cambridge: Cambridge University Press.

———. 1992. "Elites and Democratic Consolidation in Latin America and Southern Europe: An Overview." In *Elites and Democratic Consolidation in Latin America and Southern Europe*, ed. John Higley and Richard Gunther, 323–48. Cambridge: Cambridge University Press.

Camau, Michel. 1978. *Pouvoir et Institutions au Maghreb*. Tunis: Cérès Productions.

Çavdar, Tevfik. 1983. "Serbest Fırka." *Cumhuriyet Dönemi Türkiye Ansiklopedisi*, vol. 8:2052–59. İstanbul: İletişim Yayınları.

Cohen, Amnon. 1982. *Political Parties in the West Bank under the Jordanian Regime, 1949–1967*. Ithaca, N.Y.: Cornell University Press.

Cohen, Mark I., and Lorna Hahn. 1966. *Morocco: Old Land, New Nation*. New York: Frederick A. Praeger.

Collier, Ruth Berins, and David Collier. 1991. *Shaping the Political Arena: Critical Junctures, the Labor Movement, and Regime Dynamics in Latin America*. Princeton, N.J.: Princeton University Press.

Connelly, Matthew. 2001. "Rethinking the Cold War and Decolonization: The Grand Strategy of the Algerian War for Independence." *International Journal of Middle East Studies* 33, no. 2:221–45.

Cox, Gary W. 1997. *Making Votes Count: Strategic Coordination in the World's Electoral Systems*. Cambridge: Cambridge University Press.

Cumhuriyet Halk Partisi (CHP). 1948. *C.H.P. Ankara Merkez İlçesi 1947 Kongresi*. Ankara: Çankaya Matbaası.

Dahl, Robert A. 1971. *Polyarchy: Participation and Opposition*. New Haven, Conn.: Yale University Press.

Dann, Uriel. 1989. *King Hussein and the Challenge of Arab Radicalism: Jordan, 1955–1967*. New York: Oxford University Press.

Davis, Helen Miller. 1947. *Constitutions, Electoral Laws, Treaties of States in the Near and Middle East*. Durham, N.C.: Duke University Press.

———. 1953. *Constitutions, Electoral Laws, Treaties of States in the Near and Middle East*. Durham, NC: Duke University Press.

Davison, Roderic H. 1966. "The Advent of the Principle of Representation in the Government of the Ottoman Empire." In *Beginnings of Modernization in the*

Middle East, ed. William R. Polk and Richard L. Chambers, 93–108. Chicago: University of Chicago Press.

Demirel, Ahmet. 1995. *Birinci Meclis'te Muhalefet: İkinci Grup*. İstanbul: İletişim Yayınları.

Devereux, Robert. 1963. *The First Ottoman Constitutional Period: A Study of the Midhat Constitution and Parliament*. Baltimore: Johns Hopkins University Press.

Devlin, John F. 1976. *The Ba'th Party: A History from Its Origins to 1966*. Stanford, Calif.: Hoover Institution Press.

Diamond, Larry. 1992. "Economic Development and Democracy Reconsidered." In *Reexamining Democracy: Essays in Honor of Seymour Martin Lipset*, ed. Gary Marks and Larry Diamond, 93–128. Newbury Park, Calif.: Sage Publications.

Dodd, C. H. 1991. "Atatürk and Political Parties." In *Political Parties and Democracy in Turkey*, ed. Metin Heper and Jacob M. Landau, 24–41. London: I. B. Tauris.

Downing, Brian M. 1992. *The Military Revolution and Political Change: Origins of Democracy and Autocracy in Early Modern Europe*. Princeton, N.J.: Princeton University Press.

Downs, Anthony. 1957. *An Economic Theory of Democracy*. New York: Harper and Row.

Dresch, Paul. 2000. *A History of Modern Yemen*. Cambridge: Cambridge University Press.

Drysdale, Alasdair, and Gerald H. Blake. 1985. *The Middle East and North Africa: A Political Geography*. New York: Oxford University Press.

Duverger, Maurice. 1954. *Political Parties: Their Organization and Activity in the Modern State*. Trans. Barbara North and Robert North. London: Methuen.

Entelis, John P. 1980. *Comparative Politics of North Africa: Algeria, Morocco, and Tunisia*. Syracuse, N.Y.: Syracuse University Press.

———. 1986. *Algeria: The Revolution Institutionalized*. Boulder: Westview.

———. 1989. *Culture and Counterculture in Moroccan Politics*. Boulder: Westview.

Entelis, John P., and Lisa Arone. 1995. "Democratic and Popular Republic of Algeria." In *The Government and Politics of the Middle East and North Africa*, ed. Bernard Reich and David E. Long, 394–422. 3rd ed. Boulder: Westview.

Eppel, Michael. 1998a. "The Decline of British Influence and the Ruling Elite in Iraq." In *Demise of the British Empire in the Middle East*, ed. Michael J. Cohen and Martin Kolinsky, 185–97. London: Frank Cass.

———. 1998b. "The Elite, the Effendiya, and the Growth of Nationalism and Pan-Arabism in Hashemite Iraq, 1921–1958." *International Journal of Middle East Studies* 30, no. 2 (May): 227–50.

———. 1999. "The Fadhil Al-Jamali Government in Iraq, 1953–1954." *Journal of Contemporary History* 34, no. 3 (July): 417–42.

Ertman, Thomas. 1998. "Democracy and Dictatorship in Interwar Western Europe Revisited." *World Politics* 50, no. 3:475–505.

Farouk-Sluglett, Marion, and Peter Sluglett. 1991. "The Social Classes and the Origins of the Revolution." In *The Iraqi Revolution of 1958: The Old Social Classes Revisited*, ed. Robert A. Fernea and Wm. Roger Louis, 118–41. London: I. B. Tauris.

Fernea, Robert A., and Wm. Roger Louis. 1991. "Introduction." In *The Iraqi Revolution of 1958: The Old Social Classes Revisited*, ed. Robert A. Fernea and Wm. Roger Louis, vii–xxiv. London: I. B. Tauris.

Finefrock, Michael M. 1979. "The 'Second Group' in the First Turkish Grand National Assembly." *Journal of South Asian and Middle Eastern Studies* 3, no. 1 (Fall): 3–20.

Frey, Frederick W. 1965. *The Turkish Political Elite.* Cambridge, Mass.: M.I.T. Press.

Fry, Michael Graham. 1997. "Decolonization: Britain, France, and the Cold War." In *The End of Empire? The Transformation of the USSR in Comparative Perspective*, ed. Karen Dawisha and Bruce Parrott, 121–54. Armonk, N.Y.: M. E. Sharpe.

Gallagher, Charles F. 1956. "A Moroccan Political Party: The Istiqlal." *American Universities Field Staff Report Service: North Africa Series* 2, no. 2.

———. 1959. "The Evolving Moroccan Political Scene: Ben Barka and the National Union." *American Universities Field Staff Report Service: North Africa Series* 5, no. 5.

Gause, Gregory F., III. 1995. "Republic of Yemen." In *The Government and Politics of the Middle East and North Africa.*, ed. Bernard Reich and David E. Long, 150–72. 3rd ed. Boulder: Westview.

Gavin, R. J. 1975. *Aden Under British Rule 1839–1967.* New York: Barnes and Noble Books.

Gerber, Haim. 1987. *The Social Origins of the Modern Middle East.* Boulder: Lynne Rienner.

Ghods, M. Reza. 1989. *Iran in the Twentieth Century: A Political History.* Boulder: Lynne Rienner.

Gordon, David C. 1966. *The Passing of French Algeria.* London: Oxford University Press.

Gordon, Joel. 1989. "The False Hopes of 1950: The Wafd's Last Hurrah and the Demise of Egypt's Old Order." *International Journal of Middle East Studies* 21, no. 2 (May): 193–214.

———. 1992. *Nasser's Blessed Movement: Egypt's Free Officers and the July Revolution.* New York: Oxford University Press.

Grassmuck, George. 1960. "The Electoral Process in Iraq, 1952–1958." *Middle East Journal* 14, no. 4:397–415.

Güneş, İhsan. 1992. "1912 Seçimleri ve Eskişehir 'de Meydana Gelen Olaylar." *Belleten* 56, no. 216 (August): 459–82.

Haddad, George M. 1971. *Revolutions and Military Rule in the Middle East: The Arab States*. Part 1, *Iraq, Syria, Lebanon, and Jordan*. Vol. 2. New York: Robert Speller and Sons.

Haj, Samira. 1997. *The Making of Iraq, 1900–1963: Capital, Power, and Ideology*. Albany: State University of New York Press.

Halliday, Fred. 1974. *Arabia Without Sultans: A Survey of Political Instability in the Arab World*. New York: Vintage Books.

Hammoudi, Abdellah. 1997. *Master and Disciple: The Cultural Foundations of Moroccan Authoritarianism*. Chicago: University of Chicago Press.

Hamza, Hassine-Raouf. 1991. "Le Mouvement National Tunisien de 1945 à 1950: Hégémonie et institutionnalisation du Néo-Destour." *Actes du Ve Colloque International sur La Tunisie de l'après-guerre (1945–1950)*. Tunis: Publications de l'Institut Supérieur d'Histoire du Mouvement National.

Harik, Iliya F. 1975. "Political Elite of Lebanon." In *Political Elites in the Middle East*, ed. George Lenczowski. Washington, D.C.: American Enterprise Institute for Public Policy Research.

Heper, Metin. 1998. *İsmet İnonu: The Making of a Turkish Statesman*. Leiden: Brill.

Hermassi, Elbaki. 1972. *Leadership and National Development in North Africa: A Comparative Study*. Berkeley: University of California Press.

Heydemann, Steven. 1999. *Authoritarianism in Syria: Institutions and Social Conflict, 1946–1970*. Ithaca, N.Y.: Cornell University Press.

Heyworth-Dunne, J. 1951. *Political and Constitutional Development in Syria, 1918–1951*. Near and Middle East and Muslim World Briefing Papers No. 16. FAO/51/8/1832.

Hinnebusch, Raymond A. 1989. *Peasant and Bureaucracy in Ba'thist Syria: The Political Economy of Rural Development*. Boulder: Westview.

Hobsbawm, E. J. 1968. *Industry and Empire: The Making of Modern Society*. Vol. 2, *1759 to the Present Day*. New York: Pantheon.

Hourani, Albert. 1966. "Ottoman Reform and the Politics of the Notables." In *Beginnings of Modernization in the Middle East*, ed. William R. Polk and Richard L. Chambers, 41–68. Chicago: University of Chicago Press.

Huntington, Samuel P. 1991. *The Third Wave: Democratization in the Late Twentieth Century*. Norman: University of Oklahoma Press.

Hurewitz, J. C. 1956. *Diplomacy in the Near and Middle East, A Documentary Record: 1535–1914*. Vol. 1. Princeton, N.Y.: D. Von Nostrand.

Ibrahim, Saad Eddin. 1995. "Liberalization and Democratization in the Arab World: An Overview." In *Political Liberalization and Democratization in the Arab*

World. Vol. 1, *Theoretical Perspectives*, ed. Rex Brynen, Bahgat Korany, and Paul Noble, 29–60. Boulder: Lynne Rienner.

İnalcık, Halil. 1964. "The Nature of Traditional Society: Turkey." In *Political Modernization in Japan and Turkey*, ed. Robert E. Ward and Dankwart A. Rustow, 42–63. Princeton, N.J.: Princeton University Press.

Inglehart, Ronald. 1988. "The Renaissance of Political Culture." *American Political Science Review* 82, no. 4:1203–30.

———. 1997. *Modernization and Postmodernization: Cultural, Economic, and Political Change in 43 Societies.* Princeton, N.J.: Princeton University Press.

Inkeles, Alex, and David H. Smith. 1974. *Becoming Modern: Individual Change in Six Developing Countries.* Cambridge, Mass.: Harvard University Press.

Interview A. April 1998. Former ND/PSD militant, parliamentarian, and cabinet member. Tunis.

Interview B. April 1998. RCD official. Tunis.

Interview C. May 1998. ND/PSD/RCD militant and current government official. Tunis.

Interview D. May 1998. ND/PSD militant and party official. Tunis.

Interview E. May 1998. Former Tunisian Communist Party militant. Tunis.

Interview F. May 1998. Opposition party leader. Tunis.

Ismael, Tareq Y., and Jacqueline S. Ismael. 1986. *The People's Democratic Republic of Yemen: The Politics of Socialist Transformation.* Boulder: Lynne Rienner.

Issawi, Charles. 1956. "Economic and Social Foundations of Democracy in the Middle East." *International Affairs* 32, no. 1 (January): 27–42.

Jackson, Robert H. 1990. *Quasi-States: Sovereignty, International Relations, and the Third World.* New York: Cambridge University Press.

Jankowski, James P. 1975. *Egypt's Young Rebels: "Young Egypt" 1933–1952.* Stanford, Calif.: Hoover Institution Press.

Kabasakal, Mehmet. 1991. *Türkiye'de Siyasal Parti Örgütlenmesi (1908–1960).* İstanbul: Tekin Yayınevi.

Kahler, Miles. 1984. *Decolonization in Britain and France: The Domestic Consequences of International Relations.* Princeton, N.J.: Princeton University Press.

Kalyvas, Stathis N. 1996. *The Rise of Christian Democracy in Europe.* Ithaca, N.Y.: Cornell University Press.

Kamrava, Mehran. 1992. *The Political History of Modern Iran: From Tribalism to Theocracy.* Westport, Conn.: Praeger.

Karpat, Kemal H. n.d. "The Impact of the People's Houses on the Development of Communication in Turkey, 1931–1951." *Die Welt des Islams* 15, 1–4:69–84.

———. 1959. *Turkey's Politics: The Transition to a Multi-Party System.* Princeton, N.J.: Princeton University Press.

———. 1964. "The Mass Media: Turkey." In *Political Modernization in Japan and Turkey*, ed. Robert E. Ward and Dankwart A. Rustow, 255–82. Princeton, N.J.: Princeton University Press.

———. 1966. "The Land Regime, Social Structure, and Modernization in the Ottoman Empire." In *Beginnings of Modernization in the Middle East*, William R. Polk and Richard L. Chambers, 69–90. Chicago: The University of Chicago Press.

———. 1970. "The Military and Politics in Turkey, 1960–1964: A Socio-Cultural Analysis of a Revolution." *American Historical Review* 75, no. 6:1654–83.

———. 1972. "The Transformation of the Ottoman State, 1789–1908." *International Journal of Middle East Studies* 3, no. 3 (July): 243–81.

———. 1991. "The Republican People's Party, 1923–1945." In *Political Parties and Democracy in Turkey*, ed. Metin Heper and Jacob M. Landau, 42–64. London: I. B. Tauris.

Katznelson, Ira. 1986. "Working-Class Formation: Constructing Cases and Comparisons." In *Working-Class Formation: Nineteenth-Century Patterns in Western Europe and the United States*, ed. Ira Katznelson and Aristide R. Zolberg, 3–41. Princeton, N.J.: Princeton University Press.

Kaylani, Nabil M. 1972. "The Rise of the Syrian Ba'th, 1940–1958: Political Success, Party Failure." *International Journal of Middle East Studies* 3, no. 1:3–23.

Kedourie, Elie. 1992. *Democracy and Arab Political Culture*. Washington, D.C.: Washington Institute for Near East Policy.

Keyder, Çağlar. 1987. *State and Class in Turkey: A Study in Capitalist Development*. New York: Verso.

Khadduri, Majid. 1960. *Independent Iraq 1932–1958: A Study in Iraqi Politics*. 2nd ed. London: Oxford University Press.

———. 1969. *Republican 'Iraq: A Study in 'Iraqi Politics Since the Revolution of 1958*. London: Oxford University Press.

Khader, Bichara. 1984. "Le Parti Ba'th." Cahier 5. Louvain-la-Neuve: Centre de Recherches sur le Monde Arabe Contemporain.

Khoury, Philip S. 1987. *Syria and the French Mandate: The Politics of Arab Nationalism, 1920–1945*. Princeton, N.J.: Princeton University Press.

Kili, Suna. 1971. *Turkish Constitutional Developments and Assembly Debates on the Constitutions of 1924 and 1961*. İstanbul: Menteş Matbaası.

Kinross, Lord. 1965. *Ataturk: A Biography of Mustafa Kemal, Father of Modern Turkey*. New York: William Morrow.

Kirişçi, Kemal, and Gareth M. Winrow. 1997. *The Kurdish Question and Turkey: An Example of a Trans-state Ethnic Conflict*. London: Frank Cass.

Kohli, Atul, and Vivienne Shue. 1994. "State Power and Social Forces: On Political Contention and Accommodation in the Third World." In *State Power and Social Forces: Domination and Transformation in the Third World*, ed. Joel S. Migdal, Atul Kohli, and Vivienne Shue, 293–326. New York: Cambridge University Press.

Kostiner, Joseph. 1984. *The Struggle for South Yemen*. New York: St. Martin's Press.

Kraiem, Mustapha. 1985. "Le Néo-Destour: Cadres, militants, et implantation pendant les années trente." *Actes du 3e Séminaire sur l'Histoire du Mouvement National: Les mouvements politiques et sociaux dans la Tunisie des années 1930*. Tunis: Programme National de Recherche d'Histoire du Mouvement National.

———. 1997. *Le Parti Communiste Tunisien pendant la période coloniale*. Tunis: Institut Supérieur d'Histoire du Mouvement National.

La Palombara, Joseph, and Myron Weiner. 1966. "The Origin and Development of Political Parties." In *Political Parties and Political Development*, ed. Joseph La Palombara and Myron Weiner, 3–42. Princeton, N.J.: Princeton University Press.

Lackner, Helen. 1985. *P.D.R. Yemen: Outpost of Socialist Development in Arabia*. London: Ithaca Press.

Lerner, Daniel. 1958. *The Passing of Traditional Society*. Glencoe, Ill.: Free Press.

Lewis, Bernard. 1968. *The Emergence of Modern Turkey*. 2nd ed. London: Oxford University Press.

———. 1996. "Islam and Liberal Democracy." *Journal of Democracy* 7, no. 2 (April): 52–63.

Limbert, John W. 1987. *Iran: At War with History*. Boulder: Westview.

———. 1995. "Islamic Republic of Iran." In *The Government and Politics of the Middle East and North Africa*, ed. Bernard Reich and David E. Long, 41–61. 3rd ed. Boulder: Westview.

Ling, Dwight L. 1967. *Tunisia from Protectorate to Republic*. Bloomington: Indiana University Press.

Linz, Juan J. 1978. *The Breakdown of Democratic Regimes: Crisis, Breakdown, and Reequilibration*. Baltimore: Johns Hopkins University Press.

Lipset, Seymour M. 1959. "Some Social Requisites of Democracy: Economic Development and Political Legitimacy." *American Political Science Review* 53, no. 1 (March): 69–105.

Lipset, Seymour M., and Stein Rokkan. 1967. "Cleavage Structures, Party Systems, and Voter Alignments: An Introduction." In *Party Systems and Voter Alignments: Cross-National Perspectives*, ed. Seymour M. Lipset and Stein Rokkan, 1–64. New York: Free Press.

Longrigg, Stephen Hemsley. 1953. *'Iraq, 1900 to 1950: A Political, Social, and Economic History*. London: Oxford University Press.

Luciani, Giacomo. 1987. "Allocation vs. Production States: A Theoretical Framework." In *The Rentier State*, ed. Hazem Beblawi and Giacomo Luciani, 63–82. London: Croom Helm.

Luebbert, Gregory M. 1991. *Liberalism, Fascism, or Social Democracy: Social Classes and the Political Origins of Regimes in Interwar Europe*. New York: Oxford University Press.

Ma'oz, Moshe. 1972. "Attempts at Creating a Political Community in Modern Syria." *Middle East Journal* 26, no. 4 (Autumn): 389–404.

Mahoney, James, and Dietrich Rueschemeyer, eds. 2003. *Comparative Historical Analysis in the Social Sciences*. New York: Cambridge University Press.

Mainwaring, Scott, and Timothy R. Scully. 1995. "Introduction: Party Systems in Latin America." In *Building Democratic Institutions: Party Systems in Latin America*, ed. Scott Mainwaring and Timothy R. Scully, 1–34. Stanford, Calif.: Stanford University Press.

Mair, Peter, ed. 1990. *The West European Party System*. New York: Oxford University Press.

Mardin, Şerif. 1973. "Center-Periphery Relations: A Key to Turkish Politics?" *Daedalus* 102 (Winter): 169–90.

Marr, Phebe. 1985. *The Modern History of Iraq*. Boulder: Westview.

———. 1995. "Republic of Iraq." In *The Government and Politics of the Middle East and North Africa*, ed. Bernard Reich and David E. Long, 90–112. 3rd ed. Boulder: Westview.

———. 2004. *The Modern History of Iraq*. 2nd ed. Boulder: Westview.

McDowall, David. 1996. *A Modern History of the Kurds*. London: I. B. Tauris.

Meric, Edouard. 1973. "The Destourian Socialist Party and the National Organizations." In *Man, State, and Society in the Contemporary Maghrib*, ed. I. William Zartman, 285–95. New York: Praeger.

Micaud, Charles A. 1964. "Social and Economic Change." In *Tunisia: The Politics of Modernization*, ed. Charles A. Micaud, Leon Carl Brown, and Clement Henry Moore, 131–86. New York: Praeger.

Michels, Robert. 1962. *Political Parties: A Sociological Study of the Oligarchical Tendencies of Modern Democracy*. Trans. Eden Paul and Cedar Paul. New York: Free Press.

Mitchell, Richard P. 1993. *The Society of the Muslim Brothers*. New York: Oxford University Press.

Moalla, Mansour. 1992. *L'Etat tunisien et l'indépendance*. Tunis: Cérès Productions.

Moore, Barrington, Jr. 1966. *Social Origins of Dictatorship and Democracy: Lord and Peasant in the Making of the Modern World*. Boston: Beacon Press.

Moore, Clement Henry. 1964. "The Era of the Neo-Destour." In *Tunisia: The Pol-*

itics of Modernization, ed. Charles A. Micaud, Leon Carl Brown, and Clement Henry Moore, 69–130. New York: Praeger.

———. 1965. *Tunisia Since Independence: The Dynamics of One-Party Government.* Berkeley: University of California Press.

———. 1970. *Politics in North Africa: Algeria, Morocco, and Tunisia.* Boston: Little, Brown.

Murphy, Emma C. 1999. *Economic and Political Change in Tunisia: From Bourguiba to Ben Ali.* New York: St. Martin's Press.

n.a. n.d. *Le Neo-Destour: Son esprit, Ses méthodes, Ses hommes.* Document No. 3463. Tunis: Archives Nationales de Tunisie. [According to AMAE documents (638/297/155 and 652/319/47), this document was prepared in 1952 by the French resident-general in Tunis at the request of the French foreign affairs minister. The latter was concerned that U.S. policymakers viewed ND leaders as "authentic democrats" and wanted to argue to the Americans that the party was actually quite dictatorial in its methods.—M.A.]

Naylor, Phillip C. 2000. *France and Algeria: A History of Decolonization and Transformation.* Gainesville: University Press of Florida.

O'Donnell, Guillermo. 1973. *Modernization and Bureaucratic-Authoritarianism: Studies in South American Politics.* Berkeley: University of California Institute of International Studies.

O'Donnell, Guillermo, and Philippe C. Schmitter. 1986. *Transitions from Authoritarian Rule: Tentative Conclusions about Uncertain Democracies.* Baltimore: Johns Hopkins University Press.

Okruhlik, Gwenn. 1999. "Rentier Wealth, Unruly Law, and the Rise of Opposition: The Political Economy of Oil States." *Comparative Politics* 31, no. 3 (April): 295–315.

Olson, Mancur, Jr. 1965. *The Logic of Collective Action: Public Goods and the Theory of Groups.* Cambridge: Harvard University Press.

Ordeshook, Peter C., and Olga V. Shvetsova. 1994. "Ethnic Heterogeneity, District Magnitude, and the Number of Parties." *American Journal of Political Science* 38, no. 1:100–123.

Ottaway, David, and Marina Ottaway. 1970. *Algeria: The Politics of a Socialist Revolution.* Berkeley: University of California Press.

Owen, Roger, and Şevket Pamuk. 1998. *A History of Middle East Economies in the Twentieth Century.* London: I. B. Tauris.

Özbudun, Ergun. 1976. *Social Change and Political Participation in Turkey.* Princeton, N.J.: Princeton University Press.

Patai, Raphael. 1958. *The Kingdom of Jordan.* Princeton, N.J.: Princeton University Press.

Payaslıoğlu, Arif T. 1964. "Political Leadership and Political Parties: Turkey." In

Political Modernization in Japan and Turkey, ed. Robert W. Ward and Dankwart A. Rustow, 411–33. Princeton, N.J.: Princeton University Press.

Picard, Elisabeth. 1980. "La Syrie de 1946 à 1979." In *La Syrie D'Aujourd'hui*, ed. André Raymond. Paris: Centre National de la Recherche Scientifique.

Plascov, Avi. 1981. *The Palestinian Refugees in Jordan, 1948–1957*. London: Frank Cass.

Posusney, Marsha Pripstein, and Michele Penner Angrist, eds. 2005. *Regimes and Resistance: Authoritarianism in the Middle East*. Boulder: Lynne Rienner.

Prather, George Martin. 1978. *Movement, Structure, and Linkage: The Rise of the Turkish Democrat Party*. Ph.D. dissertation, University of California, Los Angeles.

Przeworski, Adam. 1986. "Some Problems in the Study of the Transition to Democracy." In *Transitions from Authoritarian Rule: Comparative Perspectives*, ed. Guillermo O'Donnell, Philippe C. Schmitter, and Laurence Whitehead, 47–63. Baltimore: Johns Hopkins University Press.

———. 1988. "Democracy as a Contingent Outcome of Conflicts." In *Constitutionalism and Democracy*, ed. Jon Elster and Rune Slagstad, 59–80. Cambridge: Cambridge University Press.

———. 1991. *Democracy and the Market: Political and Economic Reforms in Eastern Europe and Latin America*. New York: Cambridge University Press.

Przeworski, Adam, and Fernando Limongi. 1993. "Political Regimes and Economic Growth." *Journal of Economic Perspectives* 7, no. 3 (Summer): 51, 65.

———. 1997. "Modernization: Theories and Facts." *World Politics* 49, no. 2 (January): 155–83.

Przeworski, Adam, and John Sprague. 1986. *Paper Stones: A History of Electoral Socialism*. Chicago: University of Chicago Press.

Putnam, Robert D. 1993. *Making Democracy Work: Civic Traditions in Modern Italy*. Princeton, N.J.: Princeton University Press.

Pye, Lucian W. 1990. "Political Science and the Crisis of Authoritarianism." *American Political Science Review* 84, no. 1 (March): 3–18.

République Tunisienne. n.d. *Constitution de la République Tunisienne*. Tunis: Imprimerie Officielle de la République Tunisienne.

Rivlin, Benjamin. 1952. "The Tunisian Nationalist Movement: Four Decades of Evolution." *Middle East Journal* 6 (Spring): 167–93.

Rosenstone, Steven, J., and John Mark Hansen. 1993. *Mobilization, Participation, and Democracy in America*. New York: Macmillan.

Rudebeck, Lars. 1967. *Party and People: A Study of Political Change in Tunisia*. Stockholm: Almqvist and Wiksell.

Ruedy, John. 1992. *Modern Algeria: The Origins and Development of a Nation*. Bloomington: Indiana University Press.

Rueschemeyer, Dietrich, Evelyne Huber Stephens, and John D. Stephens. 1992. *Capitalist Development and Democracy*. Cambridge: Polity Press.

Rustow, Dankwart A. 1959. "The Army and the Founding of the Turkish Republic." *World Politics* 11 (1959): 513–52.

———. 1960. "The Politics of the Near East." In *The Politics of Developing Areas*, ed. Gabriel A. Almond and James Coleman, 369–454. Princeton, N.J.: Princeton University Press.

———. 1964. "The Military: Turkey." In *Political Modernization in Japan and Turkey*, ed. Robert E. Ward and Dankwart A. Rustow, 252–388. Princeton, N.J.: Princeton University Press.

———. 1966. "The Development of Parties in Turkey." In *Political Parties and Political Development*, ed. Joseph LaPalombara and Myron Weiner, 107–33. Princeton, N.J.: Princeton University Press.

———. 1970. "Transitions to Democracy: Toward a Dynamic Model." *Comparative Politics* 2, no. 3 (April): 337–63.

———. 1991. "Political Parties in Turkey: An Overview." In *Political Parties and Democracy in Turkey*, ed. Metin Heper and Jacob M. Landau, 10–23. London: I. B. Tauris.

Saikal, Amin. 1980. *The Rise and Fall of the Shah*. Princeton, N.J.: Princeton University Press.

Salibi, Kamal. 1993. *The Modern History of Jordan*. London: I. B. Tauris.

Sani, Giacomo, and Giovanni Sartori. 1983. "Polarization, Fragmentation, and Competition in Western Democracies." In *Western European Party Systems: Continuity and Change*, ed. Hans Daalder and Peter Mair, 307–40. London: Sage Publications.

Sartori, Giovanni. 1976. *Parties and Party Systems: A Framework for Analysis*. Vol. 1. Cambridge: Cambridge University Press.

Satloff, Robert B. 1994. *From Abdullah to Hussein: Jordan in Transition*. New York: Oxford University Press.

al-Sayyid-Marsot, Afaf Lutfi. 1977. *Egypt's Liberal Experiment: 1922–1936*. Berkeley: University of California Press.

Schaar, Stuart. 1973. "King Hassan's Alternatives." In *Man, State, and Society in the Contemporary Maghrib*, ed. I. William Zartman, 229–44. New York: Praeger.

Schattschneider, E. E. 1942. *Party Government*. New York: Rinehart.

Schmitter, Philippe C., and Terry Lynn Karl. 1991. "What Democracy Is . . . and Is Not." *Journal of Democracy* 2, no. 3:75–88.

Seale, Patrick. 1965. *The Struggle for Syria: A Study of Post-War Arab Politics 1945–1958*. New Haven, Conn.: Yale University Press.

Serbest Cümhuriyet Fırkası (SCF), Umumî Kâtipliği. 1930a. *Serbes, lâyık, Cümhuriyet fırkasının Yasası*. İstanbul: Cumhuriyet Matbaası.

———. 1930b. "Serbest Cumhuriyet Fırkası'nın Programı." In Tunçay, *Tek Parti Yönetimi'nin Kurulması*. İstanbul.

Sezgin, Ömür, and Gencay Şaylan. 1983. "Terakkiperver Cumhuriyet Fırkası." *Cumhuriyet Dönemi Türkiye Ansiklopedisi*. Vol. 8, 2043–51. İstanbul: İletişim Yayınları.

Sharabi, Hisham. 1960. "Parliamentary Government and Military Autocracy in the Middle East." *Orbis* 4, no. 3:338–55.

———. 1988. *Neopatriarchy: A Theory of Distorted Change in Arab Society*. New York: Oxford University Press.

Shaw, Stanford J. 1969. "The Origins of Representative Government in the Ottoman Empire: An Introduction to the Provincial Councils, 1839–1876." In *New York University Near Eastern Round Table I, 1967–1968.*, ed. R. Bayly Winder, 53–142. New York: New York University.

———. 1970. "The Central Legislative Councils in the Nineteenth Century Ottoman Reform Movement Before 1876." *International Journal of Middle East Studies* 1, no. 1 (January): 51–84.

Shaw, Stanford J., and Ezel Kural Shaw. 1977. *History of the Ottoman Empire and Modern Turkey*. Vol. 2, *Reform, Revolution, and Republic: The Rise of Modern Turkey, 1808–1975*. Cambridge: Cambridge University Press.

Silvera, Victor. 1960. "Conferences sur 'L'évolution du régime politique de la Tunisie.'" Mémoires du Centre de Hautes Etudes Administratives sur l'Afrique et l'Asie Modernes, XXème Stage, 1959–1960. Paris: Centre de Hautes Etudes Administratives sur l'Afrique et l'Asie Modernes.

———. 1966. Notes et Etudes Documentaires No. 3331: Les Institutions Tunisiennes. Paris: La documentation française.

Sivan, Emmanuel. 1997. "Constraints and Opportunities in the Arab World." *Journal of Democracy* 8, no. 2 (April): 103–13.

Skocpol, Theda. 1979. *States and Social Revolutions: A Comparative Analysis of France, Russia, and China*. Cambridge: Cambridge University Press.

Skocpol, Theda, and Margaret Somers. 1980. "The Uses of Comparative History in Macrosocial Inquiry." *Comparative Studies in Society and History* 22, no. 2 (April): 174–97.

Sluglett, Peter, and Marion Farouk-Sluglett. 1993. "Sunnis and Shi'is Revisited: Sectarianism and Ethnicity in Authoritarian Iraq." In *Iraq: Power and Society*, ed. Derek Hopwood, Habib Ishow, and Thomas Koszinowski, 75–90. Reading, N.Y.: Ithaca Press.

Spruyt, Hendrik. 2000. "The End of Empire and the Extension of the Westphalian System: The Normative Basis of the Modern State Order." *International Studies Review* 2, no. 2 (Summer): 65–92.

Stephens, John D. 1998. "Historical Analysis and Causal Assessment in Comparative Research." *APSA-CP Newsletter of the APSA Organized Section in Comparative Politics* 9, no. 1:22–25.

Stookey, Robert W. 1982. *South Yemen: A Marxist Republic in Arabia.* Boulder: Westview.

Stork, Joe. 1982. "State Power and Economic Structure: Class Determination and State Formation in Contemporary Iraq." In *Iraq: The Contemporary State*, ed. Tim Niblock, 27–46. London: Croom Helm.

Tanör, Bülent. 1990. "The Place of Parliament in Turkey." In *Turkish State, Turkish Society*, ed. Andrew Finkel and Nükhet Sırman, 139–58. London: Routledge.

———. 1992. *Türkiye'de Yerel Kongre İktidarları (1918–1920).* İstanbul: AFA Yayıncılık.

Tekeli, Şirin. 1983. "Cumhuriyet Döneminde Seçimler." *Cumhuriyet Dönemi Türkiye Ansiklopedisi.* Vol 7, 1798–1809. İstanbul: İletişim Yayinlari.

Terry, Janice J. 1982. *The Wafd, 1919–1952: Cornerstone of Egyptian Political Power.* London: Third World Centre for Research and Publishing.

Tessler, Mark A. 1982. "Morocco: Institutional Pluralism and Monarchical Dominance." In *Political Elites in Arab North Africa*, ed. William Zartman et al., 35–91. New York: Longman.

Tessler, Mark A., John P. Entelis, and Gregory W. White. 1995. "Kingdom of Morocco." In *The Government and Politics of the Middle East and North Africa*, ed. David E. Long and Bernard Reich, 369–93. 3rd ed. Boulder: Westview.

Thelen, Kathleen. 1998. "Historical Institutionalism in Comparative Politics." Paper presented at the Annual Meeting of the American Political Science Association, Boston, September 1998. In *The Annual Review of Political Science* 2, 1999 (Palo Alto, Calif.: Annual Reviews).

Thompson, Elizabeth. 1993. "Ottoman Political Reform in the Provinces: The Damascus Advisory Council in 1844–45." *International Journal of Middle East Studies* 25, no. 3 (August): 457–75.

Tibawi, A. L. 1969. *A Modern History of Syria, including Lebanon and Palestine.* London: Macmillan.

Tlili, Ahmed. 1988. *Lettre à Bourguiba: Janvier 1966.* Tunis: Imprimeries Réunies.

Toker, Metin. 1970. *Tek Partiden Çok Partiye.* Milliyet Yayınları.

Torrey, Gordon H. 1964. *Syrian Politics and the Military: 1945–1958.* Columbus: Ohio State University Press.

———. 1969. "The Ba'th—Ideology and Practice." *Middle East Journal* 23, no. 4: 445-70.

Tripp, Charles. 2000. *A History of Iraq*. Cambridge: Cambridge University Press.

Tunaya, Tarık Z. 1952. *Türkiye'de Siyasi Partiler, 1859–1952*. İstanbul: Doğan Kardeş Yayınları A. Ş. Basımevi.

Tunaya, Tarık Zafer. 1988. *Türkiye'de Siyasal Partiler, Cilt 1: İkinci Meşrutiyet Dönemi, 1908–1918*. 2nd ed. İstanbul: Hürriyet Vakfı Yayınları.

Tunçay, Mete. 1983. "Cumhuriyet Halk Partisi (1923–1950)." *Cumhuriyet Dönemi Türkiye Ansiklopedisi*. Vol. 8, 2019–24. İstanbul: İletişim Yayinlari.

Turan, İlter. 1994. "The Turkish Legislature: From Symbolic to Substantive Representation." In *Parliaments in the Modern World: Changing Institutions*, ed. Gary W. Copeland and Samuel C. Patterson, 105–28. Ann Arbor: University of Michigan Press.

Usta, Veysel. 1994. "Trabzon'da Terakkiperver Fırka'nın Kuruluşu." *Tarih ve Toplum* 21, no. 126 (June): 27–31.

Üstel, Füsun. 1997. *İmparatorluktan Ulus-Devlete Türk Milliyetçiliği: Türk Ocakları (1912–1931)*. İstanbul: İletişim Yayınları.

Van Dusen, Michael H. 1972. "Political Integration and Regionalism in Syria." *Middle East Journal* 26, no. 2:123–36.

Vatikiotis, P. J. 1967. *Politics and the Military in Jordan: A Study of the Arab Legion, 1921–1957*. London: Frank Cass.

———. 1978. *Nasser and His Generation*. New York: St. Martin's Press.

———. 1991. *The History of Modern Egypt: From Muhammad Ali to Mubarak*. 4th ed. London: Weidenfeld and Nicolson.

Vitalis, Robert. 1995. *When Capitalists Collide: Business Conflict and the End of Empire in Egypt*. Berkeley: University of California Press.

Waldner, David. 1999. *State Building and Late Development*. Ithaca, N.Y.: Cornell University Press.

Waterbury, John. 1970. *The Commander of the Faithful: The Moroccan Political Elite—A Study in Segmented Politics*. New York: Columbia University Press.

———. 1997. "Fortuitous By-Products." *Comparative Politics* 29, no. 3 (April): 383–402.

Wedeen, Lisa. 2002. "Conceptualizing Culture: Possibilities for Political Science." *American Political Science Review* 96, no. 4: 713–28.

Weiker, Walter F. 1973. *Political Tutelage and Democracy in Turkey: The Free Party and Its Aftermath*. Leiden: E. J. Brill.

Yashar, Deborah J. 1997. *Demanding Democracy: Reform and Reaction in Costa Rica and Guatemala, 1870s–1950s*. Stanford, Calif.: Stanford University Press.

Yerasimos, Stéphane. 1987. "The Monoparty Period." In *Turkey in Transition: New Perspectives*, ed. İrvin C. Schick and Ertuğrul Ahmet Tonak, 66–100. New York: Oxford University Press..

Yeşil, Ahmet. 1992. *Türkiye Cumhuriyeti'nde İlk Teşkilatlı Muhalefet Hareketi: Terrakiperver Cumhuriyet Fırkası*. Ph.D. thesis, Hacettepe University, Ankara.

Yetkin, Çetin. 1987. *Atatürk'ün Başarısız Demokrasi Devrimi: Serbest Cumhuriyet Fırkası*. İstanbul: Toplumsal Dönüşüm Yayınları.

Yılmaz, Hakan. 1996. "The International Context of Regime Change: Turkey, 1923–1960." Ph.D. dissertation, Columbia University.

Zartman, I. William. 1963. *Government and Politics in Northern Africa*. New York: Praeger.

———. 1973. "Political Pluralism in Morocco." In *Man, State, and Society in the Contemporary Maghrib*, ed. I. William Zartman, 245–59. New York: Praeger.

Zubaida, Sami. 1991. "Community, Class, and Minorities in Iraqi Politics." In *The Iraqi Revolution of 1958: The Old Social Classes Revisited*, ed. Robert A. Fernea, and Wm. Roger Louis, 197–210. London: I. B. Tauris.

Zürcher, Erik J. 1984. *The Unionist Factor: The Role of the Committee of Union and Progress in the Turkish National Movement, 1905–1926*. Leiden: E. J. Brill.

———. 1991. *Political Opposition in the Early Turkish Republic: The Progressive Republican Party, 1924–1925*. Leiden: E. J. Brill.

———. 1994. *Turkey: A Modern History*. London: I. B. Tauris.

INDEX

Abbas, Ferhat, 48, 49, 117
Abdallah, Ridha, 213n8
Abdülhamit II (sultan), 88
Abdullah (king of Jordan), 61, 137, 138
Abdülmecit (sultan), 80
Abu al-Huda, Tawfiq, 141
Abu Jaber, Kamel S., 61, 141
Abu Nuwar, Ali, 141–42
Achour, Habib, 111
Aden Association (AA), 44, 46
Aden College, 115
Aden Trade Unions Congress (ATUC), 115
administrative council system (late Ottoman Empire). *See* provincial administrative council system (late Ottoman Empire)
adul, 36
Agwani, M. S., 214n13
Ahâli Fırkası (late Ottoman Empire), 91
'Ahd Party (Iraq), 60
Ahmad, Feroz, 93
Aldrich, John H., 13, 76
Aleppo, 70
Alexander, Gerard, 207n13
Algeria, 13, 14, 15; establishment of immediate, one-party founding regime in, 117–20; making of a single preponderant party in, 47–51; relative ease of party building in, 104–6
Algerian People's Party (PPA), 49
Amir Kabir, 97
Anderson, Lisa, 39
Anglo-Egyptian Treaty (1936), 66
Anglo-Jordanian Treaty (1948), 142
Anglo-Persian Treaty (1919), 57, 58
Arab Constitutional(ist) Party (Jordan), 14, 128, 138–41
Arab-Israeli Conflict, 138, 140–41, 192, 196, 217n1
Arab Legion, 125
Arab Nationalist Movement (ANM) (Yemen), 114, 115
Arab Socialist Party (Syria), 14, 128, 143–48, 210n10
Arafat, Yasser, 4

Armée de Libération Nationale (ALN) (Algeria), 118–19
Association of the Ulama (Algeria), 48
Atatürk, Mustafa Kemal, 3, 58; and Defense of Rights societies, 216n4; and end of the Ottoman Empire, 186; and eradication of the sultanate, 186; and execution of political enemies, 169; and founding of the First Group, 163; and founding of the Republican People's Party, 165–66; and Free Republican Party, 171–74; and Grand National Assembly, 163–66; political and cultural reforms pushed by, 166; and political polarization in Turkey, 165, 175; and Progressive Republican Party, 166–69; and reforming Republican People's Party, 176–77; relationship of, to Committee for Union and Progress, 215n2; and Second Group, 164–67; and Turkish army, 186–87; and Turkish Hearths, 176; and Turkish War of Independence, 94; and the West, 193
âyan, 77–80
Avni, Şefik, 172–73

Baghdad Pact, 142
Bakdash, Khalid, 70
Banna, Hassan al-, 152
Batatu, Hanna, 60, 210n10
Ba'th Party (Iraq), 14, 128, 134–35, 137
Ba'th Party (Jordan), 14, 71, 128, 139–42, 215n16
Ba'th Party (Syria), 14, 70, 128, 143–48
Bayar, Celâl, 182
Bayraktar Mustafa Paşa, 79
ben Azouz, Mekki, 209n16
Ben Badis, Abdelhamid (sheikh), 48, 49, 117
Ben Bella, Ahmed, 119
Ben Salah, Ahmed, 110–11
Ben Youssef, Salah, 108–10, 112, 114, 212n4
bipartism, 20; and depolarization, 73, 161–62; evolution of, in Turkey, 159–84 passim; and majoritarian electoral rules, 74; origins of, in Turkey, 75, 77–96
Boumedienne, Houari, 119–20
Bourguiba, Habib, 38; and crafting of one-party rule in Tunisia, 108–14, 213nn9–10; and founding of the Neo-Destour Party, 38; and France, 108, 109; nationalist strategy of, 42; powers as president of Tunisia, 113; and Salah Ben Youssef, 108–10; as second-generation elite, 39; and silencing of political rivals, 108–11
Britain. *See* United Kingdom
Bujra, A. S., 47

caid, 35, 36, 37
caliph, 163
caliphate, 166
center-periphery conflict, 20; in Egypt, 98, 212n20; in Iran, 97; in the late Ottoman Empire and Turkey, 20, 75–97, 158–84 passim, 211n7; in Morocco, 98; in Tunisia, 99
Central Intelligence Agency (CIA), 132
challenger parties, 18; and defections from competitive norms in multiparty cases, 18, 127; failure to defect from competitive norms in Turkish case, 18, 186–87; and mobilizational asymmetry in party systems, 126–28,

154–57; and polarization in party systems, 124
class-based theories of regime formation, 5, 9–11, 198–204
cleavages, 20, 56, 68, 69–71
Cohen, Amnon, 71
Cold War, 69, 185, 192, 206n10
collective action, 20–21, 75; achieving, 76, 84, 105; and formation of political parties, 76, 104–6; among local elites in the Ottoman Empire, 85; obstacles to, 76
Collier, David, 13
Collier, Ruth Berins, 13
Comité des résistants (Tunisia), 110
Committee for Union and Progress (CUP) (late Ottoman Empire), 159, 211–12n15; and the "Big Stick" elections of 1912, 92–93; composition of, 89, 90; former members of, in Progressive Republican Party, 166–67; former members of, in Second Group, 164; and local notables in provinces, 89–93; as "new" Ottoman "center," 89–90; opposition to, during Second Constitutional Period, 91–93; origins of, 88; during Turkish War of Independence, 94
Communist Party (Algeria) (PCA), 50
Communist Party (Egypt), 15, 128, 150, 152–54
Communist Party (Iran). *See* Tudeh Party (Iran)
Communist Party (Iraq), 14, 70, 128, 134–36
Communist Party (Jordan), 14, 71, 128, 139–43, 215n16
Communist Party (Syria) (PCS), 14, 70, 128, 143–48
Communist Party (Tunisia) (PCT), 43, 112, 209nn17–18
Community Party (Jordan), 14, 128, 138–43
comparative historical analysis, 21
conservative parties, 18; and defections from competitive norms, 18, 127; and mobilizational asymmetry in party systems, 126–28, 154–57; and polarization in party systems, 124–25
Constitutional Reform Party (Egypt), 65
Constitutional Union Party (Iraq), 14, 70, 128, 135
Consultative Conference (Tunisia), 37
Cox, Gary, 68, 74, 210n2, 210n9
critical junctures, 21
culture-based theories of regime formation, 5–7, 193–94

Dahl, Robert A., 206n16
Dann, Uriel, 215n15
Defense of Rights societies, 93–95, 163, 168, 172
Demirel, Ahmet, 216nn4–5
Democrat Caucus (Iran), 14, 130
Democrat Party (DP) (Turkey), 3, 10, 15, 158–59, 178–84
Destour Party (Tunisia), 36–38, 42, 43
district magnitude, 68
Dodd, C. H., 169
Downs, Anthony, 161
Dresch, Paul, 114
Duverger, Maurice, 68, 161

East Bank, 71, 138, 141
Egypt, 13, 15; center-periphery conflict in, 98, 212n20; establishment of delayed authoritarian rule in, 149–54;

Egypt *(continued)*
explaining number of political parties in, 210n9; and Jordan, 128, 142; making of a multiparty system in, 64–67; polarization and mobilizational asymmetry in, 128; and Syria, 148
Eisenhower Doctrine, 143
elections, 16, 17, 18; in Jordan, 140; suffrage norms of, in multiparty cases, 126–28, 145–46, 156, 214n3; in Syria, 146
elections in the Ottoman Empire: "Big Stick" (1912), 92–93; for first Ottoman parliament, 87; and peripheral elite networks, 84, 85; and provincial administrative council system, 81, 211n8, 211n10; for second Ottoman parliament, 89, 90, 92; during Turkish War of Independence, 94, 163
elections in the Turkish Republic, 3, 165–66, 173, 183
electoral rules, 19, 56, 68–69, 209n7; majoritarian, 68, 73–74, 76, 210n2, 210n9; proportional representation, 68
elites, "second-generation," 19, 24, 34–35, 103–4. *See also under* Bourguiba, Habib; Hadj, Messali; National Liberation Front (FLN) (Algeria); National Liberation Front (NLF) (South Yemen); Neo-Destour Party (ND) (Tunisia)
elites, traditional, 19, 31, 32–34, 54–56
Entelis, John, 7, 51
Ertman, Thomas, 199, 200–201, 207n17
Extraordinary Assembly of Provincial Notables (late Ottoman Empire), 85

Federal Army of South Yemen, 116
fellaghas (Tunisia), 42, 110
Fernea, Robert A., 60
First Group (late Ottoman Empire/Turkey), 158, 159, 163–66, 216n5
FLN. *See* National Liberation Front (FLN) (Algeria)
founding regimes. *See* regimes, founding
France, 13, 24, 32, 207n2; and Habib Bourguiba, 108, 109; intransigence in Algeria, 49–50, 207n3; intransigence in Tunisia, 36–37, 207n3; in Morocco, 51–52; and Neo-Destour Party, 42; policies in Algeria, 47–48, 117–19; policies in Tunisia, 35–36, 42, 208n6; in Syria, 62–64, 209n3
Free Republican Party (FRP) (Turkey), 15, 159, 171–74, 176, 216nn8–10
Free-rider problem, 104–5
Frey, Frederick W., 181, 215n1, 216n5
Front des Forces Socialistes (FFS) (Algeria), 50–51
Front for the Liberation of Occupied South Yemen (FLOSY), 116
Front pour la Défense des Institutions Constitutionelles (FDIC) (Morocco), 122

Gaylani, Rashid 'Ali al-, 132
Gouvernement Provisoire de la République Algérienne (GPRA), 119
Government Council (Morocco), 52
Grand Council (Tunisia), 37
Grand National Assembly (late Ottoman Empire/Turkey), 94, 163–66
grand vizier, 79, 86, 90
Gulf States, 206n13
Güneş, İhsan, 212n18

habous, 35, 48, 112, 208n5
Hached, Farhat, 41
Hadj, Messali, 49, 117, 118
Hammoudi, Abdellah, 6
Hamza, Hassine-Raouf, 43
Hashemite(s), 61, 71, 143
Hatt-ı Şerif of Gülhane, 211n7
Hawrani, Akram al-, 145–48
Heper, Metin, 216n12
Hermassi, Elbaki, 48
Heydemann, Steven, 210n10
Hinnawi, Sami al-, 147
History of the Turkish Revolution, 175
Hizb al-Sha'b (Jordan), 61
Hizb al-Umma (Egypt), 65
Huntington, Samuel, 4, 8
Hussein (king of Jordan), 137–43 passim
Hürriyet ve İtilâf Fırkası (HİF) (late Ottoman Empire), 91–93, 159, 212n18

Ilah, 'Abd al- (prince), 133
imperial intransigence, 19, 33, 55, 207–8n3
Independence Party (Iraq). *See* Istiqlal (Iraq)
Independence Tribunals (Turkey), 169, 171
Independent Caucus (Iran), 130
Independent Wafdist Bloc (Egypt), 15, 128, 151
Individual Caucus (Iran), 130
Inglehart, Ronald, 7
İnönü, İsmet, 165, 177, 182, 216n12
interim transitional period(s), 15, 16, 18, 123–28, 206n15
Iran, 13, 14, 15; center-periphery conflict in, 97; establishment of delayed authoritarian rule in, 127–32; explaining number of parties in, 68–71; interim transitional period in, 206n15; making of a multiparty system in, 56–59; polarization and mobilizational asymmetry in, 128; and Turkey, compared, 193
Iran Party, 14, 128, 129–31
Iraq, 13, 14, 15; establishment of delayed authoritarian rule in, 132–37; explaining number of parties in, 68–70; making of a multiparty system in, 59–60; polarization and mobilizational asymmetry in, 128
Issawi, Charles, 8
Istiqlal (Iraq), 14, 70, 128, 133, 135
Istiqlal (Morocco), 51–52, 120–22
Ittihad Party (Egypt), 15, 128, 150, 151

Jabr, Salih, 70, 135, 214n8
Janissaries, 78, 79–80
Jarida, al-, 65
Jordan, 13, 14, 15; establishment of delayed authoritarian rule in, 137–43; explaining number of parties in, 68–71; making of a multiparty system in, 60–62; polarization and mobilizational asymmetry in, 128

Kabasakal, Mehmet, 171
Kabyle/Kabylia, 51
kadi, 81
Kalyvas, Stathis N., 76
Kamil, Mustafa, 64
Kamrava, Mehran, 59
Karakol, 94
Kara Vasıf Bey, 216n7
Karpat, Kemal H., 87, 180, 211n13
Katznelson, Ira, 203
Kaylani, Nabil M., 145

kaza, 80, 84
Kemal, Mustafa. *See* Atatürk, Mustafa Kemal
Kemalism, 175, 182
Khedive, 65
Khoury, Philip S., 209n3
Kostiner, Joseph, 213n14
Kraiem, Mustapha, 43

Lacheraf, Mostefa, 118
Law of Ill-Gotten Gains (Tunisia), 213n9
Law on the Maintenance of Order (Turkey), 169, 171
Law of National Indignity (Tunisia), 213n9
League of Nations, 32, 55, 59, 60, 62, 66
Lebanon, 3, 4, 206n13
Lerner, Daniel, 7, 8, 9
Lewis, Bernard, 180
Liberal Caucus (Iran), 14, 130
Liberal Constitutionalist Party (LCP) (Egypt), 15, 128, 150, 151
Liberation Party (Jordan), 14, 71, 128, 139–40
Libya, 206n13
Limongi, Fernando, 8, 9
Ling, Dwight L., 43
Lipset, Seymour M., 7, 9, 68
liva, 80
Liwa' al-, 64
Longrigg, Stephen Hemsley, 70
Louis, Wm. Roger, 60
Luebbert, Gregory, 11, 203, 204, 217nn3–4

Mahmud, Nur al-din (general), 156
Mahmut II (sultan), 79–80
Mainwaring, Scott, 161
majoritarian electoral rules. *See* electoral rules
Mardin, Şerif, 215–16n3
Marr, Phebe, 60, 70, 136
Michels, Robert, 11
Mill's "Method of Difference," 21
Mirza Hussein Khan, 97
Mitchell, Richard P., 152
Mithat Paşa, 211n13
mobilizational asymmetry in party systems, 16–18, 123–28, 154–57, 169–84
modernization theory. *See* socioeconomic development, levels of and theories of regime formation
Mohamed V (king of Morocco), 120–22
Moore, Barrington, 199
Moore, Clement Henry, 39, 40, 43, 48, 51, 208n4
Morocco, 13, 51–53, 98, 120–22, 213n15
Mossadeq, Mohammed, 131–32
Mouvement Populaire (MP) (Morocco), 122
Movement for the Triumph of Democratic Liberties (MTLD) (Algeria), 49
Mu'ayyad, al-, 65
mufti, 81
Muhammad Ali, 98
muhassıl, 80–81
multiparty systems, 54–56, 73, 123–28, 199
Muslim Brotherhood (Egypt), 15, 125, 128, 150–54, 215n23
Muslim Brotherhood (Jordan), 14, 71, 128, 139–41
Muslim Brotherhood (Syria), 70
Mustafa IV (sultan), 78
Mutedil Hürriyetperveran Fırkasi (late Ottoman Empire), 91

Nabulsi, Sulayman al-, 142–43
Nahda, al- (Jordan), 137
nahiye, 80
Naser al-Din Shah, 97
Nasser, Gamàl Abdel, 114, 213n13
National Bloc (Syria), 62–64
National Brotherhood Party (Iraq), 60
National Democratic Party (NDP) (Iraq), 14, 70, 128, 133, 135
National Front (Iran), 131–32
National Front (Iraq), 136
National(ist) Party (Syria), 14, 70, 128, 143–48
National Liberation Army (Algeria). *See* Armée de Libération Nationale (ALN) (Algeria)
National Liberation Front (FLN) (Algeria), 14, 31, 50–51, 117–20
National Liberation Front (NLF) (South Yemen), 14, 31, 46–47, 114–17, 213nn13–14
National Party (Egypt), 64–65
National Party (Iraq), 60
National Socialist Party (NSP) (Jordan), 14, 128, 139–43
National Union Caucus (Iran), 14, 130
Neo-Destour Party (ND) (Tunisia), 14, 31; approach of, to nationalist mobilization, 38–40, 208–9n14; growth and organization of, 40–41; leaders' backgrounds, 38, 39, 107; and nationalist agitation, 41–42, 208nn8–9; origins of, 38; preponderance of, 42–44; reorganization of, in 1958, 114; satellite organizations of, 40–41, 208n10; and silencing of political rivals, 108–11, 213n7; social networks key to building of, 107; and takeover of Tunisian nationalist movement, 38; and takeover of the Tunisian state, 111–14, 213n8, 213n12; and Tunisian independence, 42
Neo-Destour Youth, 208n12
networks. *See* peripheral elite networks in the late Ottoman Empire and Turkey
North Yemen, 44, 45, 47, 206n13
notables, local, in the late Ottoman Empire and Turkey, 80–82, 87, 211n7, 212n18

Okyar, Ali Fethi, 171–74
OLOS (South Yemen), 116
Osmanlı Sosyalist Fırkası (late Ottoman Empire), 91
Ottoman constitution, 86, 89, 90, 211nn12–13
Ottoman Empire: collapse of, 206n15; decline of, 78; and Egypt, 64–65, 66; geographic reach of, 207n20, 210n5; and Turkish War of Independence, 210n1
Özbudun, Ergun, 168

Pahlavi, Mohammed Reza (shah), 59, 132
Pahlavi, Reza (shah), 58, 59
Palestine/Palestinians, 62, 71, 138, 217n1
Palestine Mandate, 71, 192
Paris Peace Conference, 65
parliament(s), 16, 18; in Egypt, 64, 66, 149–54 passim, 210n9; and emergence of multiparty systems, 19, 55–56; in Iran, 55, 58–59, 71, 127–32; in Iraq, 59–60, 132–36; in Jordan, 61, 71, 137–43 passim, 215n15; lack of powerful, in pre-independence Tunisia, South Yemen, and Algeria, 33; in Ottoman

parliament(s) *(continued)*
Empire, 79, 83–93, 211n13; in Syria, 62–63, 143–48 passim, 215n20; in Turkey, 216n4. *See also* Grand National Assembly (late Ottoman Empire/Turkey)
Parti Communiste Algérien (PCA). *See* Communist Party (Algeria) (PCA)
Parti National Tunisien, 209n16
parties, political: as analytical approach of the book, 5, 11–18, 199–204; difficulty of building, 76, 104–5, 212n1; number of, 15, 19, 56, 67–72, 161–62, 190–91; roles in regime formation processes, in works of class scholars, 11, 200, 203
party system characteristics, 5, 13–21
Patriot Caucus (Iran), 14, 130
Patron-client ties, 18, 31; and challenger party formation in Turkey, 170; changes in, in Tunisia, 35–39; as characteristic of conservative parties, 126; impact of imperialists' modes of occupation on, 19, 32–35, 55–56
PDI (Morocco), 121, 122
Peker, Recep, 175, 177
People's Houses and Rooms, 177, 184
People's Party (Iraq), 60
People's Party (Syria), 14, 70, 128, 143–48
People's Socialist Party (PSP) (South Yemen), 47, 116
peripheral elite networks in the late Ottoman Empire and Turkey, 20, 75, 84–90 passim; and building of the *Hürriyet ve İtilâf Fırkası*, 92; and Democrat Party, 180–81; and Free Republican Party, 172–73; and Progressive Republican Party, 167–70; and Turkish War of Independence, 93–95
polarization in party systems, 16, 17, 18; and establishment of delayed authoritarian rule, 123–25, 128; in interwar Europe, 200; and number of parties in party systems, 161–62; reduction of, in Turkish case, 159–84; sources of, 191–92, 195–96, 217n1; types of, 18, 124–25
political culture. *See* culture-based theories of regime formation
Prather, George Martin, 217n13
Progressive Party (Iraq), 60
Progressive Republican Party (PRP) (Turkey), 15, 159, 166–71, 216n7
proportional representation electoral rules. *See* electoral rules
provincial administrative council system (late Ottoman Empire), 20, 75, 79–86, 211n14
Przeworski, Adam, 8, 9, 11, 16
public good, 76, 105, 210n3
Putnam, Robert D., 84

Qajar(s), 56–57, 58, 97

regimes, founding, 13–16, 103–4, 123–28
rentier hypothesis, 197–98
republicanism, 160, 173–74, 175, 177, 182
Republican People's Party (RPP) (Turkey), 3, 10, 15, 158–59; accession to free and fair elections in 1950, 182–84, 186, 206n10; and the army, 186–87; defections from competitive norms, 194; and Democrat Party, 178–84; and election of 1946, 183; and Free Republican Party, 171–74, 175; organizational handicaps of, relative

to its opponents, 170–71; and overcoming mobilizational asymmetry in Turkey, 176–84, 217n13; and People's Houses and Rooms, 177; and Progressive Republican Party, 166–71; reforms in the 1930s, 174–77; suppression of opposing parties, 159; and Turkish Hearths, 176
Rifa'i, Samir, 143
Rimawi, Abdullah al-, 142
Rokkan, Stein, 68
Ruedy, John, 118
Rueschemeyer, Dietrich, 11, 199, 200–201, 203, 204
Russia, 57–58, 71, 97
Rustow, Dankwart A., 16, 169

Sadiqia College (Tunisia), 107
Sa'dist Party (Egypt), 15, 128, 150, 151
Sa'id, Nuri al-, 70
sancak, 80, 84, 92
Sani, Giacomo, 161
Sartori, Giovanni, 161
Saudi Arabia, 128, 142
SAVAK, 132
Sayyid, Ahmad Lutfi al-, 65
Schattschneider, E. E., 13
Scully, Timothy R., 161
Second Constitutional Period (late Ottoman Empire), 89–93
Second Group (late Ottoman Empire/Turkey), 158, 159, 163–66, 215–16n3
secularism, 160, 173–74, 175, 176, 182
selective incentives, 106
Selim III (sultan), 78, 79
Sened-i İttifak, 79
Sèvres, Treaty of, 93
Şeyhülislam, 90
Sha'b Party (Egypt), 15, 128, 150, 151
shah, 58, 132
Sharabi, Hisham, 6, 214n1
shari'a, 36
Shaw, Stanford J., 84, 85
sheikh(s)/shaykh(s), 35, 37, 39, 61
sheikhat, 114
Shishakli, Adib, 147–48
Sidqi, Ismail, 150
Silvera, Victor, 109, 113
single preponderant parties, 15–16, 19, 31–35, 103–20 passim
Sivan, Emmanuel, 198
Sivas Congress, 94
social capital, 20, 84, 117
social cleavages. *See* cleavages
Socialist Nation Party (Iraq), 14, 70, 128, 135, 214n8
Socialist Party of Egypt. *See* Young Egypt
Society for the Study of Turkish History, 175–76
socioeconomic development, levels of, and theories of regime formation, 5, 7–9
South Arabian League (SAL) (South Yemen), 47, 116
South Yemen, 13, 14, 15; establishment of immediate, one-party founding regime in, 114–17; making of a single preponderant party in, 44–47; relative ease of party building in, 104–6
Soviet Union, 57, 128–32, 139, 185, 192, 206n10
Sprague, John, 11
Stephens, Evelyne Huber, 11, 199, 200–201, 203, 204
Stephens, John D., 11, 199, 200–201, 203, 204
suffrage norms. *See* elections

sultan (Ottoman), 64, 78, 86–90, 163, 211n7
sultanate (Ottoman), 186
Sun-Language Theory, 176
Şura-yı Devlet, 86
Syria, 13, 14, 15; establishment of delayed authoritarian rule in, 143–48; explaining number of parties in, 69–70; making of a multiparty system in, 62–64; overcoming religious and regional differences in, 210n10; polarization and mobilizational asymmetry in, 128, 215n19

Tabara, Bahjat, 143
Talal (king of Jordan), 137
Tanzimat, 85–86, 88, 89, 211n7, 211n14
tax farming in the Ottoman Empire, 77–83
Teşkilat-ı Mahsusa, 94
theories of Middle East authoritarianism, 5–11, 197–98
Third Wave, 4, 9
Thompson, Elizabeth, 85
Tibawi, A. L., 209n3
Tlili, Ahmed, 111
Toker, Metin, 182
Transjordan. *See* Jordan
Tudeh Party (Iran), 14, 71, 128, 129–32, 214n5
Tunisia, 13, 14, 15; center-periphery conflict in, 99; establishment of immediate, one-party founding regime in, 107–14; making of a single preponderant party in, 35–44; relative ease of party building in, 104–6, 212n1
Tunisian Communist Party (PCT). *See* Communist Party (Tunisia) (PCT)
Turkey, 13, 15; as case of single-party rule, according to others, 207n18; comparability of, with other cases, 23–26; depolarization and increased mobilizational symmetry in, 158–87 passim; emergence of bipartism in, 73–97; interim transitional period in, 18, 73, 158, 206n15; majoritarian electoral rules in, 73, 76, 210n2; political exceptionalism of, 190–94, 217n1
Turkish Hearths, 176, 177
Turkish War of Independence. *See* War of Independence, Turkish
Two-party system(s). *See* bipartism

ulama/ulema, 31, 33, 36, 78–79
Union Générale des Agriculteurs Tunisiens (UGAT), 40, 41, 109, 112, 208n11
Union Générale des Etudiants Tunisiens (UGET), 40, 41, 111
Union Générale des Travailleurs Algériens (UGTA), 50
Union Générale des Travailleurs Tunisiens (UGTT), 40–41, 43; and Bourguiba-Ben Youssef rift, 109; origins of, 41; relationship to Neo-Destour, 40–41, 107, 110–11, 114, 208n13, 212n5
Union Nationale des Agriculteurs Tunisiens (UNAT), 112
Union Nationale des Forces Populaires (UNFP) (Morocco), 122
Union des Travailleurs Tunisiens (UTT), 111
Union Tunisienne des Artisans et Commerçants (UTAC), 40, 111, 208n11
United Kingdom, 13, 24, 32; in Egypt, 64–67, 149–54; in Iran, 57–58, 71, 128–32; in Iraq, 59–60, 132–35; in Jor-

dan, 60–61, 138–42, 209n2; in Palestine, 192; and political polarization in Iraq and Jordan, 124–25; in South Yemen, 44–47, 116, 208n3
United States, 128–32, 194–97
University of Tunis, 213n10
U.S.S.R. *See* Soviet Union
Usta,Veysel, 168

Vatikiotis, P. J., 65
vekil, 81

Wafd Party (Egypt), 15, 64–67, 128, 149–54, 215n23
Waldner, David, 17, 124
War of Independence, Turkish, 210n1
Watani Party (Egypt), 15, 128, 150–51
Waterbury, John, 16
Weiker, Walter F., 176
West Bank, 62, 68; annexation of, by Jordan, 71, 138, 140; as distinct from the East Bank, socially, economically, and politically, 138, 214n13; and Jordanian army, 141; socioeconomic discrimination against, in Jordanian public policy, 71
wilaya, 118

Young Egypt, 15, 128, 150–56 passim
Yusuf, Ali (sheikh), 65

Za'im, Husni al-, 146–47
Zawiya(s), 107, 212n2
Zitouna, 39, 107, 112, 213n10
Zubaida, Sami, 214n1
Zürcher, Erik J., 163, 164